ABYSS TO
ABUNDANCE:

FROM RECOVERY TO DISCOVERY OF WHO YOU ARE
AS A CHRISTIAN IN THE KINGDOM OF GOD

RHONDA KAY LANDRY

copyright © 2013 Glory Gate Ministry

ISBN-10: 0988284464
ISBN-13: 9780988284463
Library of Congress Control Number: 2012948827
Glory Gate Ministry, Beaumont, Texas

I DEDICATE THIS BOOK TO MY SWEET ABBA FATHER,
MY LORD AND SAVIOR, JESUS CHRIST, AND TO THE
SWEET HOLY SPIRIT, WHO DWELLS WITHIN ME, FOR
WITHOUT THEM, THIS BOOK WOULD NOT HAVE BEEN
POSSIBLE; MY LIFE WOULD BE NOWHERE, AND I
WOULD BE NOTHING.

To my beloved Johnny Angel, for teaching me how to love
unconditionally and showing me what it *truly* means
to walk with Christ!

To Irene Breaux, because Jesus' radiance shines through her,
which helped lead me to God.

To Ruby Bennett, who held my hand as we walked in His light.

To my Pastor, Rick White, for preaching The Word.

To Pastor Carlton Sharp for preaching The Word and his
willingness to ordain me to minister The Gospel.

TABLE OF CONTENTS

INTRODUCTION

When I began to write this book, I was somewhat concerned I wouldn't have enough to say. After all, who was I? I certainly didn't have any education, credentials, or certifications to support evidence of being any type of authority on God, at least not by the world's standards. However, as I began to write, things began to happen and God began to speak to me in a multitude of ways. There are things He wants you to know—things He needs clarified and emphasized. He has given me revelation and knowledge to edify His church, His beautiful bride He will one day claim.

As His ideas and impressions began to flow forth out of me like a great rushing river, I began to wonder if there would ever be a stopping point to this book. After all, I am writing about the Almighty, the Eternal Creator of the Universe. It could go on forever. As I write this introduction, I am still writing the body of the book. I know one day He will reveal the conclusion to me because He wants this published. God spoke to me through many avenues that confirmed writing and publishing this book was part of His plan.

So, who am I to write this book? Perhaps I'm not an expert as the world would define it, but I'm an expert in my Father's eyes. He created me to bring Him glory and great pleasure. Through all the hardships, trials, suffering, grief, and sorrows, I have grown extremely close to my Father in Heaven, which has brought me a great amount of wisdom and knowledge concerning His nature. However, I must emphasize this book is not about what I have been through. I wrote it to clarify who God truly is: our Father who loves us beyond what we could ever comprehend. I also wrote it to clarify who we all truly are when we choose Him: *victorious in all situations.*

I found the more involved I became in writing this book, the deeper my intimacy with Him grew. I began to get a true revelation of just how much He loves *all* of His children! He does not play favorites; He loves us all with the same "breadth and length and depth and height" (Ephesians 3:18, KJV). His love is limitless. When you receive this revelation, you will never be the same, and the world around you will become a very different place. I pray all of you who read this book will get the same revelation of the love He has for you, just as I did when I had the great privilege to write it.

So, it is with blessings, gratitude, honor, and glory forever to His Holy Name that I have the honor to pen this book for Him, for without Him, it would not have been possible, but "with God, all things are possible" (Matthew 19:26, KJV).

It is my sincere prayer this book will give hope and instill faith in those who are lost and suffering, which was my life just a few short years ago. I was in a deep pit of despair as I wanted to die following my husband's death, but I reached up to God and He pulled me out. As the Bible tells us, "He brought me up also out of an horrible pit, out of the miry clay, and set my feet upon a rock, and established my goings" (Psalms 40:2, KJV). I was truly transformed by His tender, loving care. I had once been dead to His love and His Spirit. His precious Son, my Lord and Savior, Jesus Christ, saved me on so many levels and in so many ways. I was on a path of destruction, but now I am victorious. I am *more than a conqueror and am prospering above all things* due to the saving grace of my sweet Savior, Jesus Christ, whose Holy Spirit now dwells within me. I have to say, "Thank you, Lord for making me brand new!"

It is God's sincere desire no man shall perish, but everyone should be saved through His Son, Jesus Christ (2 Peter 3:9). I have often said to God, "Wouldn't it be wonderful if not one single person was left on this Earth and all were saved and went to Heaven? That would be the ultimate revenge on the enemy—to watch him run to and fro over the earth looking for someone to torment, but everyone would be in Heaven!" It gives me great joy when I picture that in my mind, and it gives me even greater joy to believe souls will be won after reading the words in this book. I only typed it while these divinely-inspired words, ideas, expressions, and feelings were poured out on the pages of this book. God guided my hand through this writing just as He guides my life.

It is my sincere prayer this book will turn hearts to Jesus and He will become Savior to millions. Please, accept Him into your heart so He will not have to say, "…I never knew you: depart from me…" (Matthew 7:23, KJV). That will break His heart. His heart has been broken enough through rejection and our pain, which He experiences on a very deep level.

CHAPTER ONE

THE ROAD TO HEALING

Perhaps you are in a pit and you feel like you are in so deep you can never, in any way, climb back out, nor do you have any motivation to do so. What can you do? More importantly, the question should be, what *should* you do? *Do the only thing that works—surrender to God. You can't be healed without the Great Physician; you can't receive appropriate counsel without the Wonderful Counselor; you can't be comforted without the sweet comforter—the Holy Spirit.*

I know from experience surrender may seem impossible, but *it is not just letting go of control, it is about resting in Him.* It is so amazingly wonderful to let go and rest in His big, strong, loving arms and know without a shadow of a doubt He has you in the palm of His hand. He loved you first. Knowing that is true freedom. Knowing the Creator of the Universe loves you beyond measure, beyond what you could ever completely comprehend, is the key to healing. Knowing His love will allow you to rest in Him—the work is already done. *Just let go and give Him control.* It becomes easy to do so when you finally understand He has already done everything for you. He has blessed you with every spiritual blessing in the heavenly realms (Ephesians 1:3). God created the entire Universe in six days. *He rested on the seventh day. This was His way of telling us to rest in Him.*[1] *We are to rest in Him because everything was already done.* It is ours for the taking and all we have to do is *believe it and receive it.* His abundant blessings abound because of His grace and mercy, which then enable us to be a blessing to others.

When you do not understand who God is, it is not possible to rest in Him. This is the main focus of this book: to clarify who our Father is so you will be able to receive from Him as His heart desires. When you are able to fully receive His grace and operate in His kingdom, *you will be more than a conqueror and prosper above all things!*

I used to think God was this big, powerful, entity somewhere in Heaven and He was inaccessible. Due to my previous lack of knowledge about God, I believed there was no way I had any right, in all of my heathenness, to expect Him to answer any of my prayers. I might as well have been talking to the wall for all I knew, but, was I ever wrong.

For many of us, our relationship with our Heavenly Father becomes broken because we separate ourselves from Him as we think He must be the same as our earthly parents. Mothers and fathers are supposed to be a reflection of the love our Heavenly Father has for us. Sometimes this doesn't occur when dysfunction prevails. If you have earthly parents who are hurt, distant, angry, unloving, and unavailable, then why should you expect a Heavenly Father, whom you've never seen, to be any different? But He is different from the parents many of us have. He is the opposite of everything they expressed in their fallible humanity. *He is all good things*—gentle, loving, kind, empathetic, wise, comforting, caring, compassionate, powerful, generous, and the list goes on and on.

He *waits patiently* for us to come back to Him. He is there right now waiting for you. Just run into His arms, then you'll see how great your life will be.

---

1   Living in the Balance of Grace and Faith. CD-ROM. Colorado Springs: Andrew Wommack Ministries.

I have come to understand *God's great capacity to love is only paralleled by His capacity to hurt.* Even though He has given us free will, I believe when we are not following His plan for our lives, it must upset Him because He wants the best for His children. He knows better than we do what that is. It is no different when an earthly parent sees their grown child making poor choices for their lives. They grieve over their actions because they know their lives could be much better. I recently had this revelation God hurts when we are going down the wrong path. It was revealed to me through my addiction to television. It has been the constant companion of my life. The first thing I did when I sat down was turn it on. I began to notice I felt severely depressed after watching it for hours on end. I realized the depression was originating from the grief I was causing the Holy Spirit that dwells within me. Gluing myself to a television interfered with God's great plans for me. There was no way He could see His plans carried out when I wasn't available to execute them. I noticed how drastically my state of mind improved when I gave up the television in favor of His presence. I no longer felt depressed.

When we hurt, He hurts, and He promises He will comfort us: **"Blessed are they that mourn, for they shall be comforted"** (Matthew 5:4, KJV, emphasis added). Many times, we endure trials, which lead us to diligently seek God and enter into an intimate relationship with Him. We are then given our heart's desire of unspeakable joy and peace that surpasses all understanding, which brings us more comfort than we have ever known. As the great Psalmist, David, wrote, "Delight thyself also in the LORD: and he shall give thee the desires of thine heart" (Psalm 37:4, KJV).

So, what do you do when you find yourself in the pit of despair? If you haven't accepted Jesus as your Savior, you must do so. You can do it right now, by confessing the following out loud:

"Father,

It is written in Your Word if I confess with my mouth that Jesus Christ is Lord and believe in my heart that You have raised Him from the dead, I shall be saved. Therefore, Father, I confess that Jesus is my Lord. I make Him Lord of my life right now. I believe in my heart, Father, you raised Him from the dead. I accept Jesus Christ as my personal Savior and according to your Word, I am saved right now. I renounce my past life with Satan and close the door to any of his devices.

Thank You for forgiving me of all my sins. Jesus is my Lord and Savior, and I am a new creation. Old things have passed away. Now all things become new in Jesus' mighty name.

Amen."

Now, find a local church, get baptized, and *saturate yourself with His Word,* which will make you a new creature in Christ. As the Apostle Paul has instructed us, "Therefore if any man be in Christ, he is a new creature: old things are passed away; behold, all things are become new" (2 Corinthians 5:17, KJV). "And I am certain that God, who began the good work within you, will continue his work until it is finally finished on the day when Christ Jesus returns" (Philippians 1:6, NLT).

Also, Pray. Pray God will give you a revelation of how much He loves you—that you may "know the depth, the breadth, and length, and height" of His love. Ask Him to make you like Jesus.

Do you have a rebellious streak in you? Are you saying, "I don't want to do this!" Join the club! Most of us have the same affliction, but guess what? You can pray about that, too! On this healing journey, I've discovered I can't change myself; only God can. What a relief it was to find that out. All I have to do is trust and rest in Him, and He will do all the work in me.

Increasing your prayer life, the time you spend in His Word, and fellowshipping with God may be a new lifestyle for you. But it is abso-lutely necessary to healing because it draws you into an intimate rela-tionship with Him and brings His blessing upon you, from which all other blessings flow. Again, pray and ask Him for a desire to do these things. When you pray according to His will, the answer is always yes. It has to be yes if it is what He wants, right? That is what the Scripture tell us.

When you pray, Jesus stands at the Father's right hand and intercedes on your behalf. When you pray according to God's will, He hears you: "And this is the confidence that we have in Him, that if we ask anything according to His will, He heareth us" (1 John 5:14, KJV).

In the meantime, keep your focus on how much He loves you. When you realize this, you will then love Him with everything you are, and others as yourself, which is the sum total of all the commandments. You won't be able to help yourself. Remember whatever you focus on will be magnified. If you focus on God, He will take center stage in your life. Your problems will become miniscule and no longer dominate your existence.

Ask Him to make your heart a loving heart by filling you up with His love so you can love Him and your neighbor, which not only includes those living next door to you, but everyone on this planet.

Don't expect a transformation to happen overnight. Your flesh has to become receptive to the renewing of your spirit through the new programs of God's Word. Those old worldly programs have been playing for so long, you have become brain-washed with lies that contradict who you truly are and who your Heavenly Father truly is. Transformation is an evolving process. Perhaps it has to be a process because of the constant exposure of negativity to our bodies. If we received all of God's powerful positive, loving energy at one time, we might explode. Maybe that is why He has to trickle it in little by little as we are transformed from glory to glory (2 Corinthians 3:18).

Another thing you should do to facilitate your recovery is fill your environment with praise and worship music. It ushers in the Holy Spirit and you will be lifted up. Additionally, there are some powerful lessons you can purchase from some evangelists, who are noted in the appendix. Memorize scriptures and repeat them several times per day to become rooted in God's Word. This will delete any negative programs that may be playing in your head.

These are some of the basic things to get you started on the road to recovery: whether you have a problem with addiction, abusive relationships, poor self-esteem, or are experiencing deep grief. There is one cure for any affliction. It is God. There are other roads that appear to lead to healing. I've tried many of them. They are long, winding, and fragmented. Many of them lead to a dead end. Some take you to very dark places. Some keep going and never seem to end. But the shortest road—the only one that takes you to your destination—starts and ends with God, and it is complete. It is a one-step process. You surrender and there He is, working it all out for you!

He can even heal your physical body with the very principles I describe in this book. But now I would like to tell you about who God is, so let's take a look at the next chapter, and I will introduce you to Him if you don't already know him. If you already do, perhaps seeing Him through different eyes will give you a new perspective and a deeper bond with Him.

Please be aware as you are reading, I will repeat scriptures and concepts throughout this book for two reasons. They are relevant to the topic and repetition will activate them in your spirit, which will increase your faith. Moreover, you will notice a pattern of the biblical principles I will write about as they are the foundation for every topic that will be addressed.

Remember this scripture as you are on the road to recovery and discovery: "No eye has seen, no ear has heard, and no mind has imagined what God has prepared for those who love him" (1 Corinthians 2:9, NLT).

CHAPTER TWO

UNDERSTANDING THE NATURE OF GOD AND YOUR RELATIONSHIP TO HIM

WHO IS GOD?

Before you can understand who you are and how you can obtain your heart's desire, you have to first understand who God is.

As previously mentioned, I used to think God was some big, powerful, unreachable form of energy out in the Universe somewhere in Heaven. I believed I wasn't worthy enough for Him to answer my prayers. After all, I was a big sinner and didn't have any motivation to change my behavior. I would still pray on occasion—when I was in trouble, felt really guilty about something, or when I really needed His help. But deep down inside, I felt like He wouldn't answer me because I wasn't living a Christian life.

However, one day, He did answer me. While my beloved husband was in a coma dying from leukemia, I went back to the hotel room and lie down, prostrate, in the shape of a cross, on the floor. I asked God to take my husband home so he wouldn't have to suffer any longer. I then asked Him to somehow take all of my hopelessness and turn it into something positive that could be used to help others.

I had all of this *devastating* grief that was inside of me. It was tearing me apart. Johnny and I were loners. He was my best friend and the man I had waited for my entire adult life. Not only was he my best friend, he was the best person I ever knew. He wasn't your average human walking the earth. Johnny was extraordinary. He was here on a mission: to love, heal, and protect. He touched many lives during his sixty five years.

One Christmas I came home to find several stacks of twenty dollar bills on the counter. When I asked him what he was doing with all that money, he replied he was going to give it to the homeless people for Christmas. We were far from wealthy, but Johnny was always giving away money or his time to help others in need.

I will always remember one very special moment when I looked into his eyes; it was as though I was looking into eternity. The depth of what I saw at that moment defies description. It felt like everything stood still and we were both frozen in that millisecond of time. It was the strangest thing I had ever experienced with another human.

I often wondered if Johnny had the anointing of Noah upon his life because of his extraordinary love for and protection of animals. He was always rescuing strays and finding homes for them or taking injured animals to the vet. He couldn't even kill a spider. Whenever he would see one in the house, he would scoop it up and bring it outside. He had recurring dreams of walking up a plank to an ark. At the entrance into the ark, an ancient-looking lion would greet him. The lion would ask him, "Where have you been? I have been waiting for you." The lion then would gently take Johnny's hand into his mouth and lead him into the boat.

Johnny was very special in many ways, and when he died I felt *totally* lost. I wanted to die with him because I didn't know what

I was going to do once he was gone. Soon after I prayed that one single prayer in the hotel room, I could sense deep within me God was going to do exactly what I had asked for; He was going to use all of my pain toward something good. *It was the strangest thing*—I was consumed by gut-wrenching grief, but this excitement way down deep in my spirit began to stir. *Looking back now, I can see how God takes our brokenness and lets His beautiful light shine through the cracks of our souls so we can minister to others. All I had to offer God was my grief and the culmination of a life that seemed broken beyond repair. I took my offering to Him, and He blessed it beyond what I could ever imagine.*

A couple of months following my husband's death, I began to see God through another person. She radiated love, joy, and peace. I thought to myself, "I want some of what she has." Well, what she had was God living in her, and with His Holy presence came all of His wonderful characteristics, which is what the Bible refers to as the fruit of the Spirit. I began going to the church she attended, and I felt the presence of God overwhelm me each time I went. I began to pray earnestly for God to come and fill me up with His Holy Spirit. On three separate occasions in my life, I had accepted Christ as my Savior, but I didn't live a Christian life. I, therefore, believed I needed to be filled with His Holy Spirit. I had the pastors pray over me and ask for the Holy Spirit to fill me. I could feel God doing His work within me as incredible peace washed over me after each of the services. I would go home and have the most restful sleep.

Little by little, I drew closer to God. I became hungry for Him and threw myself into His Word by reading the Bible, listening to sermons and praise and worship music, and reading inspirational books based on God's Word during the majority of my free time.

I came to realize God isn't some big, inaccessible form of divinity as I had previously thought. He is my sweet Abba Father. He was there all the time, just waiting patiently for me to come to Him. He always knew I would. I now live in celebration with my Heavenly Father as we enjoy a loving relationship.

GOD IS LOVE

As I drew closer to God, I began to learn about His character and have a deeper understanding of who He really is: "...*God is love*" (1 John 4:8, KJV). God tells us just how much He truly loves us in His word: "...I have loved you, my people, with an everlasting love. With unfailing love I have drawn you to myself" (Jeremiah 31:3, NLT).

If you think about how He gave His only Son and allowed Him to be beaten beyond human recognition and tortured beyond imagination, how could you not realize He is love, and that He loves you beyond anything you have ever known? *If you don't know that God loves you after He has done all of this, then you will never know.* If you have never seen Mel Gibson's *The Passion of the Christ,* please watch it. You will receive a deep revelation of God's love for you. It has saved and changed many lives. Many people were never the same after watching that movie—it's a fact noted in the documentary, <u>Changed Lives: Miracles of the Passion</u>.

What a wonderful God we serve. Did you know there are somewhere between three thousand and seven thousand promises in His book? There are so many it's difficult to count them all. The most amazing thing about these promises is He will fulfill all of them when we are under His blessing by accepting and receiving His Son as our Savior. As David tells us in the following verse: "He hath remembered his covenant forever, the word which he commanded to a thousand generations" (Psalms 105:8, KJV). We are also told, "For all the promises of God in him are yea, and in him Amen, unto the glory of God by us" (1 Corinthians 1:20, KJV).

God says yes to His promises because He loves us. Loving is not *what* He does, but *who* He is. He is love—love radiates from Him, which is abundantly evident in the following scriptures:

His concern for us is enduring:

> "For the mountains shall depart, and the hills be removed; but my kindness shall not depart from thee, neither shall the covenant of my peace be removed, saith the Lord that hath mercy on thee" (Isaiah 54:10, KJV).

Before He ever created us, He loved us and planned a great future for us:

> "Before I formed thee in the belly I knew thee; and before thou camest forth out of the womb I sanctified thee..." (Jeremiah 1:5, KJV).

He pays close attention to every detail of our lives:

> "Are not two sparrows sold for a farthing? and one of them shall not fall on the ground without your Father. But the ***very hairs of your head are all numbered.*** Fear ye not therefore, ye are of more value than many sparrows" (Matthew 10:29-31, KJV, emphasis added).

When I read the scriptures above, my heart just melts, and I fall more in love with my Heavenly Father. How could you not when you realize He loves you so much *His concern for you is His primary reason for existing?* This is evident to me in the way He takes such interest in the minute details of our lives. *He knows every hair on our heads!* How amazing is that? Just imagine—as much as an earthly parent can love his or her child with his or her limited capacity, which is bound by constraints of the flesh, how much more does our Heavenly Father love us? *He is love. Loving is not something He does, but is what He is.* His capacity to love is truly beyond our comprehension.

One Saturday after I had written sections of this chapter, I suddenly began to experience the presence of God's overwhelming love.

It was like I was in a state of bliss. I was totally immersed in peace, which lifted me up. I can't really put it into words. Even though my body was on the ground, I felt like the rest of me was extremely light as though I was floating. In that moment, I felt as though there was not one single thing that could detract, reduce or interfere in any way with the love that had enveloped me. It was an awesome experience that defies description. I now realize that God let me experience the full measure of His love so I could give you a glimpse of what His love is truly like and how wonderful it will be to dwell with Him in eternity.

Jesse Duplantis writes the following about the love He experienced while meeting Jesus when He was taken to Heaven:

> "The intensity of His love for us was evident in His face and voice. When I looked into His eyes, I understood the importance of what He was saying. At that instant I knew His coming is the greatest thing we can wait for. The message that Jesus is coming soon is the greatest news we can share."[2]

I know with my heart, mind, and soul that God, and His son, Jesus, loves me—loves us all—more than we will ever understand, and I can't wait to be kneeling at their feet one day. They will have to pry me away from them with a crowbar!

God is the beautiful sunset in the Blue Ridge Mountains in the fall season. This is His creation, and in its beauty is His expression of who He is. All the rays of light igniting the vibrant colors of the gold, red, and yellow maple leaves surrounded by purple velvet mountains exemplify His wonderful characteristics and loving promises that create the most beautiful place beyond what your mind could ever create, your eyes could ever hope to see, and by which your soul could ever be uplifted. How precious He is to create such breathtaking scenery to bring us great joy and exhilaration. When we draw close to our Heavenly Father, *He* becomes that beautiful scenery. *He* brings us

---

2 Duplantis, Jesse. *Close Encounters of the God Kind.* Jesse Duplantis Ministries, 1996:123.

unspeakable joy and exalts our spirits to commune with His. Thank God we have a god of infinite love!

GOD IS MERCIFUL

So what else is known about God's magnificent character in addition to His great love for us? He is truly merciful. The best way to explain this is through His tremendous sacrifice in sending Jesus to die on the cross for our sins. Can you imagine watching your child go through such horrible agony? Did you know Jesus perspired blood in the Garden of Gethsemane the night before His crucifixion (Luke 22:44)? Medical science teaches great stress can cause the capillaries, which are just below the skin, to burst.[3] I can't even imagine what Jesus must have experienced that night! *No earthly parent would have the capacity to sacrifice a beloved child in such a horrible manner, but Our Heavenly Father loves us all that much:* "***For God so loved the world,*** that he gave his only begotten Son, that whosoever believeth in him should not perish, but have everlasting life" (John 3:16, KJV, emphasis added).

Jesus came down from His throne, where He sat by His Father's right hand, and saved us all. The concept of salvation and what Jesus did for us is difficult to understand. He took all of our sins upon Himself when He hung on the cross, so we could be cleansed by His blood and become the righteousness of God and be adopted into His family.

Please know God desires to have an intimate relationship with us. He wants all of us to come home, and the only way to accomplish that is through His son. *Sacrificing His beloved Son so we could obtain righteousness is the epitome of true mercy!* So, if you have things you need to repent of, just thank your Heavenly Father for the cleansing blood of Jesus Christ and know He has already forgiven you because He is merciful! As Jesus said, "***Neither do I condemn thee.*** Go and sin no more" (John 8:11, KJV, emphasis added).

---

3   Blood, sweat and fear: A classification of hematidrosis. Journal of Medicine, 27(3-4):115.

It's imperative you know that God doesn't want *any* of us to perish. That is why He tells us through His word the following: "For **Whosoever** shall call upon the name of the Lord shall be saved" (Romans 10:13, KJV, emphasis added). Hell wasn't originally created for us; it was created for Satan and the fallen angels that followed him, which is a recorded statement by Jesus in the following scripture: "Then shall he say also unto them on the left hand, Depart from me, ye cursed, into everlasting fire, *prepared for the devil and his angels:*" (Matthew 25:41, KJV, emphasis added). According to the context of this verse, Jesus was talking about people who refuse to love Him by refusing to love others.

I have read and listened to numerous accounts of near death experiences. Many of the people who recall these events state that they ended up in the pit of Hell. Some have stated that they called upon the name of Jesus and He came and rescued them.[4] There He was at the very last minute saving them, despite their previous lifestyle. These events attest to the truth that the name of Jesus, that powerful name, can break through all barriers, including the flames of Hell. They also show God is a god of second, third, and fourth chances. These accounts support the scriptures concerning God's desire that no man shall perish, all who call upon the name of the Lord shall be saved, and Hell wasn't created for us. These near death experiences also correlate with God's word: the *only* people that are condemned to Hell are the ones who *reject* Jesus, which makes sense because He is the reigning King. There can't be any rebellion in Heaven. Satan is the product of rebellion and we all know how well that served Him; he was kicked out.

God *is* merciful and wants us *all* to come to Him so His blessing will be upon us. When I think about the idea of Jesus knowing all of our thoughts, but He forgives us regardless of what we think, I realize how truly merciful He is. I know there has been a lot of garbage in my thought life, but there He is; always loving, protecting, and guiding me into His plan for my life.

---

4 "Near Death Experience." Joni Table Talk Daystar. Dallas. 09 March 2013, 12 December 2012.

GOD IS JUST

What does this mean? It means *God will ensure His children receive restitution when appropriate.* He is on the side of the underdog. *He hates it when His children are mistreated in any way.* It grieves Him when they are cheated, taken advantage of, abused, neglected, or harmed on any level. *Rest assured: He will obtain justice for us when the need arises!* He tells us this in the following verse:

> "For I, the LORD, love justice. I hate robbery and wrongdoing. I will faithfully reward my people for their suffering and make an everlasting covenant with them" (Isaiah 61:8, NLT).

As I was writing this book, I made the mistake of revealing to someone my plans for it upon completion. That person scoffed and made a joke about it. That same night, God blessed me with one of the most wonderful dreams. The dream confirmed the reason God wanted this book written. *He showed me He is often misunderstood because people don't read His Word, which is very upsetting to Him.* The book you are now reading will clarify who He is and help others to know Him as a just god. In this book, His nature is clarified, and in the dream He gave me, and through this book's reach, I am justified. There have been many times in my life when I have felt like a failure. During those times, God always came to my rescue and has brought justice to me by presenting situations or giving me dreams that make me see myself as successful as I really am. This usually happens soon after I experience feelings of inadequacy. He absolutely cares about the souls of His children, and *He will judge accordingly and ensure justice is executed.*

I think it is prudent that we look at the word "judgment." It has a negative connotation; *however the word actually means to make a determination.* God is simply determining what He should do for you or what reward you deserve when He judges you: "…for he was looking ahead and including them in what he would do in this present time. **God did this to demonstrate his righteousness, for he himself is fair and just,** and he declares sinners to be **right in his sight** when they believe in Jesus" (Romans 3:26, NLT, emphasis added). Now, keep in mind I am writing about those who are saved: Judgment for sinners—well, that is a different ball game. So when God judges His children, it is *not* for their sins. That judgment has already been done by our precious Savior, Jesus, when He took all of our sins upon Himself at the cross. When He judges you, God is therefore simply assigning some event or blessing to you according to the situation at hand or the works you have performed. Your works include whatever He called you to do: whether it is a mechanic, a nurse, or a store clerk; work as though you are working for The Lord (Colossians 3:23). You will be judged on how well you fulfilled your calling. This judgment will determine, not *if* you spend time in eternity; that's a done deal if Jesus is your Lord and Savior, but *how* you will spend time there. The following quote is a great explanation of the judgment Christians will face:[5]

> "The judgment of the saved: I Cor. 3:10-23, II Cor. 5:10-11. It is called the BEMA judgment, which is the Greek word for "Judgment Seat." It refers to the Greek Olympic and the place where rewards were given. There would be at the end of the competition a giving of rewards. Three rewards would be given: First place for the best athlete, second and third rewards for those that came in the next two places. It was not a place of condemnation, but only a place where rewards were given. God's judgment of Christians is the same. No one at this judgment will be condemned because they are forgiven of their sins and saved, but here all will be judged accounting to their works for Christ. As Paul put it we will (be) judged according to how we ran the race of this Christian life."

God is able to judge fairly and impartially because He is able to see into our hearts and know what our true motives are. This gives me comfort. Because we live in this flesh and a world ruled by darkness (Ephesians 6:12), it is sometimes impossible to always do the thing you know is right. If you love God, it grieves you to make

---

5   Abrams, Cooper and Carolyn Abrams. "The Account We Must Give: The Positive Side of Judgments of the Lost and Saved." Bible Truth. <bible-truth. org>.

a mistake. God knows this and has compassion for your situation because of His sense of justice, wisdom, and righteousness. *He is not going to punish you for it by bringing destruction to your life.* So, the next time you make a mistake, thank God for seeing your heart and Jesus for cleansing you, and just keep pressing on and fighting the good fight of faith!

I believe my life exemplifies God is just. Even though I had turned my back on Him for the majority of my life, when I needed Him in my darkest hour, He was there. He didn't judge me based on my past. He could see I had a good heart, despite the sin in my life. I am sure He knew my poor choices were due to a culmination of negative influences. He, therefore, decided to deliver me from the grief and the other bondages that kept me out of His perfect will.

GOD IS GRACIOUS

In addition to being loving and merciful, God is also gracious. When we receive Jesus as our Savior, His grace is upon our lives. What is grace? It is undeserved favor. Scripture tell us grace is, in fact, Jesus. In all of our sinfulness, did we deserve the great gift of His Son, Jesus Christ? No, we surely did not, but God gave Him to us anyway. *If you are saved, then pay special attention to His favor in your life.* You might not have recognized it before. It is evident when you get a good parking place; when it stops pouring down rain just before you get out of the car; when you buy something and didn't have a coupon for it, but the sales clerk pulls one out and gives it to you; when you get that job you have been hoping for; or you get a raise just before a salary freeze goes into effect, etc. His grace can show up in a multitude of ways. It is there in your personal gifts: a beautiful voice, the ability to write poetry, the ability to comfort those who are hurting, and so on. Whatever your gifts are, thank your Heavenly Father for them. Thanking Him for the grace in my life is always included in my prayers to Him. I have been without His favor upon me, and I can definitely see the difference in my life, and I ***never*** want to be without it again.

In the following scripture, God tells us He will give us more than enough. We will have so much that we will be able to bless others. This has certainly been evident in my life. It truly is a blessing to be a blessing: "And God is able to make all grace abound toward you; that ye, *always having all sufficiency in all things, may abound to every good work*:" (2 Corinthians 9, KJV, emphasis added).

GOD IS WISE

God, of course, is wise. Pray for His wisdom to operate in your life. Whenever you have to make difficult decisions or you need to advise someone, you definitely want to have His wisdom flow through you. *You know without a doubt His wisdom is operating when suddenly the right decision becomes clearly evident.* Many times you may find yourself astounded. You know you couldn't have thought it up by yourself. It comes without effort—no more brain wracking or wringing your hands to try to come up with a solution: it is just there and you know with absolute certainty the decision is correct. Moreover, a peace washes over you. That, in my mind, is the definitive sign God's wisdom is working through you. Several times, I have prayed for solutions when treating my patients. Without fail, the answer came to me with great clarity. I knew these answers came from God because my mind doesn't work that way without His help.

King Solomon prayed for wisdom. He felt he didn't have the adequate skills to properly rule his subjects. God came to him in a dream and asked him what blessings he'd like to receive. Solomon asked for a wise and discerning heart in order to properly lead his people. The Lord was extremely pleased with Solomon's response and answered, "Behold, I have done according to thy words: lo, I have given thee a wise and an understanding heart; so that there was none like thee before thee, neither after thee shall any arise like unto thee. And I have also given thee that which thou hast not asked, both riches, and honour: so that there shall not be any among the kings like unto thee all thy days" (1 Kings 3:12-13, KJV).

Our Father understands wisdom is a great blessing and it will lead to other blessings in our lives. *Pray for His wisdom to be manifested in your life. You will be blessed beyond measure!*

GOD IS A HEALER

God is a healer. He is called *The Great Jehovah Rophi,* which means *the Lord who heals you.* God actually tells us this: "for I am the Lord that healeth thee" (Exodus 15:26, KJV). *He does and He will.* Every time someone came to Jesus in the Bible and asked for healing, His answer was always yes—always! He never said "maybe;" or "no;" or "you are a sinner and don't deserve it;" or "if you repent, I will." He said, "*I will come and heal him*" (Matthew 8:7, KJV, emphasis added). He healed the blind, the lepers, the lame, those possessed by demons, and He raised the dead. How awesome is that? You may be thinking, "He did all that two thousand years ago when He was walking around on the Earth so He could gather believers." That is what I used to believe—but not anymore because I am living proof Jesus heals today. He is the same healer today as He was two thousand years ago: "*Jesus Christ the same yesterday, and to day, and for ever*" (Hebrews 13:8, KJV, emphasis added). "*For I am the Lord, I change not...*" (Malachi 3:6, KJV, emphasis added).

He healed others and He will heal you, too! He does *not* show partiality or favoritism: "*...God is no respecter of persons*" (Acts 10:34, KJV, emphasis added). He healed me more than once and on all levels: mentally, spiritually, emotionally, and physically. Right after I was saved, I began to feel in my spirit God was going to help me lose weight. I lost one hundred and ten pounds in twenty-seven months! I had been overweight since I was five years old and addicted to sugar since I was a teenager. But God, in all of His goodness and mercy, delivered me. It was a one-step program! I was an outcast most of my life—my classmates made fun of me as an adolescent, and my peers continued to reject me as an adult. I couldn't go swimming because I didn't want to wear a bathing suit. As I became heavier, I was in severe pain. I couldn't walk very far or stand up very long. I usually avoided social gatherings as I felt uncomfortable around people and hated the way I looked when I tried to dress up. My life had almost come to a standstill until the Lord healed me from this lifelong struggle. We have a great God and He is good all the time!

He also delivered me from a mental disorder, which I suffered from for most of my life. I was plagued daily with anxiety, severe depression, as well as paranoid and suicidal thoughts. I lived like this between the ages of fifteen and fifty-three. I had grown so accustomed to this mental state I thought it was simply a normal part of life. After I was saved, I began to experience unspeakable joy and peace that surpasses all understanding (1 Peter 1:8; Philippians 4:7). God healed my mind through His Word. After you receive Jesus as your Savior, you have to *work out your salvation by renewing your mind through the Word of God, which is found in the following scripture,* "And be not conformed to this world: but be ye **transformed** by the renewing of your mind, that ye may prove what is that good, and acceptable, and perfect, will of God" (Romans 12:2, KJV, emphasis added). Please note the scripture says "renewing," which means it is an ongoing process.

In addition to addictive behaviors, there is also mental illness on both sides of my family, so I had a double dose of the enemy. *You didn't think these things came from God, did you?* Oh, I know, false doctrine can lead you to believe God brings things into your life to punish or test you. God may allow certain things to happen because in His infinite wisdom, He knows it will create great character in you, but He certainly doesn't cause it. That would contradict the purpose for Jesus' descension. Jesus said, "...I am come that they might have life, and that they might have it more abundantly (John 10:10, KJV). In Isaiah's prophetic vision, he tells us exactly what Jesus came to do:

> "The Spirit of the Lord GOD is upon me; because the LORD hath anointed me to preach good tidings unto the meek; he hath sent me to bind up the brokenhearted, to proclaim liberty to the captives, and the opening of the prison to them that are bound;

To proclaim the acceptable year of the LORD, and the day of vengeance of our God; to comfort all that mourn; To appoint unto them that mourn in Zion, to give unto them beauty for ashes, the oil of joy for mourning, the garment of praise for the spirit of heaviness; that they might be called trees of righteousness, the planting of the LORD, that he might be glorified" (Isaiah 61:1-3, KJV).

Jesus has already done every single thing for us; all we have to do is believe and receive. He became a curse for us and took on all diseases, illnesses, and all manner of infirmities when He hung upon the cross (Deuteronomy 21:23; Galatians 3:13, KJV). *In the old covenant, a curse would come upon those who sinned; now there is a new, redemptive covenant through His Son, Jesus Christ. When we are saved, we are no longer living under the curse but in the fullness of His blessing, which includes healing.*

You may not have His favor or His hand protecting you if you are not saved, and then the enemy will wreak havoc upon you. You may be attacked by the enemy, and God may not deliver you right away because He might use this attack to strengthen your faith and build your character, but He certainly doesn't create these attacks. He took affliction away when Jesus became a curse for us. Hopefully that clears up where we all are or can be in our walk with God. *God has been extremely misrepresented by erroneous doctrine. We are living under God's grace and are redeemed by the blood of Jesus Christ. When we accept Jesus as our Lord and Savior, God has His loving hand upon us. We are protected, and His blessing, including healing, will flow in our lives.*

GOD IS HUMOROUS

Did you know God has a great sense of humor? Well, He does! Remember He created us in His image. We all have the capacity for humor. I will give you a couple of examples of His wonderful sense of humor.

One Saturday, Ben, his wife, Kathy, and Ben's dad, Joe, were fishing on a big lake. Kathy dropped Ben's favorite rod and reel in the water. They both became really upset, so Kathy began to pray:

She heard God ask her, "Kathy do you trust me?"

She replied, "Yes, I trust you, Lord."

He said, "Well then, just pick up your rod and reel and go back to fishing like nothing happened. Just have faith and everything will be okay."

That is what she did and within a short time everyone was happy again. She told Ben and Joe about her conversation with God.

The very next week they went back to the same big lake. The very first cast Ben made resulted in a catch. Can you guess what he caught? It was the same rod and reel Kathy had dropped in the water the week before! Now, what makes the story funny is there were two people in that boat that were unsure of God's existence. When Ben caught that rod and reel it appeared God was saying, "Look here, fellas. I really do exist, and I can make anything happen, big or small, including catching a rod and reel in this huge lake you thought was lost forever."

Another story includes a dream I had. God has spoken to me in dreams for many years. In this particular dream, I was honking this guy's nose—and it was a great big nose. I kept doing this while I was saying, "Honk! Honk!" This was something I always did to my dog. I woke up, and I was laughing and telling God how funny He was, which made me laugh even more. Even as I write this, I am laughing. If you don't think it's that funny—well, I guess you had to be there. As I stated, it was a great big nose! God was speaking to me about knowledge (symbolic for nosey, for wanting to know). He could have given me any symbol, but He chose one that made me laugh, brought me joy, and represented my playful nature with my dog. He definitely has a sense of humor.

GOD IS A PROTECTOR

Another one of God's wonderful characteristics is that He is a mighty protector of His children. He promises to make footstools of our enemies: "***Until I make thy foes thy footstool***" (Acts 2:35, KJV, emphasis added). Just so you understand—God is speaking to Jesus in this scripture, but in essence He is speaking to all His children because we are all sitting at God's right hand with Jesus: "***...as he is, so are we in this world***" (1 John 4:17, KJV, emphasis added). *The scripture in Acts tells us that God will fight our enemies.* This is one of His great promises, which is noted throughout the Old Testament battles God won for His chosen people. For specific examples, check out the books of Exodus, Joshua, and Samuel. God helped David slay a giant with nothing but a rock, simply because David called upon His name and trusted Him. Yeah, I know what you may be thinking, "Oh, that was thousands of years ago." *Yes, but, as previously stated, God says He is the same today, yesterday, and tomorrow* (Hebrews 13:8), and "God is not a man, that he should lie..." (Numbers 23:19, KJV). *He delivered His chosen then and He does today!* From what giants do you need to be protected—depression, addiction, rejection? *Call on His name—He will help you slay them all! He promises us this:* "...Thus saith the LORD unto you, Be not afraid nor dismayed by reason of this great multitude; ... ***for the battle is not yours, but God's.*** To morrow go ye down against them... ***Ye shall not need to fight in this battle: set yourselves, stand ye still***, and see the salvation of the Lord with you, O Judah and Jerusalem: fear not, nor be dismayed; to morrow go out against them: ***for the Lord will be with you***" (2 Chronicles 20:15-16, KJV, emphasis added). From the context of this scripture, we are told the Israelites had formed an army and God instructed them to go *stand* against their enemies. We can derive from this instruction that we have to do our part in battle. This includes applying the strategies of spiritual warfare, which will be discussed in subsequent chapters, and then trusting God to take care of the rest. However we are not to battle in the flesh, including verbal and physical assault, because Scripture tells us it is not flesh that we are dealing with.

God loves all of *His children* so much He will seek out those who harm us: *"And whosoever shall offend one of these little ones that believe in me, it is better for him that a millstone were hanged about his neck, and he were cast into the sea"* (Mark 9:42, KJV, emphasis added). Do you have any idea how big a millstone is?

God states He will rebuke our enemies for us when we are walking with Him. I don't know about you, but I find it very comforting to know when someone has hurt me God will handle it: "But if thou shalt indeed obey his voice, and do all that I speak; *then I will be an enemy unto thine enemies, and an adversary unto thine adversaries"* (Exodus 23:22, KJV, emphasis added). In this verse, God was speaking about one of His angels who would lead the Israelites into the Promised Land. Now we have the Holy Spirit, who guides us into righteousness and kingdom living. This is the voice we are to listen to so that we follow the two greatest commandments of loving God and our neighbor. When we are walking in love, we are in His light and His protective hand is upon us.

God tells us through His Word: *"For he shall give his angels charge over thee, to keep thee in all thy ways"* (Psalms 91:11, KJV, emphasis added) and *"The angel of the LORD encampeth round about them that fear him, and delivereth them"* (Psalms 34:7, KJV, emphasis added). *We are also told angels are in our presence and we don't realize it:* "...*entertained angels unawares"* (Hebrews 13:2, KJV, emphasis added).

When I think of His angels surrounding me, I don't worry about anything. I'm sure you have heard at least one angel story, right? I have an elderly friend who is one of my spiritual mentors. She said she was in the hospital one night and was very ill. She was praying to be healed when suddenly an angel quickly flew across the ceiling and sprinkled some type of gold dust over her. She began to feel better; she recovered quickly, and went home.

Once when I was driving to the nursing home where I worked, a car that was at a stop sign began to turn onto the road at the precise time I was entering the intersection. My heart dropped into my stomach. There was no way I had time to stop—it happened so quickly. Then suddenly, it seemed as though the other car went right through my vehicle. When I looked in my rearview mirror as I passed the intersection, the driver had already turned and was driving behind me. This *had* to be angelic intervention. That car should have plowed right into me on the driver's side. I guess God thought it was more important I go and take care of all those residents in the nursing home instead of being laid up in a hospital somewhere.

Another time, I had been driving about eighty miles per hour in a sixty-five mile-per-hour zone on a country highway. I heard a voice inside me say, "Slow down and put on your seatbelt," which I did immediately. A couple of minutes later, an oncoming car turned to cross the highway. I slammed on my brakes but couldn't avoid hitting the car. Thank God I had listened to that voice, or I would have been dead or very seriously injured. Obviously, God wasn't ready for me yet and had other plans for me here on Earth.

One of my church members recently had back surgery. Prior to the procedure, I was praying for her speedy recovery. I had a vision of her being surrounded by angels in the operating room. I knew in my spirit God wanted me to tell her what I had seen. She seemed to be encouraged by what I shared with her. She recovered quickly and resumed her role as our worship leader in church. She later revealed to me several others shared the same vision with her soon after I had described to her what I had seen. I truly believe angelic intervention, under God's direct order, was one of the key ingredients to her complete recovery.

Think of all those stories you hear about a mother's intuition. Where do you think that comes from? That is God protecting His children. When my son was an infant, I laid him down and then left the room. Something told me to go check on him. *I am so grateful for God's voice.* When I returned to the room, my baby was choking on the milk he had regurgitated. I quickly turned him over, and he was able to clear his throat. I had gotten there just in time, thanks to God's protection. What a great protector He is!

God has always had His hand on me; He has always watched over me. I left home when I was fifteen and hitchhiked all over the country. I got into cars with strangers like it was nothing. I slept in abandoned buildings, in bushes, in the homes of strangers, and underneath overpasses. It's amazing some serial killer didn't pick me up. I was on the California and Washington highways at the same time the Zodiac Killer and Ted Bundy were in those areas murdering people. I actually stayed in a suburb of Seattle for several weeks when Ted Bundy was on his killing rampage. *I know now God has great plans for me and there was no way He was going to just hand me over to the enemy.* He doesn't hand *any* of His children over to the enemy. *Even though I was not living for the Lord most of my life, I had given my life to God when I was just nine years old, so I was definitely His, and He wasn't going to let anyone else have me.*

Additionally, I truly believe God protects us by instructing us to turn away from sin, which is destructive. If you block the saving grace of your Lord, sin will completely destroy you. Sin also opens the door to the enemy. Once the door is opened, he will gain a foothold on you that can turn into a death grip and choke the life out of you.

One point I feel I need to emphasize is God's protection is *much more powerful than anything* the enemy can use to attack you when you are walking with the Lord. I have heard many preachers and Christians say the enemy attacks you when you receive Jesus as your Savior. I have even heard some preachers say if you're not being attacked, there is something really wrong; if he leaves you alone, you must not be a threat to him.

After I was saved, the majority of the time, I experienced joy and peace. However, I had fleeting moments of negativity in my life, but I didn't *allow* it for very long. In fact, the Word tells us to prevent his evil strategies from affecting us: "Neither **give** place to the devil" (Ephesians 4:27, KJV, emphasis added). I combat his tactics by praising God, saturating my environment with His Word, and putting on the whole armor of God (Ephesians 6:10-18). When you do this the enemy flees. The more practice I had with these techniques, the less time I would spend in "the pit of despair." I also found the closer I drew to God, the trials I did experience were far and few between. They became miniscule compared to my magnificent Heavenly Father. I simply sailed right through any adversary that came my way. I had a deep revelation He will always take care of me. Even though my head was trying to make me look at the facts of the situation, my heart *knew nothing* could harm me because I had the Almighty Defender on my side and I was standing firm on His truths and partnering with Him through His Word. I am His child and He is my Father.

Yes, the enemy will do what he can to attack you because he doesn't want you walking with God. However, *immediate and consistent* use of God's armor will quickly defeat the enemy's strategies. When you defeat him, you bring God glory, which helps lead others to Christ. This is why you were created.

Keep in mind the enemy tries to come and steal the Word as soon as it's revealed to you. The Word says this, but he flees as soon as you rebuke him by the authority given to you as a Christian by Jesus Christ: **"Submit yourself therefore to God. Resist the devil, and he will flee from you"** (James 4:7, KJV, emphasis added). When you have the power of the Holy Spirit living in you, do you actually believe the enemy has any power over you? He definitely wants you to think that. The scripture states: **"...for he is a liar, and the father of it"** (John 8:44, KJV, emphasis added). However, you can combat him with the Word following one of his attacks. Saturate your environment with the Word and worship music, praise God, speak scriptures, pray, and rebuke him in Jesus' name. You will then be back on track.

I know when you are under God's blessing, He is not going to allow any harm to come to you when you stand as the spiritual warrior He created you to be and partner with Him through His Word. *You have been given the power over the enemy. This is the key: you take authority over the situation! You call forth the power Jesus placed within you when He gave you His Holy Spirit.* First, you need to realize it *is warfare* and then you need to know the enemy has no authority over you when you belong to Christ: "***Behold, I give unto you power to tread on serpents and scorpions, and over all the power of the enemy: and nothing shall by any means hurt you***" (Luke 10:19, KJV, emphasis added). He doesn't say "some," but "over *all* the power of the enemy." It's totally up to you. You can *allow* the enemy to attack you, or you can rebuke him by the power that lives within you and the blood of Jesus Christ. The attack won't last but for a moment. If you are not being attacked, that does not mean anything is wrong with you, though some preachers would have you believe otherwise. It simply means God has His hand on you, and He is telling the enemy not to touch you.

Read the book of Job. It illustrates God's protective hand. When God took it away, the enemy attacked Job. Before that, he had been extremely blessed with prosperity in every area of his life. God allowed him to be tested when the enemy accused Job of being a man of integrity only because of God's blessing that was upon Him. When Job passed the test, however, God restored him sevenfold. This attack occurred before Jesus was the Savior, and the enemy was "…the accuser of the brethren…" (Revelation 12:10, KJV). Now we have Jesus who sits at the right hand of God (Hebrews 12:2). *Jesus has cleansed it with His blood* (Hebrews 9:22-23). The enemy can no longer stand there and accuse us (Romans 8:33). Jesus' blood has totally wiped out his ability to do so, "…***for the accuser of our brethren is cast down,*** which accused them before our God day and night. And ***they overcame him by the blood of the Lamb***, and by the ***word of their testimony…***" (Revelation 12:10-11, KJV, emphasis added). *We were judged on the cross. The enemy can't harm us when we take authority over him. This authority was given to us by Jesus. It is our divine birthright as children of God.* We are protected from all of his accusations. So, the next time you hear the devil *trying* to accuse you, *immediately* demand that he flee. You are sealed with Jesus' Spirit and are seated in heavenly places with Christ (2 Corinthians 1:22; Ephesians 2:6).

When a trial comes, use the whole armor and praise God. The trials will simply diminish. If Christians are being *relentlessly* pursued by the enemy, they are not *consistently and immediately* using the whole armor of God for protection. Don't *allow* the enemy to attack. He definitely will if you don't stop him. That is his purpose. I can only speak from my experience, which has been exactly the opposite of all the things I have heard.

GOD IS CREATIVE

God is also an awesome creator. Just stop and think about the intelligent design of the human body. God created DNA, which consists of encoded genetic information and results in making each person unique. What about the majesty of a beautiful mountain; the pounding of the ocean waves against the shore; or, my favorite, the whispering pines that sway in the wind? There is so much variety in the beauty of His many creations. Whenever I see a hawk floating with an air current, I feel such reverence for and an intense connection to God. I know I can soar with His power under my wings. It is then I realize He can and will create all good things for my life. Because we are co-heirs with Christ (Romans 8:17), we also have the power to create our own realities, which is part of the road to healing. Some would argue this simply means inheriting the treasures of Heaven. However, I believe it means inheriting all the things God is. Jesus said, "If ye had known me, ye should have known my Father also: and from henceforth ye know him, and have seen him" (John 14:7, KJV). Jesus is God in the flesh. We inherit our earthly parents' attributes. Why would it be any different with our Heavenly Father, who says it is His good pleasure to give us the kingdom (Luke 12:32)? Living in His kingdom includes more than material prosperity. If you are to be prosperous, you must first create wealth on the inside. When we speak the Word of God, we become co-creators with Him. His Word has the power to create. When you come into agreement with Him and say what He says, it is very powerful.

GOD IS GENEROUS

We are told in Scripture about God's great generosity:

"Fear not, little flock; for it is your Father's good pleasure to give you the kingdom" (Luke 12:32, KJV).

"But my God shall supply *all* your need according to his *riches* in glory by Christ Jesus" (Phillipians 4:19, KJV, emphasis added).

The blessing of the LORD, it maketh *rich,* and he addeth *no sorrow* with it" (Proverbs 10:22, KJV, emphasis added).

How awesome is this? *God owns everything in this universe and He wants to give it to* you, but He doesn't want you to work yourself into a frazzle in order to obtain it. He sent Jesus here for this reason: "*...I have come that they may have life and have it more abundantly*" (John 10:10, KJV, emphasis added). God's instruction also reveals His generous nature: "*let them have dominion...over all the earth*" (Genesis 1:26, KJV, emphasis added). He has given us this Earth to rule over, and He fully expects us to take it back from the enemy. He is just waiting for us to activate our faith and claim our divine inheritance.

God gave the greatest gift in the form of His precious Son, Jesus Christ. This is the ultimate expression of generosity—to sacrifice His beloved child so He could have an intimate relationship with a sinner like me. *Because of God's gracious generosity, I am the righteousness of God through His Son Jesus and so are you!* (1 Corinthians 1:30).

The second greatest gift He has given us is the Holy Spirit, which comes and lives within us when we accept Jesus as our Savior. As the Bible tells us," *...he has identified us as his own by placing the Holy Spirit in our hearts as the first installment that guarantees everything he has promised us*" (2 Corinthians 1:22, NLT, emphasis added). If He gives us His Holy Spirit, will He not give us His kingdom? He wants to give us everything. *His greatest desire is to lavish abundance on us!*

What an amazing gift—God's Spirit is living right inside of you. He is there to bring you comfort, truth, and guidance whenever you need it. His Spirit also bears wonderful fruit and gifts: "but the *fruit* of the Spirit is love, joy, peace, forbearance, kindness, goodness, faithfulness, gentleness and self-control" (Galatians 5:22-23, NIV, emphasis added). When you receive His Spirit and operate in it, these characteristics become manifest in your life. *The Holy Spirit can and will change you into the person God intended you to be when He created you!*

The *gifts* of the Holy Spirit demonstrate God's amazing generosity when they manifest themselves in your life including wisdom, knowledge, healing, discernment, and faith (1 Corinthians 12:8-10). I truly believe with all my heart *God doesn't give because of who you are but because of who He is.*

God is generous and He gives to all of His children. He does not play favorites. Now, that doesn't mean there are no consequences when we sin, but God still loves us and wants to lavish His treasures upon us. In fact, He thinks of us as *His treasures:* "...and a book of remembrance was written before him for them that feared, the Lord, and that thought upon his name. And they shall be mine, saith the Lord of hosts, in that day when I make up my jewels; and I will spare them, as a man spareth his own son that serveth him" (Malachi 3:16-17, KJV). In case you may be wondering, fear of the Lord means to reverence Him; it means to be in awe of Him and understand His power and all of His wonderful characteristics. It also means to honor Him and do your best for Him, which includes making Him the priority of your life by surrendering to His will. When you are His child, there is no reason to be afraid of Him. He would never harm you. I had a revelation of this before I fully understood the concept of fearing God. I simply couldn't be afraid of a Father who loved me the way He does. However, *sinners* who reject God their entire lives should, and will one day, be afraid of Him.

Jesus tells us about our Father's generosity in Scripture: "If ye then, being evil, know how to give good gifts unto your children, **how much more** shall your Father which is in heaven give good things to them that ask him?" (Matthew 7:11, KJV, emphasis added). Please note that evil doesn't necessarily mean some type of demonic influence, but can simply refer to anything that does not line up with God's Word.

God has great treasures stored up for us. All we have to do is believe by thanking Him for what He has already supplied and then expect Him to deliver: "Ask, and it shall be given you; seek, and ye shall find; knock, and it shall be opened unto you: For every one that asketh receiveth; and he that seeketh findeth; and to him that knocketh it shall be opened" (Matthew 7:7-8, KJV). This point is emphasized in James 4:2: "*yet ye have not because ye ask not.*" You also have to show faith after asking because "*...faith without works is dead...*" (James 2:26, KJV, emphasis added). You can demonstrate your faith by speaking it and/or preparing for the blessing you are waiting for.

GOD IS FAITHFUL

I think one of the most important things to know about God is that He is faithful, which is noted all throughout the Bible:

> "And the Lord gave unto Israel **all the land** which he sware to give unto their fathers; and they possessed it, and dwelt therein. And the Lord gave them rest round about, according to all that he sware unto their fathers: and there stood not a man of all their enemies before them; the Lord delivered **all** their enemies into their hand. There failed not ought of **any** good thing which the Lord had spoken unto the house of Israel; all came to pass" (Joshua 21:43-45, KJV, emphasis added).

God always comes through on His promises. However, He may not come through when you are expecting it, and it may take longer than you anticipate. God has His own time frame. I like to joke with Him and say, "Papa knows best," because He really does. He has a plan for your life. If He gave you something you weren't ready for, you could have a disaster on your hands, which could have a domino effect and ruin all kinds of things. So, be patient. Pray for God to help you tap into and develop the patience the Holy Spirit has placed within you. *God wants this for you, so He will help you with developing this attribute. Tell God you have great expectations He is going to deliver what you are asking for because it lines up with His will.* Additionally, when you develop patience and exhibit great faith while you are waiting, sometimes the waiting periods grow shorter and shorter. I think sometimes the waiting period may be to develop our patience and faith, so when we pass the test, there is no reason to make us wait any longer. God then delivers because He is faithful to His Word and His children.

One of God's great promises is to restore His children. There are numerous passages in the Bible where God makes this great promise. He has surely done a mighty restoration in me. I had a dream a few months ago He was going to heal my rejection issues, which have been a lifelong problem. Two months after the dream, the issues resurfaced. I felt myself sinking back into the pit. My earthly father phoned and spoke very healing words to me. An instant healing took place and an incredible sense of peace, acceptance, and love washed over me. God delivered on His promise to restore! He restores on all levels—physically, emotionally, spiritually, mental, relationally, and financially.

One of my favorite promises is "Blessed are they that mourn: for they shall be comforted" (Matthew 5:4, KJV). This is one of the Beatitudes Jesus taught on the Sermon on the Mount. A beatitude is defined as extreme happiness and inner peace; bliss or blessedness. I have heard numerous interpretations of all the Beatitudes, but I believe the literal interpretation of the aforementioned scripture because I am experiencing it. God has consistently comforted me whenever the grief surfaces and I am in need of the Father's love. I am extremely blessed because of His great faithfulness.

GOD IS A PROVIDER

God is also an *awesome* provider. *He is called Jehovah Jireth, which means "the Lord who provides."* He is our true source for *every good thing* we have. You may not have thought of that before, but it is the truth. For example, every material thing I have is because the Lord called me into service to be a therapist to help others. One day, when I was in my late twenties, I was sitting at my desk where I worked as a receptionist. Suddenly, I began to have this overwhelming desire to go to college. The thought consumed me. I would sit and daydream about it. Within a few short months, I enrolled in college. I know this was all part of God's plan for me—not only did He provide for me, but through me He also provides for others whom I serve. Because of His gracious provision, I am able to bless others.

He called me, I answered, and He blessed me greatly for it. I have to say again, *God is awesome. His grace, which allowed me to become a therapist, has blessed me repeatedly.* When you are under His blessing, there is no end to His benevolence. *God is truly a divine cycle of blessings.*

God has always taken care of me, even when I wasn't living the life He had planned for me. I have never been without anything I needed, not once in my entire life. Even when I was raising a child alone on a limited income, my needs were always met. We always had a roof over our heads, a car, clothes, and whatever else we needed.

Recently, God reminded me what a great provider He is. While I was sitting by the river under a tree, a big blackbird came and sat in a branch right above me. He stayed there for a long time, making his strange noise. I felt in my spirit God wanted me to read the story of Elijah. God instructed him to go live by a brook where he would be fed by a raven that was under God's direct orders. This occurred during a great famine in the land. I knew the blackbird was God's way of reminding me of His great promise to always provide, no matter what situation may occur. *He will often surprise you with His provision. You may never know where it comes from, it may come when you least expect it, but it will come just when you need it, all thanks to God!*

GOD IS PATIENT

God is exceptionally patient. He is described as being *long-suffering.* There are several scriptural references that attest to this wonderful characteristic, but the Apostle Paul's testimony epitomizes God's enduring patience. Paul relentlessly pursued Christians, which led to their heinous murders, before Jesus appeared to Him. He then became a great apostle, who wrote more than half of the New Testament. Paul writes about God's enduring patience: "But God had mercy on me so that Christ Jesus could use me as a ***prime example of his great patience with even the worst sinners.*** Then others will realize that they, too, can believe in him and receive eternal life" (1 Timothy 1:16, NLT, emphasis added). I know this is true. I lived as a sinner as He patiently waited for me to return to Him. He could have turned His back on me many years ago. After all, that is basically what I did to Him. I lived in sin and darkness and put Him way on the back burner, even though I had committed to Him when I was younger. *I backslid and when I got to the bottom of the hill, He was there to catch me, take me in His arms, and make everything wonderful! Even though I was not living the life He had planned for me, He never left me. He was always there waiting patiently for me to come to Him. He waits patiently for all His children. He longs for us to return to Him.*

His loving patience can be illustrated by a dream I had. In the dream there was a refreshing spring. It came from a hill and trickled down into a lush, green pasture. When I woke up, I knew God was telling me He had been waiting for me. He wanted to know what was taking me so long. He was there waiting to restore and refresh me with His living waters. He was waiting patiently for me. It was an awesome dream. For some reason, I forgot to log it into my dream journal, but I'll never forget the meaning of it, which clearly conveyed the intensity of our Heavenly Father's love. *His kindness and patience is truly overwhelming.*

GOD IS RIGHTEOUS

"He is the Rock; his deeds are perfect. Everything he does is just and fair. He is a faithful God who does no wrong; how just and upright he is!" (Deuteronomy 32:4, NLT, emphasis added). His righteousness is the sum of all of His other characteristics: truth, justice, light, love, compassion, generosity, faithfulness, mercy, grace, protection, and patience. Because He possesses all of these loving characteristics, it is *impossible for Him to do anything wrong.* That's what makes Him God. That's what makes Him righteous. *Isn't it wonderful to know we have a Father who loves us beyond measure and won't ever make any mistakes when He guides us?*

GOD IS A MIRACLE WORKER

There are an estimated 2.1 billion Christians on this Earth. That is one-third of the population. That statistic is a true miracle. The religious leaders had Jesus crucified by the Roman soldiers and tried their best to kill Christianity, but He rose from the dead. *He lives and so does His Word!*

The intense love I feel from my Heavenly Father and my Lord and Savior, Jesus Christ, is the greatest miracle to me. *When I think about the intimate relationship I have with someone I have never seen in this physical realm; I am astounded.* I have never felt such love, such trust, such security, such healing, such peace, or such joy in my entire life—and it all comes from an unseen source. All of my faith, my entire life, and my whole world revolve around a being I have never met on Earth. Yet I know without a shadow of a doubt He is real and loves me beyond measure. Even though I can't feel Him next to me or see Him in front of me, *I know without a doubt He is right there.* He is part of me, and *nothing can ever separate us!* Now, *that,* in my mind, is the greatest miracle—with the exception of His great sacrifice of the crucifixion and resurrection. Yes, Jesus performed miraculous feats in biblical times, and He performs them today. His resurrection was the most miraculous feat of all, and I am in no way trying to minimize any of His great miracles, but *I am in true awe of the miracle of His love and the wonder of His presence in my life.* He does create miracles in all kinds of ways, on all kinds of levels, including the past, present, and future; but in my heart, there is no comparison with the true miracle of having such an intense relationship with the most awesome being in the universe, whom I cannot even see.

GOD IS COMMANDER-IN-CHIEF

For many nonbelievers, the theory of creation rests on a natural cause. However, if you know anything about the miracle of DNA or other biological processes, or even the wonder of the universe; you should find it hard to believe that everything just simply created itself. There is no way genetic coding, cellular replication, or chromosomal alignment during embryonic development just happens randomly. Did you know every living thing on Earth shares the same exact six elements? Carbon, hydrogen, nitrogen, oxygen, phosphorous, and sulfur are found in trees, plants, animals, and humans.[6]

Because of the complexities of the design of the Universe and living organisms, a theory of intelligent design has been proposed. The following quotes are conclusions based on research from proponents of the intelligent design theory. Stephen Meyer and William Dembski, who are part of a think tank of the Discovery Institute for Science and Culture, have made the following statements.

Stephen Meyer, philosopher of science and Director for Discovery Institute's Science and Culture Center states: "Because we know intelligent agents can (and do) produce complex and functionally specified sequences of symbols and arrangements of matter (i.e., information content), intelligent agency qualifies as a sufficient causal explanation for the origin of this effect. Since, in addition, naturalistic scenarios have proven universally inadequate for explaining the origin of information content, mind or creative intelligence now stands as the best

---

6 Gardiner, Lisa. "The Elements of Life."Windows To The Universe. 25 June 2013. www. windows2universe.org

and only entity with the causal power to produce this feature of living systems."[7]

William Dembski, an American philosopher, proponent of intelligent design, and a theologian, states: "But the conceptual soundness of the theory can in the end only be located in Christ."[8]

In an interview by Hank Hanagraff from the Christian Research Institute, Dembski states,

> "...that God could create a world like this that obeys certain scientific principles that where you see the exquisite organization intricacies, nanotechnology-sized cells—all speaks to the wonderful intelligence of the Creator."[9]

I think of the creative process by our Almighty God this way. He is composed of powerful energy and He infuses that divine intelligent energy into every single atomic molecule that He creates, which seems to be supported in the following scripture:

> "For by Him all things were created both in the heavens and on earth, visible and invisible, whether thrones or dominions or rulers or authorities—all things have been created through Him and for Him. He is before all things, and in Him *all things hold together*" (Colossians 1:16-17, NASB, emphasis added).

Because in Him all things hold together, I believe when He instructs those six basic elements of carbon; hydrogen; nitrogen; oxygen; phosphorous; and sulfur to come together as a tree; a plant; an animal; or a human, they follow His command. If His own creations are infused with His divine energy, *then we are truly all connected.* That is why we have

7 Meyers, Stephen C. "DNA and Other Designs." Evangelical Philosophical Society. 09 June 2013. <http//www.arn.org>.
8 Dembski, William. *Intelligent Design; the Bridge Between Science and Theology*. Downers Grove, Il. InterVarsity Press,1999:210.
9 Dembski, William. Interview with Hank Hanegraff. You Tube Video.18 July 11. Accessed 09 June 2013. <.http://www.youtube.com/watch>.

the ability to feel His presence in other people, when we are in nature, or even when we share a great love with one of our pets. If you slow down and smell the roses, I can assure you that you will find God there. He is in the fragrance of the beautiful flower you are admiring. He is swaying in the tall tree you are sitting under. He is in the warm smile of a caring friend. He is even in the joy of your dog that is wagging his tail.

I believe God's divine energy is in all of creation. It, therefore, stands to reason that everything God created has the ability to respond not only to each other, but to Him as well. Perhaps this is what the Apostle Paul was alluding to when he stated, "… *all of creation is groaning for Him:*"

> "Against its will, ***all creation*** was subjected to God's curse. But with eager hope, ***the creation*** looks forward to the day when ***it*** will ***join God's children*** in glorious freedom from death and decay. For we know that ***all creation*** has been groaning as in the pains of childbirth right up to the present time. ***And we believers also*** groan…" (Romans 8:20-23 NLT, emphasis added).

Please note Paul didn't say some of creation or most of it, but *all* of it. It seems apparent when he referenced creation, he was writing about nature. If he were only writing about humanity, then these verses would contradict God's Word. This is clearly evident if you replace the phrase "the creation" with the word "non-believers" in the second verse, which would oppose the truth of the redemptive covenant. Non-believers will not experience eternal salvation and the relief from suffering which it will encompass. Furthermore, Paul specifically mentions believers as an addendum with the use of the word "and," rather than an inclusion to all creation, which is further evidence he was writing about nature.

The Psalmist, David, also writes about all of creation praising our Lord:

> "…Let the sea and everything in it shout his praise! Let the fields and their crops burst out with joy! Let the trees of the forest rustle with praise" (Psalms 96:11-12, NLT).

Due to the verses written by Paul and David, I believe nature does have the ability to respond not only to God, but also to its environment. The following example further supports my belief: My house was previously surrounded by woods until the land was developed with new homes. My husband said he could actually hear the trees screaming as they were being cut down. It broke his heart. This may sound crazy, but my husband was totally sane, and he was extremely in tune with nature. He spent the majority of His life on the ocean as a fisherman. Moreover, he was a man of integrity. I know what he told me was the absolute truth. My husband's experience, coupled with the aforementioned scriptures written by Paul and David, reveal *that all God's creation is waiting to be in His majestic presence and relieved from the sinful nature of this world. It is, therefore, absolutely clear to me God is the one and only creator of this entire Universe and the true Commander-in-Chief! How else would all of creation respond to Him?*

GOD IS FATHER

Above all, you need to know God as your Father. I saved the best for last. This is truly the very best thing about our wonderful God. He relates to us as His children. *He has adopted us into His family, which gives us the right to call Him Abba, which is Greek for daddy:* "For ye have not received the spirit of bondage again to fear; but ye have received the Spirit of adoption, whereby we cry, Abba, Father" (Romans 8:15, KJV). *How precious is that?*

Since He created us, it only seems natural *His greatest desires center around our welfare because* we are His children. He is our protector, nurturer, deliverer, and healer. He holds us right there in the palm of His great, big powerful hand: "See, I have written your name on the palms of my hands..." (Isaiah 49:16, NLT).

Another scripture that tells us of our Father's great concern for us is found in the book of Psalms: "How precious also are thy thoughts unto me, O God! how great is the sum of them! If I should count them, they are more in number than the sand…" (Psalms 139:17-18, KJV). Our father spends His existence living for us. His thoughts must be stayed upon us continually. The number of grains of sand on the beach is countless.

Jesus clearly instructs us if you know Him, then you will know the Father (John 14:7). When we know our Father, our heart will be filled and the desires of the flesh will fade away: "Show us the father, then we will be satisfied" (John 14:8, NLT). This is the ultimate truth. Whenever I am in His presence, the whole world just falls away, and nothing else matters. *There is nothing in this world that can fill a void like our Heavenly Father can;* not money, material objects, relationships, hobbies, food, drugs, sex, or any other form of entertainment. Oh, they might appear to, but just for a fleeting moment. Then, the gnawing emptiness comes rushing back in. That's why people become addicts. They are continually trying to fill that big gaping hole inside of them. It can't be done outside of yourself. *It only comes from within. Once you are saved by accepting Jesus Christ as your Lord and Savior, and ask for His Holy Spirit to continually fill you, then there will be no more empty spaces.*

It is our Father's greatest desire for everyone to be saved so we can live as His children: "The Lord is not slack concerning his promise, as some men count slackness; but is long-suffering to us-ward, **not willing that any should perish**, but that **all** should come to repentance" (2 Peter 3:9, KJV, emphasis added). As you can see from this scripture, our Heavenly Father patiently waits for us to come to Him and repent of our worldly ways. When we do this, we receive His great promise of eternal salvation and a life filled with His loving promises. He wants all of us to receive Jesus as our Lord and Savior so we can be adopted into God's family and we can all call Him "Father."

Being with the Father is being home, and there is no place like home. You can run to that big, beautiful place somewhere outside of yourself that seems to be the fulfillment of all your dreams, but you will still long for the desires of your heart: peace and joy. There is only way one to obtain them—by allowing Jesus to live inside you. He promised us before He ascended:

*"**Peace I leave with you**, my peace I give unto you..."* (John 14:27, KJV, emphasis added).

"Nevertheless I tell you the truth; It is expedient for you that I go away: for if I go not away, *the Comforter* will not come unto you; but if I depart, I will send him unto you" (John 16:7, KJV, emphasis added).

Pray to God to know Him as your sweet Abba Father. Unfortunately, many of us come from broken homes and did not get the security of nurturing parents. *Let God be the parent you never had. It's not too late. Let Him love you, caress you, and teach you the way of life.* Pray He will help you to receive Him as the parent you never had so you can help others with this issue. They are all around you. That is one of the major reasons people behave in ungodly ways—they did not have parents to love them. Pray God will heal their broken souls.

God is now the new man in my life. He is my husband, my father, my best friend, my partner—the one I run to in times of trouble and in good times, too. He is my confidant and my protector. He fills me with everything I need. I trust Him with all I have and with all I am. I am so in love with Him and I will be His for eternity. I can't wait to sit in His lap and feel His loving arms around me. He often gives me visions of this. He holds me tight and we snuggle and laugh. It is truly wonderful! *I know there is nothing like being surrounded in the Father's love. He fills me with more love than I've ever known. He's everything I have ever wanted and have searched for my entire life and He can also be everything for you.*

WHO ARE YOU?

Who you truly are when you are adopted into God's family can best be summarized in the following scriptures:

"...Even for this same purpose have I raised thee up, that I might *shew my power in thee*, and that my name might be declared throughout all the earth" (Romans 9:17, KJV, emphasis added).

> **"…what the riches of the glory** of his inheritance in the saints, And what is the **exceeding greatness of his power to us-ward** who believe, according to the working of his mighty power" (Ephesians 1:18-19, KJV, emphasis added).

> "And of his **fullness** have all **we received, and grace for grace**" (John 1:16, KJV, emphasis added).

> "Whereunto he called you by our gospel, to the **obtaining of the glory** of our Lord Jesus Christ" (2 Thessalonians 2:14, KJV, emphasis added).

Just stop and reflect on these scriptures, and pay close attention to the phrases in boldface. God is telling us He has filled us with His grace, glory, and power so He is manifested within us! *This is who you truly are. If you have been saved, the glory of the Lord is upon you.* Do not allow yourself to go back to the past, wallow in self-pity, and be consumed by regrets. *All you need to do is trust in Him and receive it now!*

Two very important scriptures tell us not only who we are, but we have specific roles to fulfill as children of God:

> "And I have put my words in thy mouth, and I have covered thee in the shadow of mine hand, **that I may plant the heavens, and lay the foundations of the earth**, and say unto Zion, Thou art my people" (Isaiah 51:16, KJV, emphasis added).

> "Your eyes saw my unformed body; **all the days ordained for me** were written in your book before one of them came to be" (Psalms 139:16, NIV, emphasis added).

God is telling us He has created us for His purpose. We are the fulfillment of God's divine plan. He states we will bring His plan forth into the heavens and the earth. How inspiring is that? Just thinking of the fact I am part of His divine plan boggles my mind. So, the next time you are thinking you are *less than a child of a King because* your insecurities and fears consume you, *think about what God says about you.* He planted you here for a reason. Divinity is your destiny—*when you step into your purpose, no devil in hell can stop you!*

You are a triune being, just like God. You are soul, body, and spirit. Your soul consists of your mind, will, and emotions.[10] Your physical body provides the vehicle for transportation and the metabolic processes for the energy you need to function and execute God's will. Your spirit provides wisdom (1 Corinthians 2:10, NIV) and the ability to commune with God (John 4:24).

Your spirit is who you truly are, which is evident in Scripture. God breathed you into life when you were born (Genesis 2:7). According to the Hebrew translation for breath, the word "ruach" means spirit, breath or wind.[11] Therefore, God's breath is synonymous with His spirit. The Psalmist, David, tells us God's spirit is what begins and ends your life (Psalms 104:29-30). These scriptures reveal we are spirits in bodies, not bodies with spirits. The good news, at least for the believer, is that we don't die. Only our bodies wear out. We then move on to the eternal realm. This is not such good news, however, if you never receive Jesus as your Savior.

While you are on the road to discovering who you truly are, just remember, you're a work in progress. It won't happen overnight. So, look at the progress you've made and where you've come from. You may not be expressing everything God has created you to be at this very moment, but, you have come a long way from where you were— you've made a whole lot of progress! So just keep pressing forward into His kingdom, into His Word. Keep pressing forward into the person He created you to be. One day, you will get there, and it's going to happen, little by little. You're going to turn around, and you will

---

10 Von Buseck, Craig. "The Three Parts of Man." Christian Broadcast Network. 07 July 2013. <cnb.com>

11 Parallel Bible. Bible Hub. 9 June 2013.< http://biblehub.com>.

say, "Wow, look how far, I've come!" You're going to make so much progress! You may not even recognize the "new you" because *little by little, "the old man" is going to fade away, and the "new man" is going to take over* (2 Corinthians 5:17, emphasis added).

Every day, little by little, you are becoming a new person and you are stepping forward into the kingdom. God is making you new with His Word, so just keep praying. He will give you what you ask, if it lines up with His will.

This is who we are when we are adopted into His family - *the child that God loves.* He called me *down* to the altar at age nine to save me. He has always sent His angels to watch over me in times of trouble. He delivered me from bondage.

After everything I have been through, including addiction, abuse, violence and devastating grief; I *should* be dead, but God had other plans for me because *I am the child that God loves!* "***For I know the plans I have for you" declares the Lord, "They are plans for good and not for disaster, to give you a future and a hope***" (Jeremiah 29:11, NLT, emphasis added). How wonderful is this? If you are wondering if this is true, rest assured, it is the absolute truth because I am living it right now and so are many other Christians.

I now realize God was waiting for me; He was always waiting for me to come to Him, just as He is waiting for you to come to Him. He is our sweet Abba Father with His arms wide open. Go! Run! Jump into His arms. He will catch you and give you love like you never experienced because you are the child that God loves.

You are the child God loves. I want you to know deep in your heart you are loved unconditionally. Now start confessing it out loud several times every day. When I do this, I began to feel peace and joy, and a smile comes upon my face. It helps me to tap into all of His goodness and the Holy Spirit living within me because *I am the child that God loves!* Knowing this creates stability, power, and a sense that "***I can***

do all things through Christ which strengtheneth me," because "...
If God be for us, who can be against us?" (Philippians 4:13; Romans
8:31, KJV, emphasis added).

I am the child that God loves. It is December 31, 2011. As I write
this, I know this revelation of His love for me is going to create a great
new year. It is no coincidence He is planting this in my spirit at this
very moment. Over the last year, He nurtured and watered me. His
seed is now producing a great harvest of all the good things for which
He created me because *I am the child that God loves.*

You are the child that God loves. What does God say about you?

> "And the Lord shall make thee the head, and not the tail; and
> thou shalt be above only, and thou shalt not be beneath..."
> (Deuteronomy 28:13, KJV).

> You are "...fearfully and wonderfully made:" (Psalms 139:14,
> KJV).

> "Before I formed thee in the belly I knew thee..." (Jeremiah
> 1:5, KJV).

This is the message I want to convey to you—you are loved deeply,
more than you will ever know. This is who you truly are—a child of
the God of infinite love. How could you *not* be loved?

When you belong to God, He lifts you up from feelings of unworthiness because you are esteemed in all His glory. You are the child of
The King, the Creator of the Universe. *You have royal blood pumping
through your veins:* "**But you are a chosen generation, a royal priesthood, a holy nation, His own special people, that you may proclaim
the praises of Him who called you**" *(*1 Peter 2:9, NKJV, emphasis
added*).*

You are a co-heir with Jesus Christ: "**And if children, then heirs;
heirs of God, and joint-heirs with Christ; if so be that we suffer with**

him, so that we may be also glorified together" (Romans 8:17, KJV, emphasis added). This gives us the divine right to expect God's blessing will flow in our lives. *Once His blessing is upon you, all blessings will begin to flow like a tidal wave of goodness.*

One morning when I woke up, Whitney Houston's song, "I Will Always Love You," was playing in my head. This is one of the ways God frequently communicates to me. I had been asking Him what my anointing is. I asked for clarification about the song that was playing in my head. The Holy Spirit revealed to me *God's love is the anointing.* His love for us is like a river from which all the blessings flow. So, when God loves you for eternity, you will be eternally blessed.

However, you have to receive His love and you have to walk in the anointing to develop a *deep*, intimate relationship with Him. He called you for a specific purpose. If you don't know what it is, ask Him to reveal it to you and begin to tap into it. *Your purpose is the bridge that connects you to Him.* You will be amazed *how well* you can communicate with Him once you begin to fulfill what He called you to do.

As co-heirs with Christ, we are seated in heavenly places with Him. This is one of the great mysteries of God. We are in Him, and He is in us. I think of it like an exchange of our spiritual energy. Because we are seated at the throne of God along with our Lord and Savior, Jesus Christ, we are exalted as He is "...*because as he is, so are we in this world*" (1 John 4: 17, KJV, emphasis added). Don't let your flesh (anything that is against God's will) tell you otherwise. *Your mind, especially if controlled by the enemy, will try to make you believe just the opposite of who you truly are: a child of the Most High God.* The enemy can oppress you by making you think you are less than who you truly are. He will try to keep you from the truth that God has placed power within you as His child. Don't let him get away with that. Start meditating upon these scriptures, speaking them aloud, and you will believe who God says you *truly* are. You are "...an heir of God through Christ" (Galatians 4:7, KJV).

You are more valuable than you know: "For you are a people holy to the LORD your God. The LORD your God has chosen you out of all the peoples on the face of the earth to be his people, ***his treasured possession***" (Deuteronomy 7:6, NIV, emphasis added). Now, if you have been dealing with self-esteem issues—and most of us do on some level at some time in our lives—then this scripture needs to become a revelation to you. If you truly know in your heart you are God's valuable child, then nothing else will matter. People can say what they want, behave as they will, but you are God's special child, the gem of His heart, and the apple of His eye. *When His favor is upon your life and you take authority over the enemy, nothing can harm you. It is impossible.* I know because I am living it. I am amazed every day at His protective, loving concern that shows up in my life in a multitude of ways. Whenever I truly need Him, there He is with a word of encouragement or wisdom.

Who are you? *You are chosen by God to be saved and sanctified by His beautiful Spirit*: "But we are bound to give thanks always to God for you, brethren beloved of the Lord because God hath from the beginning ***chosen you to salvation through sanctification of the Spirit and belief of the truth***" (2 Thessalonians 2:13, KJV, emphasis added). After reading this, you should receive a revelation of God's love for you. *Do you think He would just place His own Spirit in someone He did not highly esteem and greatly love? You are the child that God loves. He has called you to be filled with a very special part of Him!*

You are like a tree planted by a river: "***And he shall be like a tree planted by the rivers of water, that bringeth forth its fruit in its season; his leaf also shall not wither; and whatsoever he doeth shall prosper***" (Psalm 1:3, KJV, emphasis added). This scripture is the absolute truth. Many Christians, including myself, are experiencing it. When you get rooted in God's love, you grow within a fertile foundation that makes you as strong as you could ever be. Because God created you and placed you within His will, He will provide more than you will ever need. *He put you here for His purpose. Do you think He would do that if He had no intention of caring for you?* Do you think He would destroy you after taking such care in creating you and placing you here? No! He will feed you, water you, and take great delight as you blossom into the majestic oak He knew you would become when He planted you. You will have an abundant harvest of all the good things God has planned for you. You will continue to grow and produce wonderful things throughout your entire life. You will flow in the Spirit, just as a tree sways in the wind. As you age, you won't wither away; instead, you'll be productive all your life. When a storm comes your way, you may sway with the wind, you may bend a bit, you may even crack, but you will never be destroyed. Just as a majestic oak that has stood for a hundred years weathers a hurricane, so will you stand firm on God's Word and in His loving, protective arms. You will have God's favor upon you, and it will be evident to all those around you.

This biblical truth is analogous to the life of Joseph found in the book of Genesis. His brothers were jealous of him and threw him in a pit to die. As his brothers sat down to eat, they suddenly had a change of heart and sold him to the Ishmaelites, who then sold him into Egyptian slavery. *The story tells us Joseph honored God and God was with Joseph.* Joseph went through many trials during his bondage, *but he was extremely blessed and highly favored by the Lord.* He became a great leader directly under Pharaoh, and every single thing Joseph did was successful. Even though he went through many storms, he was rooted in God's love. God more than provided for him, and Joseph led a blessed life.

You are blessed and highly favored. There are numerous scriptures throughout the Bible that tell us this. You will see it in your life when you walk closely with God as noted in the life of Joseph in the preceding story and Mary, the mother of Jesus:

> "*But the LORD was with Joseph*, and shewed him mercy, and gave him *favour* in the sight of the keeper of the prison" (Genesis 39:21, KJV, emphasis added). "And the angel came in unto her, and said, Hail, thou that art *highly favoured*, the Lord is with thee: *blessed* art thou among women" (Luke 1:28, KJV, emphasis added).

You are more than a conqueror: "…in all these things we are **more than conquerors** through him that loved us" (Romans 8:37, KJV, emphasis added). In this scripture, the Apostle Paul tells us we are mighty, spiritual warriors. *When we are covered with the blood of Jesus Christ and are filled with His Holy Spirit, we can overcome anything in this life!* His power lives in us, and we are mighty to withstand the battle with God as our Commander in Chief. Whatever comes our way, God is on our side. So hold up your shield of faith and your two-edged sword with His Word, and prepare to win the battle! When you do this, each victory becomes shorter and easier to endure because *when you tap into that unseen power Christ has placed within, you truly are more than a conqueror.*

You need to know you are the seed of Abraham, which means you are adopted into the Jewish bloodline when you accept Jesus Christ as your Lord and Savior:

> "For ye are all the Children of God by faith in Christ Jesus. And if ye be Christ's, then are ye Abraham's seed, **and heirs according to the promise**" (Galatians 3:26, 29, KJV, emphasis added).

God made an everlasting covenant with Abraham:

> "And I will establish my covenant between me and thee and thy seed after thee in their generations for an **everlasting** covenant, to be a God unto thee, and to thy seed after thee. And in thy seed shall **all the nations of the earth be blessed;** because thou hast obeyed my voice" (Genesis 17:7, 22:18, KJV, emphasis added).

Do you have any idea what that entitles you to? This promise ensures you will inherit God's estate when Jesus comes back to reign, which will include the Earth, as well as God's treasures He has stored up for you. It also includes His blessing upon your life right now, at this moment, and all the wonderful things that come with His favor upon you. As we read in the Lord's Prayer: "**On earth as it is in**

Heaven," which means you can manifest God's kingdom *right now* in your life.

God promised to bless *all* of Abraham's descendants. *He also promised to bless those who bless you and curse those who curse* you: "And I will bless them that bless thee, and curse him that curseth thee: and in thee shall all families of the earth be blessed" (Genesis 12:3, KJV). Do you have an enemy? All you have to do is sit back and let God fulfill His promise. He will handle it. In the meantime, pray for them to be blessed. Pray their hearts will turn to Jesus so they no longer hurt others.

Your cup runneth over. When you follow God, He will open up the windows of Heaven and pour out a blessing on you that will overflow. *When you cleave to your Heavenly Father, He will cleave to you. This in itself is the blessing.* This is where the blessing comes from and all other blessings flow. *When you have a close relationship with Him, He will lavish His love upon you.* When you are in this state of grace, every good thing will come your way. Everywhere you turn, you will see blessings, from the ordinary to the extraordinary. God just can't help Himself. He *absolutely* loves His children, and it gives Him great pleasure to lavish gifts upon us. *We are truly blessed and highly favored.*

TALKING WITH GOD

So now that you know a little more about God and who you are as His child, how do you communicate with Him? I know, you might think this is impossible, but I can promise you that it's not. The main thing is when you begin to pay attention, the lines open up wide, and all kinds of amazing things begin to happen. I think He is trying to speak with us all the time, but we are not always aware of it. However, when you get in touch with Him, you will be extremely glad you did!

One of the ways God speaks to us is through nature. Yesterday, someone began to tell me about a hawk he had observed around his house. A few hours later, on the other side of the county, I saw a magnificent hawk standing at the side of a road, eating his prey. I felt in my spirit God was reminding me His Word is food to our spirit, and when we focus on Him and His Word, we are empowered to operate in His kingdom and can rise above anything just as a hawk soars above the air currents: "Thy words were found and I did eat them; and Thy word was unto me the joy and rejoicing of my heart..." (Jeremiah 15:16, KJV). When we study, which is not just reading but also meditating upon His Word, and we digest it, it changes who we are. It enables us to become the person God created, as the "old man" is replaced with the "new one."

As I was writing one morning about God being the awesome creator He is, specifically in reference to seeing a soaring hawk which usually brings me into His divine presence, I heard a song on the radio about soaring under His wings. Later that day as I was driving home, I turned onto my street and there was a hawk soaring as it floated on an air current. I felt God was confirming all of those thoughts and feelings I am now conveying in this book. You may think this is a coincidence, but I don't believe in coincidences. I knew God was telling me through these three separate hawk incidences He created me to soar—to do wonderful and mighty things for His kingdom. I felt in my spirit He was speaking directly to me, saying, "Rhonda, you can fly as high as your wings will take you, and I have created them for limitless journeys!"

My life is a testament to that fact. With my life history, I could have ended up in the gutter. But I live a successful life and am using the spiritual gifts God placed within me. I did it with His power, His amazing plan for my life, and the hope He instilled within me, which is confirmed in the following scripture:

> *"For my thoughts are not your thoughts, neither are your ways my ways, saith the Lord. For as the heavens are higher than the earth, so are my ways higher than your ways, and my thoughts than your thoughts"* (Isaiah 55:8-9, KJV, emphasis added).

As I write these words for you, my spirit leaps with joy, and I feel this indescribable excitement as though my insides are on fire. These sensations are confirming what I write is the absolute truth, and God wants you to know at this very moment it is true for you also. *He is speaking to you right from this very page, from this book. He wants you to know how much He loves you! He has a special plan just for you!* He wants you to have the very best of who He is. You are His child, and He ordained you for a special purpose before He even created you (Psalms 139:16, NLT). Have you given your life to Him yet? If not, please do it now. He is speaking to you! Don't wait any longer. If you have been a backslider, (not living for Christ after declaring He is your Savior) like I was, then rededicate yourself to Him now. Say the prayer of salvation I included in Chapter One.

Another mode of communication includes the use of repetition. *Many times when God speaks to us, He will speak to us in twos or threes.* You may feel He is telling you something, and this feeling will be confirmed through a second or third communication. For example, the story I just told you of the hawk was something I shared with my church congregation. After I shared this story, there were several people that testified they had recently experienced similar hawk sightings and felt God was communicating with them as well.

As previously mentioned, another way *God speaks to me is through songs.* Frequently, I will awaken with a song playing in my head with lyrics that are relevant to something He is confirming or He would like me to notice. For example, I was going through this very difficult trial not too long ago. When it first began, I was very emotional, and I cried out to God for His help. I heard the Christian song that has a scripture as the chorus, "All things work together for good," playing in my head. I knew God was telling me it was going to be okay and He would work it out for me. That's exactly what He did. Within a few days, it was all okay, just as He said in the song lyrics.

God also speaks through scriptures. He may give you a specific scripture, which you will suddenly recall that is relevant to your situation, or you may be reading a chapter and a scripture may jump out at you. Once I was reading a chapter in which the scripture says borrowing and not returning something is akin to stealing. I put down the Bible and asked myself if I had ever done this. Immediately, I thought of a man to whom my husband owed money. I called the man's father, since I didn't have his phone number. The father was astonished, as he told me he was planning to call me that night. He intended to ask if I knew about the loan and was able to pay it back, as his son was having some financial difficulty. When I told him God told me to call him so I could pay it back, he was floored, and so was I! I definitely knew God was speaking to me through His Word.

God will also speak through a pastor or a sermon. There have been several times when I have felt God was speaking to me through this avenue, as the topic of the sermon was directly relevant to my current issue. On New Year's Eve we had a special service to welcome in the New Year. The reverend prophesied that we would go through some trials in the upcoming year, but we were going to get through them and be strengthened by them. Upon arising on New Year's Day, I heard a song playing in my head that includes a passage from Revelation: "And they overcame him by the blood of the Lamb, and by the word of their testimony…" (Revelation 12:11, KJV). I turned on the television, and heard a preacher refer to the same scripture in his sermon. I knew God was confirming what I had heard at church the night before. Looking back now as I write this, there were a couple of things I faced and overcame, which alleviated my fears, strengthened my faith, and made me totally reliant on the grace of God.

God will also speak through people He puts into your life. While I was writing this book, I felt I was being lead to be an ordained evangelist of the Gospel so I began praying for confirmation. The next morning, I turned on the television and heard a pastor preaching that John the Baptist announced Jesus' ministry to the world when He baptized him. A couple of hours later I received a phone call from my spiritual mentor. She said, "I have a word from God for you. He says He wants you to become ordained." *When God begins to speak, He makes sure that you know He's talking!* If he speaks once, He will speak to you again and you will definitely know the communication is from Him.

My ability to listen to God opened up dramatically when I began talking to Him as though I were speaking to a friend. All throughout the day I would just say little things to Him like, "Well look at this, God. I forgot to buy some oranges." Or, "Look at that car, God. I love the color! What do you think? Do you like it?" Whatever you might say to a friend or spouse, you can also say to God. He wants to have fellowship with us. He desires it even more than we do. He created us to bring Him great pleasure: "*...for it is God which worketh in you both to will and to do of His good pleasure*" (Philippians 2:13, KJV, emphasis added). Now, I'm not knocking ritualistic prayer. I'm sure God likes those also—when spoken with a pure heart—but I really believe He loves it when we speak to Him like a friend or a loved one. Just think about that for a moment. Would you want your child or friend speaking to you formally in every conversation? I know that would surely make me feel lonely and isolated from my loved one. How could you develop a close bond like that? I noticed a great shift in the degree of intimacy with my Heavenly Father when I began speaking to Him as a friend.

So, when you are talking to Him like a friend, lay it all on the table. Tell Him your desires, your fears, your needs, your weaknesses, or anything else that is on your mind. He won't stop loving you, no matter what you say. He loves you unconditionally. He already knows what is in your heart. This is what Jesus did in the Garden of Gethsemane— He poured out His Heart to God. His close communication with the Father strengthened Him for what He was about to face. Go ahead. Pour your heart out to Him. You will be amazed how much better you feel when you do this and how much closer you will become to Him.

As I mentioned earlier, God has a sense of humor. When I was writing about His generosity, I asked Him if He would like me to write anything else. I heard Him say, "What are you trying to do, put me on a pedestal?" I replied, "Well, you are on the throne." We both began to laugh. It was very precious. He often makes me laugh through silly little conversations or ideas.

Once, I was really having a hard time with the grieving process after the death of my husband. The small church I attended wasn't meeting my expectations of fellowship and I was feeling extremely lonely. I heard God speak inside my head: "Be still and know that I am God and this too shall pass." I knew it was Him because I don't talk that way. He was right, of course. I trusted Him and peace soon returned to my life.

In another instance, I was going to take my car into a shop to have an air conditioner installed. I heard a voice inside me say, "Don't take it there." At the time I wasn't walking closely with God; I thought it was my imagination. I wish I would have listened to that voice because I ended up getting ripped off and having to take the owners to court. Even after winning the case, I never received any restitution.

In case you are wondering—when I hear God speaking, it is a voice inside my head. I know it is Him because He uses different words than I would use. His loving, authoritative, nature is very evident during the conversation. Sometimes, however, it is like a gentle, whisper. There are other times when the Holy Spirit is revealing something to me, which is manifested as this deep knowing inside of me, and nothing has the power to convince me otherwise. There are no doubts and total peace comes with this knowing.

Sometimes God speaks to us through unanswered prayers. God's answer was no when I tried to publish a book I wrote over a decade ago. This is actually the third rewriting of that book. I had written the first version over ten years ago, with most of the focus on my past, but with sections that highlighted God's healing love. I received many positive comments from publishers, but those came in the context of rejection letters. The second time I tried to write it, I included more about God, but the focus was still my past. There was also quite of bit of information about the enemy and how he operates. I finally realized God wanted me to leave most of the negativity out and focus on Him in order to let others gain clarity about His loving nature and His plans for His children.

God will also speak to you in visions. Once I asked God what the mansion He has prepared for me looks like. Immediately, this wonderful picture popped into my head. I was standing in the middle of a big, Grecian-style home. The floors were polished marble. One of the walls was made of a series of continuous French doors that were opened. Sheer curtains were pushed back from the doors and flowed gently in the breeze. Past the doors, the mansion was surrounded by a marble patio, which was encompassed by a marble banister. As far as I could see beyond the patio was a manicured lawn that was bordered by very tall, slender evergreen trees. I couldn't have planned it better myself. You may be thinking it was merely my imagination, but it was too real. It was as though as I was there. My imagination never creates the details I experienced in this vision. It was wonderful and I can't wait to get there! Oh, how He loves us! He suffered on that cross, and now He is busy preparing a beautiful place for His faithful children to live. As the scripture tells us: "***In my Father's house are many mansions: if it were not so, I would have told you. I go to prepare a place for you***" (John 14:2, KJV, emphasis added).

I have heard more than one person say that they don't need a mansion; a small home is fine with them. I think many of us have been conditioned to believe that being materially blessed is wrong. I believe just the opposite. I am a child of the King. I have royal blood pumping through my veins and so do you! We were born to be prosperous. Our real home, Heaven, is made of opulent materials. The Word says so. Our Heavenly Father wants to bless us when we go Home. He has prepared wonderful homes for all of His faithful children.

Once when I was praying, I was totally filled with love for God. I began to tell Him how much I loved Him. My eyes were closed. Suddenly, in my mind's eye, two celestial beings appeared. They were identical and were dressed in matching white robes. They were surrounded by the whitest light. It was like nothing I had ever seen before. Their hair was like spun threads of iridescent silver. They were both smiling at me. Mere words cannot express the intense joy and love I felt at that moment. I thought at first it was my imagination, so I opened my eyes and looked around the room. When I closed my eyes, they were waiting for me with the same loving smiles upon their faces. That was over twenty years ago, but I remember it as if it were yesterday. I believe that vision was God's way of saying, "I love you too!"

As the scripture tells us, *"**And it shall come to pass in the last days, saith God, I will pour out of my Spirit upon all flesh: and your sons and your daughters shall prophesy, and your young men shall see visions, and your old men shall dream**"* (Acts 2:17, KJV, emphasis added). I definitely felt His Spirit was poured upon me that night. I felt as though I could fly, like I wanted to go on the mountaintop and shout to the world our love for each other. Jesus has told us in the Beatitudes, "Blessed are the pure in heart: for they shall see God" (Matthew 5:8, KJV). I know I had this vision because of the pure love that was in my heart for my Heavenly Father. I believe these two beings may have been Jesus and God. Jesus said the pure in heart shall see God. My heart was never as pure as it was at that moment. The two beings were identical. Jesus said, "…he that hath seen me hath seen the Father…" (John 14:9, KJV, emphasis added).

Now, I also know the Bible states no man can look upon God's glory and live. Moses had to hide in the cleft of a rock and see God's glory as He passed by. But I was not actually in God's physical presence. This was a vision in my mind's eye, so perhaps the two celestial beings were representations of God and Jesus. I know Jesus has been depicted with brown hair, olive skin, etc., which is the way we visualize Him in human form. Perhaps in His pure celestial form, He does look like the vision I saw. In Revelation 22:4, we are told we shall see His face. Whoever they were, it was the most wonderful experience I have ever had, and they were beautiful inside and out—beyond description! I know when I get to Heaven I will never want to leave their side!

I feel strongly God showed himself to me that night so I could share it with you at this very moment. What better way is there to testify for Him than such a glorious vision of Him and His Son? What better way is there to draw you closer to Him? I can definitely and honestly declare without the smallest of doubts I have only experienced love such as that one other time. It occurred as I was writing about God's love in the second chapter of this book. His love defies description. As sure as I write these words, I know the Father and the Son love us light years beyond what we can begin to imagine. It is amazing, awesome, and exalting!

In addition to visions, another way God will communicate with you is through dreams. He actually tells us this in the following verse:

"In a dream, in a vision of the night, When deep sleep falls upon men, While slumbering on their beds, Then He opens the ears of men, And seals their instruction" (Job 33:15-16, KJV).

However, it is important that you never rely solely on your dreams for guidance. If God speaks, He will speak again and confirm that the message is coming from Him. "Dreams are important pieces to the puzzle, but not the only pieces."[12]

Dreams that have the messages repeated or recurring dreams about something means the message from the dream has been established. This is what happened in the story of Joseph, who interpreted a dream for pharaoh in the book of Genesis:

"And it came to pass at the end of two full years, that Pharaoh dreamed: and, behold, he stood by the river. And, behold, there came up out of the river seven well favoured kine and fat fleshed; and they fed in a meadow. And, behold, seven other kine came up after them out of the river, ill favoured and lean fleshed; and stood by the other kine upon the brink of the river. And the ill favoured and lean fleshed kine did eat up the seven well favoured and fat kine. So Pharaoh awoke. And he slept and dreamed the second time: and, behold, seven ears of corn came up upon one stalk, rank and good. And, behold, seven thin ears and blasted

12 Thomas, Benny. *Exploring the World of Dreams*. Springdale: Whitaker House, 1990:66-69.

with the east wind sprung up after them. And the seven thin ears devoured the seven rank and full ears. And Pharaoh awoke, and, behold, it was a dream." (Genesis 41:1-7, KJV).

"And Joseph said unto Pharaoh, The dream of Pharaoh is one: God hath shewed Pharaoh what he is about to do. The seven good kine are seven years; and the seven good ears are seven years: the dream is one. And the seven thin and ill favoured kine that came up after them are seven years; and the seven empty ears blasted with the east wind shall be seven years of famine. This is the thing which I have spoken unto Pharaoh: What God is about to do he sheweth unto Pharaoh. Behold, there come seven years of great plenty throughout all the land of Egypt: And there shall arise after them seven years of famine; and all the plenty shall be forgotten in the land of Egypt; and the famine shall consume the land; And the plenty shall not be known in the land by reason of that famine following; for it shall be very grievous. And for that *the dream was doubled unto Pharaoh twice; it is because the thing is established by God, and God will shortly bring it to pass*" (Genesis 41:25-32, KJV, emphasis added).

As you can see, Pharaoh's dreams had recurring symbols of seven, and the dream was repeated twice. This is how Joseph knew God was about to do something and it would be established. If you read a little further in the book of Genesis, you will find there were indeed seven years of plenty followed by seven years of famine.

Prior to the death of my late husband, I had recurring dreams he would leave me for a younger woman. This went on for several years. Following his death, the dreams suddenly stopped, and I realized God had been trying to warn me. My husband did leave me for a younger woman. Upon his death, he was reunited with his late wife in Heaven. She had been younger than me when she died.

I have been studying my dreams for over fifteen years. I keep a tape recorder by my bed. As soon as God wakes me up, which I believe He does after a dream so I won't forget them, I record what I can remember while it is still fresh. The other morning, I woke up coughing because of a tickle in my throat. As soon as I woke up, I remembered my dream.

Most dreams include different sections or topics, which is the way I write them down after listening to the recording. It is important to remember God speaks to you in symbols that mean something to you. For example, a storm may mean a difficult time or a dog may represent a friend or some type of protection. Dreams that seem to jump around or that have poor clarity in the details are not usually from God since He is not the author of confusion (1 Corinthians 14:33).

I believe God uses dreams to give us direction when we're going down the wrong path or when we're uncertain of the road to take. He also gives us dreams about things we may need to work on or let go of. Dreams from God can also serve as a warning. For example, there was a time in my life when I was thinking about getting back together with my ex-husband as he had claimed a new life, which included abstinence from alcohol. This was a time in my life when I didn't have a close relationship with my Heavenly Father, and I was extremely afraid of loneliness. I dreaded the thought of being alone. So, when my ex-husband told me he had quit drinking, I really wanted to believe him. We were living about fifteen hundred miles apart at that time, so we began a relationship over the phone. One day, I was expecting his call, but never received it. I waited all day by the phone. I was somewhat put out by this because it was a gorgeous day, and I had wasted it indoors. That night I dreamed my ex-husband was getting drunk. The next day, he called, and he let it slip he'd been getting drunk at the very time I was dreaming about it. I thanked God as I received His time-sensitive warning, which helped me avoid disaster.

Sometimes God gives me dreams to teach me something. One day, I was watching a sermon about grace on television. Some of the concepts were somewhat new to me so God gave me a message in a dream to confirm what I was learning was the truth. That night I went to bed and dreamed I was telling a friend from my youth (she represented my past sins), about the concept of grace versus the law. She wrote it down in some type of reference book she had. Later, I looked in her book and saw three scriptures that were written down. I looked up the scriptures when I woke up, which was the central message of the dream. In 1 Timothy 1:9, Paul writes about the law being given to those who are extremely disobedient: for the ungodly and the sinners. It was never intended for the righteous man. God's grace is for the righteous man: the man who has a pure heart and desires to repent, but is still affected by sin because of Adam and Eve's legacy of sin.

As you can see, God will speak to you in a variety of ways. Just yesterday morning I was driving down the highway. One of my favorite gospel songs came on the radio and I became overwhelmed with His presence. As I put my hand up to worship God, a tanker truck drove by. On the side of the truck was the word "Grace" written in huge black letters. How often do you see that on an eighteen-wheeler? *Never!* I knew God was answering my prayer concerning a situation I was facing. This was His way of telling me He is always watching over me. *He truly amazes me with all the different ways He breaks through this thick skull of mine!*

Last, but certainly not least, is prayer. This says it all: "…The effectual fervent prayer of a righteous man availeth much" (James 5:16, KJV). One day I was praying a very heartfelt prayer. I was wracked with emotion and cried out to God. He replied with this scripture concerning fervent prayer. I knew it was God because it was not a scripture I had committed to memory, although I was somewhat familiar with it. I looked it up and discovered He left out the word "effectual." When I pondered this fact, I realized I was already praying effectually because I prayed the scriptures while reminding Him of His great promises. What was missing was the fervency. *Fervent* is defined as follows: moved by or showing great warmth or intensity, as of emotion or enthusiasm.[13] *Fervent prayer is crying out to God from the depths of your soul.*

---

13 Landau, Sidney, et al. Funk and Wagnalls Standard Desk Dictionary. Lippincott and Crowell, 1980:235

Think of it this way—how can you connect with God if you can't connect with your own heart and soul? We are triune beings, just as our Father is. Our soul, body, and spirit are connected. If we are disconnected from parts of ourselves, then we can't connect to Him. After all, it is our spirit that communicates with His. So, before you pray, search the depths of your heart and soul and allow your spirit to fill with passion for your petition to the Father.

I learned this concept directly from conversations I had with God. Immediately before He spoke to me through the scripture concerning fervency, I heard Him say, "You have not because you ask not." I replied I didn't understand, as I had repeatedly asked Him for the same thing, and I couldn't understand why He wasn't answering my prayer. I was praying according to His will. Then He replied with the scripture about fervency. He told me because I had prayed fervently during this particular prayer, it would be answered. He said I always need to pray with a pure heart. He said that is what He meant by, *"Blessed are the pure in heart: for they shall see God"* (Matthew 5:8, KJV, emphasis added). He *will show up in your life*, when you pray effectually and fervently. Prayers *will* be answered and *His presence* will be manifested in your life just as His presence was manifested in the vision I had of the two celestial beings as I prayed fervently to express my love for Him. This is the only true way to ask; it is the most effective way to pray. Your whole being, including your mind; will; thoughts; and emotions has to be focused on the issue for which you are praying. Remember He has promised *"that whatsoever ye shall ask of the Father in my name, he may give it you"* (John 15:16, KJV, emphasis added). This is true if you are praying according to His will. So, get your Bible and find out what He wants for your life. It is all good things, and remember…tap into your purpose. This will develop a deeper intimacy with your Heavenly Father, which will enable you to know His loving nature.

FOCUS ON HIS LOVE FOR YOU

Jesus prayed the most beautiful prayer before His crucifixion. I weep when I read it because I can feel *just how much He truly loves us all.* His heartfelt prayer speaks of unity. He is not only praying for His twelve original disciples, but all those who believe in Him. *You can feel the sincerity of His desire for us to be sanctified and protected from the evil in this world.* It is very healing when I read it in times of trouble. It brings immediate relief and comfort to me. Try reading it out loud. It will touch the depths of your heart and soul:

> "Father, the hour has come. Glorify your Son, that your Son may glorify you. For you granted him authority over all people that he might give eternal life to all those you have given him. Now this is eternal life: that they know you, the only true God, and Jesus Christ, whom you have sent. I have brought you glory on earth by finishing the work you gave me to do. And now, Father, glorify me in your presence with the glory I had with you before the world began."

Jesus Prays for His Disciples

> "I have revealed you to those whom you gave me out of the world. They were yours; you gave them to me and they have obeyed your word. Now they know that everything you have given me comes from you. For I gave them the words you gave me and they accepted them. They knew with certainty that I came from you, and they believed that you sent me. I pray for them. I am not praying for the world, but for those you have given me, for they are yours. All I have is yours, and all you have is mine. And glory has come to me through them. I will remain in the world no longer, but they are still in the world, and I am coming to you. Holy Father, protect them by the power of your name, the name you gave me, so that they may be one as we are one. While I was with them, I protected them and kept them safe by that name you gave me.

None has been lost except the one doomed to destruction so that Scripture would be fulfilled."

"I am coming to you now, but I say these things while I am still in the world, so that they may have the full measure of my joy within them. I have given them your word and the world has hated them, for they are not of the world any more than I am of the world. My prayer is not that you take them out of the world but that you protect them from the evil one. They are not of the world, even as I am not of it. Sanctify them by the truth; your word is truth. As you sent me into the world, I have sent them into the world. For them I sanctify myself, that they too may be truly sanctified."

Jesus Prays for All Believers

"My prayer is not for them alone. I pray also for those who will believe in me through their message, that all of them may be one, Father, just as you are in me and I am in you. May they also be in us so that the world may believe that you have sent me. I have given them the glory that you gave me, that they may be one as we are one— I in them and you in me—so that they may be brought to complete unity. Then the world will know that you sent me and have loved them even as you have loved me."

"Father, I want those you have given me *to be with me where I am, and to see my glory, the glory you have given me because you loved me* before the creation of the world."

"Righteous Father, though the world does not know you, I know you, and they know that you have sent me. I have made you known to them, and will continue to make you known in order that the *love you have for me may be in them and that I myself may be in them*" (John 17, NIV, emphasis added).

Can you feel how much you are loved after reading Jesus' sincere prayer for you? It is His love that changes you. You can't change yourself, but He can and will. So when trouble comes, or you are expecting something from Him, don't focus on your problem or all the good works you have done. Instead, focus on His love for you. *It is because of who He is, not who you are or what you have done or haven't done, which results in the blessing upon your life as His child.* He loves you beyond measure and wants to bless you for eternity. Believe it, know it, and get it firmly planted as the seed drops from your mind into the fertile ground of your heart, which is your transformation center—then His grace will flow like a tidal wave into your life. Magnify His love, and His love will forever surround you like the Universe surrounds the Milky Way.

When you get a true revelation of the depth, the breadth, and the height of His love, you will be like the eagle. You will soar on a current, floating, higher and higher above all the turbulence of this world. Nothing will touch you. You will be like a phoenix rising out of the ashes.

Please visit the following website: FathersLoveLetter.com. Read this love letter out loud. You will be overwhelmed by the Father's love for you.

CHAPTER THREE

OVERCOMING OBSTACLES

FEAR

The following scriptures instruct us on the truth concerning fear:

> "For God hath not given us the spirit of fear; but of power, and of love, and of a sound mind" (2 Timothy 1:7, KJV).

> "***...but perfect love casteth out fear***" (John 4:18, KJV, emphasis added).

When you know who you are in Christ and you are loved infinitely by your Heavenly Father, you can conquer anything. You need to rebuke the spirit of fear and claim you only need God's approval. He is the one guiding, directing and providing for you, not man. Don't allow fear to rule your life. When you do, the enemy gets a stronghold on you. It opens up the door for him and his legion of warrior enemies to wreak havoc on your life. *Fear is the opposite of love.* God operates from love—the enemy operates from fear. The enemy will sneak up on you with some subtle suggestion of insecurity, failure, lack, etc. If you dwell upon it, it will snowball out of control, and you definitely won't be living the blessed life. *Remember all of the things God has done for you in the past.* When fear tries to come into my head, I start reviewing every single time God protected me. The fear immediately leaves when I do this. Some of you may be thinking God has never done a single thing for you. Ask God to reveal it to you. If you look back, His divine intervention will become evident.

When you are living in fear, you are not trusting God. The Word instructs us:

> **"Trust in the LORD with all thine heart; and lean not unto thine own understanding. In all thy ways acknowledge him, and he shall direct thy paths"** (Proverbs 3:5-6, KJV, emphasis added).

When the fear creeps in, cast it down. Rebuke the thought in the name of Jesus and keep looking up. Otherwise, you will be looking down and soon find yourself in a deep abyss: a place you don't want to be.

Fear is a dense negative emotion and prevents you from receiving God's blessing. God has revealed this concept to me through prayer. It is as though your receiver is malfunctioning. It is unable to catch the positive charges of God's light and energy. Bind up the enemy, throw him into the pit of hell, and burn him up because he has no authority over you! Do it every morning before your feet hit the floor: "**Behold, I give unto you power to tread on serpents and scorpions, and over all the power of the enemy: and nothing shall by any means hurt you**" (Luke 10:19, KJV, emphasis added). This is my favorite warrior scripture—and it works! I feel the power when I speak it. Declare your right as Christian with the following truth: "I call for the the power of the Holy Spirit, the same power that raised Christ from the dead to squash the enemy and eliminate all his devices!" *Use the power of the tongue and put on the whole armor of God.*

That old saying, "There is nothing to fear, but fear itself" is the absolute truth. The things I fear never manifest; it's all wasted energy for nothing. Have you ever noticed how much energy it takes when you worry about something? It totally wipes you out.

I love the Sermon on the Mount. Jesus spoke some beautiful words that are filled with the most excellent advice for living a fearless life:

> "Therefore I say unto you, Take no thought for your life, what ye shall eat, or what ye shall drink; nor yet for your body, what ye shall put on. Is not the life more than meat, and the body than raiment? Behold the fowls of the air: for they sow not, neither do they reap, nor gather into barns; yet your heavenly Father feedeth them. Are ye not much better than they? Which of you by taking thought can add one cubit unto his stature? And why take ye thought for raiment? Consider the lilies of the field, how they grow; they toil not, neither do they spin: And yet I say unto you, That even Solomon in all his glory was not arrayed like one of these. Wherefore, if God so clothe the grass of the field, which to day is, and to morrow is cast into the oven, shall he not much more clothe you, O ye of little faith? Therefore take no thought, ***saying,*** What shall we eat? or, What shall we drink? or, Wherewithal shall we be clothed? (For after all these things do the Gentiles seek:) for your heavenly Father knoweth that ye have need of all these things. But seek ye first the kingdom of God, and his righteousness; and all these things shall be added unto you. Take therefore no thought for the morrow: for the morrow shall take thought for the things of itself. Sufficient unto the day is the evil thereof" (Matthew 6:25-34, KJV, emphasis added).

It is obvious from the scriptures above that if God takes care of the animals and plants in this world, He surely will take care of His beloved children, who He has ordained for specific purposes. As the scripture tells us, "...I know whom I have believed, and am persuaded that he is able to keep that which I have committed unto him against that day" (2 Timothy 1:12, KJV).

Rest in Him, and let it all go! Have faith He will answer your prayers and trust in the Lord. He came to this Earth and made the great sacrifice because of His immense love for you. He told us so with His own lips. There are no limits on what He will do for you. Believe this truth and *your ever-increasing faith will crush the fear!*

PROTECTION

The following verse may sound frightening, but when you know who you are in Christ and trust God with all your heart, you will have a deep revelation of the intense protection that surrounds you like a shield: God warns us to be careful: "Be sober, **be vigilant**; because your adversary the devil, as a roaring lion, walketh about, seeking whom he may devour" (1 Peter 5:8, KJV, emphasis added). God wants you to be careful by guarding your heart, which is your faith center. The measure of faith God has placed in you will comfort you as your belief in His great concern for you provides ultimate protection. Your faith in Him and His victory on the cross will overcome any of the enemy's strategies. Jesus destroyed all the evil forces, which gives us authority over the enemy when we implement the strategies of spiritual warfare.

In Ephesians, Paul instructs us to put on the whole armor of God to protect ourselves against the principality of darkness:

> "Finally, my brethren, be strong in the Lord, and in the power of his might. Put on the whole armour of God, that ye may be able to stand against the wiles of the devil. For we wrestle not against flesh and blood, but against principalities, against powers, against the rulers of the darkness of this world, against spiritual wickedness in high places. Wherefore take unto you the whole armour of God, that ye may be able to withstand in the evil day, and having done all, to stand. Stand therefore, having your loins girt about with truth, and having on the breastplate of righteousness; And your feet shod with the preparation of the gospel of peace; Above all, taking the shield

of faith, wherewith ye shall be able to quench all the fiery darts of the wicked. And take the helmet of salvation, and the sword of the Spirit, which is the word of God: Praying always with all prayer and supplication in the Spirit, and watching thereunto with all perseverance and supplication for all saints" (Ephesians 6:10-18, KJV).

Paul is telling us to stand firm in the truth of God's Word so we won't fall victim of the enemy's lies. When you put on the helmet of salvation, you protect your mind by thinking God's thoughts. Wearing the helmet of salvation means we keep our minds focused on God and our Lord and Savior, Jesus Christ. If we keep our sight on the eternal prize of Heaven and living with our sweet Abba Father for eternity in the mansion He has already built for us, then our minds are not an open battlefield for the enemy. *Our minds will always be filled with something.* Which would you rather have? You can choose thoughts the enemy plants, which will allow him to gain a foothold and cause havoc and destruction in your life, or you can choose thoughts of eternal divinity. *You have the power to cast down all thoughts that are not of God and replace them with His Word.* In fact, the Apostle Paul tells us to do just that:

> "(For the weapons of our warfare are not carnal, but mighty through God to the pulling down of strong holds;). Casting down imaginations, and every high thing that exalteth itself against the knowledge of God, and bringing into captivity every thought to the obedience of Christ;" (2 Corinthians 10:4-5, KJV).

You can't control thoughts that pop into your head, but you can control what you choose to dwell upon. Cast down the negative and replace it with God's Word. Paul also instructs us with the following: "And be not **conformed** to this world: but be ye **transformed** by the **renewing** of your mind, that ye may prove what is that good, and acceptable, and perfect, will of God" (Romans 12:2, KJV, emphasis added). Look at the word "renewing." He doesn't say renew or renewed, but *renewing*, which implies *this is an ongoing process.* So, stay strong while remaining in the Word. Saturate yourself in the Word as often as possible, and you will defeat the strategy of the enemy. Remember, he doesn't have anything on you. He will, however, try as he might, to control you. He uses subtle strategies that can include playing the old programs in your head of poor self-worth, having regrets, or living in the past. You can recognize his strategies by lining up your thoughts and feelings with The Word. If it doesn't line up, you can bet he is doing his dirty, rotten work.

We all experience those negative thoughts in our heads: I am not good enough; I can't do it; He doesn't love me; I'll never get that job or promotion, etc. *If we are walking with God and truly know who we are in Christ, we believe what the Word says about us.*

Do you know what the Word says about you? I will repeat it:

> You can do **all** things through Christ who strengthens you (Phillipians 4:13).

> You are the head and not the tail. You are above and not below (Deuteronomy 28:13).

> You are like a tree planted by the **rivers** of water, that brings forth your fruit in your season; your leaf will **never wither**; and **whatsoever** you do will prosper (Psalms 1:3).

And that's just for starters. God thinks of you as His treasure, so start treasuring yourself!

David wrote the most inspiring Psalm about God's protection. Make it part of your daily profession:

> "I will say of the LORD, He is my refuge and my fortress: my God; in him will I trust" (Psalms 91:2, KJV)

Paul also instructs to put on the breastplate of righteousness. It will guard your heart from the enemy's worldly influence and keep you pure and holy. When you are in God's presence, you stand in righteousness and the enemy can't touch you! Furthermore, when you seek His presence, temptation and sin will be far from your mind, so it's a win-win situation. Believe you are the righteousness of God through the faith of Jesus Christ (1 Corinthians 1:30). When this truth becomes alive in your spirit, you will become the great warrior that God created you to be. You will stand tall and gird your loins from all evil influences. The world will see your strength and the enemy will flee from your presence. You will be like a shadow of our Almighty Defender, The Great El Gibbor.

We are also told to put on the shoes of peace. This will provide a pathway to protection from the enemy. It is like having an invisible shield around you. If you encounter negativity of any kind during the day, you will respond to it in a positive way—with love, patience, wisdom, understanding, and compassion. On the flip side, if you begin your day in a state of anxiety, and something bad comes your way, you probably will react in a negative way—perhaps with anger, frustration, impatience, etc. This will open the door for more problems, which could create a snowball effect. Therefore, putting on peace will protect you from the enemy's strategies by shifting the atmosphere so you will avoid conflict.

In addition to wearing the shoes of peace, you have to hold up the shield of faith. This will enable you to walk in the Spirit and believe what God says about Himself and you. Not only do you have to believe it, but you need to put it into action. So when the enemy throws a fiery dart of doubt, denial, and/or deceit, put up your shield, and the dart will bounce right off. You may be wondering, "What do you mean by putting up a shield?" First, you visualize holding the shield and seeing the darts bounce off as you speak God's words aloud. Start every recitation with, "The Scriptures say…" This is what Jesus did in the wilderness when the enemy tempted Him. Some of the things you might say could include:

"I am a child of God. I am His special treasure. I belong to Him, not you! I rebuke you by the blood of Jesus Christ. I have been given the authority over all the power of the enemy so that I can tread upon serpents and scorpions and crush them underneath my feet. Nothing can in any way ever hurt, injure, or harm me."

When you say this and call Jesus' name, the enemy tucks his little scrawny tail in and scurries off. That's because the enemy has no power over Jesus or any of those who belong to Him. Now, to those who are not living under God's protective hand, the enemy may look like some fierce demon and the scariest creature known to man, but for a Christian, he is nothing when you have Jesus on your side. That is how you need to see him—as nothing. *He has no power over you, so demand he leave.*

Paul also tells us to fight the enemy with the two-edged sword. The sword is God's Word. Find scriptures that relate to your issue, and start speaking them out loud. The best strategy is to have scriptures memorized that apply to particular problems or issues. This way, you'll be ready when the enemy comes against you. Then you can pull the sword out immediately and make him flee. Remember, God promises: **"*For I the LORD thy God will hold thy right hand, saying unto thee, Fear not; I will help thee*"** (Isaiah 41:13, KJV, emphasis added).

Paul also instructs us to stand firm. That means to stand on God's Word by having strong faith and believing what God says. Believe you will be victorious in all things because that is what God created you to do. Believe "... ***the battle is not yours, but God's***" (2 Chronicles 20:15, KJV, emphasis added). All you have to do is rest after you have applied the principles mentioned above, and God *will* take care of everything else, as that is what He has promised us. Because God only speaks the truth, you can rest assured He will deliver on all of His promises.

Finally, Paul instructs us to pray: "Praying always with all prayer and supplication in the Spirit, and watching thereunto with all perseverance and supplication for all saints" (Ephesians 6:18, KJV). Always be mindful, *when we pray, our High Priest, Jesus Christ, acts as our advocate and keeps us in communication with our Father.* Not only are we instructed to pray for ourselves, but God instructs us to pray for others, especially those who can't or don't pray for themselves. Pray for them to be covered with the blood of Jesus Christ and to be surrounded with an encampment of angels. Pray God will send other Christians into their lives and their hearts will be opened to receive Jesus as their Lord and Savior and they will have an intimate relationship with Him.

Paul tells us to *always pray.* This means to stay in an attitude of prayer. Have God in the forefront of every thought. This will enable you to offer Him thanks, praise, and acknowledgement of His awesomeness, provision, and blessing upon your life.

I frequently pray for non-believers that God will send a big, beautiful angel who will manifest its presence to him or her so that person will no longer doubt the existence of God. When you see a twenty foot angel standing in front of you, how could you doubt any longer? You can also pray for others that their wills and minds will be aligned with God's. *Pray they will come to know how much God truly loves them.* If they are already saved, pray they will remain strong in Christ and will be a soul winner for Him.

Always put on the whole armor of God first thing in the morning by making these declarations:

> "I put on the breast plate of righteousness. I will stand upright and dwell in God's presence and no good thing will be withheld from me. I am the righteousness of God through the blood of Jesus Christ so there is no condemnation in me. I put on the girdle of truth so I won't be a victim to the enemy's lies. I put on the helmet of salvation so he can't enter my thoughts. I put up my shield of faith so the fiery darts of the enemy will bounce right off. I carry my two-edged sword. I'm a verbal partner with God. I speak His word. It is stronger than any weapon of mass destruction and is a catalyst for the most powerful, creative construction. I put on the shoes of peace. Wherever I go, I will shift the atmosphere and allow God's divine light to shine bright which will destroy all darkness and usher in the Holy Spirit."

TRIALS AND TRIBULATIONS

"These things I have spoken unto you, that in me ye might have peace. In the world ye shall have tribulation: but be of good cheer; I have overcome the world" (John 16:33, KJV, emphasis added). So can you. Jesus is telling us to model after Him. You will be *more than a conqueror in Christ.* The Holy Spirit will provide you with strength, courage, and great faith to be victorious in all situations.

When you accept Jesus as your Savior, He can save you from all things. Just claim it with thanksgiving and expect it to happen. Perhaps you have some type of family or financial struggle. The fact is you may be in a pit, but the truth is you are seated in heavenly places with Christ (Ephesians 2:6). Ask God to pull you out and lift you up to the place where you are in Christ. Sometimes, our greatest trials bring God the greatest glory, and bring us into His perfect will, which become our greatest moments. Jesus refers to this in the following scriptures:

> "Neither this man nor his parents sinned," said Jesus, "but this happened so that the **works of God might be displayed in him**. After saying this, he spit on the ground, made some mud with the saliva, and put it on the man's eyes. "Go," he told him, "wash in the Pool of Siloam" (this word means "Sent"). So the man went and washed, and came home seeing. (John 9:3, 6-7, NIV, emphasis added).

> "Now my soul is troubled, and what shall I say? 'Father, save me from this hour'? No, it was **for this very reason** I came to this hour. Father, glorify your name!" Then a voice came from heaven, "I have glorified it, and will glorify it again" (John 12:27-28, NIV, emphasis added).

Whenever you are going through a trial, instead of looking at the circumstances, focus on how you may bring glory to God and win souls for Him by being victorious. When you obtain this mindset, you will move through your trial more quickly and smoothly.

As I mentioned earlier, when I received Jesus as my Savior, He delivered me from a life-long battle of obesity, which began at the age of five and ended at age fifty-three. I always give God the glory. Whenever people ask me about it, I tell them God did it all. I couldn't do it. All the expensive diets, doctors, and men in the world couldn't rescue me from this terrible prison I had built around myself—but God could and did! So, the obesity set me up for a manifestation of God's glory, which is illustrated by the following verse: "And call upon me in the day of trouble: I will deliver thee, and thou shalt glorify me" (Psalms 50:15, KJV).

Have you been going around the same mountain, just like the Israelites did for forty years after God delivered them out of Egyptian slavery? He was bringing them to the Promised Land, and all they did was murmur and complain. He created numerous miracles for their protection and needs: He parted the Red Sea during their escape; He made food rain down from the sky and water pour out of a rock when they were in the desert; they wore the same shoes for forty years without wearing them out! *He never left their side:*

> "And the Lord went before them by day in a pillar of a cloud, *to lead them the way*; and by night in a pillar of fire, *to give them light*; to go by day and night: *He took not away* the pillar of the cloud by day, nor the pillar of fire by night, from before the people" (Exodus 13:21-22, KJV, emphasis added).

He promises to be with us in every situation:

> "But now thus saith the Lord that created thee, O Jacob, and he that formed thee, O Israel, *Fear not: for I have redeemed thee, I have called thee by thy name; thou art mine*. When thou passest through the waters, *I will be with thee*; and through the rivers, they shall not overflow thee: *when thou walkest through the fire, thou shalt not be burned*; neither shall the flame kindle upon thee. For I am the Lord thy God, the Holy One of Israel, thy Saviour: I gave Egypt for thy ransom, Ethiopia and Seba for thee" (Isaiah 43:1-3, KJV, emphasis added).

I am overwhelmed by the revelation of God's love as I write this. No matter what trial we are going through, *He never, ever leaves us.* You may think He has, but if you just look up, you will find Him; He is always there leading, guiding, and protecting you. The Israelites only needed to keep their eyes focused on God instead of complaining. He was supplying all their needs. This is His great promise: "***he will be with thee, he will not fail thee, neither forsake thee: fear not, neither be dismayed***" (Deuteronomy 31:8, KJV, emphasis added). This promise is repeated in Isaiah 41:10, Matthew 28:30, and Hebrews 13:5. I have found whenever I *really* need Him; there He is with a timely message of inspiration, guidance or deliverance. I recently experienced some fear, and I was reminded of the scripture, "...My grace is sufficient for thee, for my strength is made perfect in weakness" (2 Corinthians 12:9, KJV). Those words, which I regularly meditate upon now, are extremely powerful. *Whenever* the enemy comes at me with negativity, I simply claim this truth, which has become part of me, and the fear vanishes.

God wants to bless us, just like He wanted to bless the Israelites, but as previously mentioned, His blessings can't flow when we are blocked with negative emotions. Science has proven our bodies work from an intricate system of electricity with positive and negative charges, which create an electromagnetic field around us.[14] The Holy Spirit has revealed to me when this gets out of balance and is negatively charged, it blocks the flow of blessings to us. From a *physiological* perspective, the human body can't handle extreme shifts in energy. This is a fact that can best be illustrated in severe diabetic cases where the patient has excessive elevations in blood sugar levels. The attending physician has to slowly bring the blood sugar levels down to avoid rapid electrolyte shifts, which could result in cerebral edema from massive fluid shifts.[15]

---

14 Rubick, Beverly, Phd, "Measurement of the Human Biofield and Other Energetic Instruments." Foundation for Alternative and Integrative Medicine. Foundation for Alernative and Integrative Medicine.org. 06 June 2013. <http://www.faim.org>.

15 Mensing, Carole, et al. "Hyperglycemia". *The Art and Science of Diabetes Self-Management Education.* Chicago, Ill: American Association of Diabetic Educators, 2006:173.

I believe a rapid shift of electrical charges in our spiritual and emotional body would be just as detrimental. It seems evident this is the reason God instructed the Levitical priests in the correct ritual of exiting His presence from the inner sanctuary:

> "When they return to the *outer* courtyard where the people are, they must take off the clothes they wear while ministering to me. They must leave them in the sacred rooms and put on other clothes so they do not *endanger anyone by transmitting holiness to them* through this clothing" (Ezekiel 44:19, NLT, emphasis added).

The holiness of God is certainly all positive energy, which is beyond our comprehension because of His vast power and incomprehensible love. Some commentators interpret the aforementioned scripture to mean that it serves as a reminder that no one can enter God's presence through their own goodness.[16] On a deeper level, I believe the wording supports the concept that people who are "negatively charged" would be endangered by rapid energy shifts. This concept is further supported in the book of Leviticus. It's written that Aaron's two sons died after they approached the Lord while they were intoxicated, which made them ceremonially *unclean.* Following this tragedy, God instructed the Levitical priests about the danger of death upon and the proper preparation before entrance into the Holy of Holies.

It is a scientific fact that when positive energy meets negative energy, there is a huge surge of electricity. This can be illustrated when battery cables are incorrectly connected to positive and negative terminals, which could result in an explosion. These laws of electrical properties lead me to conclude that we have to *prepare ourselves, just as the priests had to prepare themselves, to receive the positive energy from God's grace by switching from a negative to a positive state.* Otherwise His energy would destroy us. God certainly wouldn't transfer anything to us if He knew it would result in destruction.

---

16 Henry, Matthew. "Concise Commentary. Online Parallel Commentaries." Bible Hub. <biblehub.com>. 27 June 2013.

Furthermore, the scripture in Ezekiel makes reference to the people in the *outer* courtyard being endanger of His holiness from the clothes worn by the priests. This portion of the scripture reveals two things: people who don't have an *intimate* relationship with God have not been transformed into a more positive state by His loving energy. It also alludes to the characteristic of the intensity of His power. Just being near His loving energy or near those who have been transformed by Him, has the power to transform you. Additionally, the intensity of His power has to be incrementally administered to us. I know this is true because I had to repeatedly ask to be filled with the Holy Spirit after rededicating myself to Him. This filling didn't occur all at once, but was given to me over a period of time. Moreover, His divine energy in us is only a small measure of the Godhead. There is no way our flesh could contain the vastness of His power.

God is there waiting to release the blessings He has already provided for you (Ephesians 1:3). Let His love and grace flow by being an open channel to His blessings. You can accomplish this by focusing on His love for you and your love for Him and others, which will facilitate letting go of negativity.

In essence, *it is our choice to lead a blessed life.* We can flip the switch to positive and allow God's blessing to flow, or we can stay in the negative mode, and close the door to God's grace while we continue to live in torment for most of our lives. The way to be positive is quit complaining; speak to the situation, not about it; renew your mind with His Word; and, most of all look up. *He is there waiting for you to praise Him even in the tough times. That's when you will really feel His presence. When you do this, you will move through your trial much quicker and His grace will flow in your life.*

Sometimes we get the same lesson over and over and over again, especially when we complain and murmur like the Israelites did. It might come wrapped in a different package, but nevertheless, the core concept still remains. *If we could just realize if we conquer the problem early on, we wouldn't have to deal with it any longer.* Recognize it for what it is: an opportunity for growth. Tackle it and move on. You will be glad you did. The next time another one comes your way, it will be easier to process it.

When you find yourself in a difficult situation, do the best you can. Speak scriptures related to the issue; pray; stand on God's Word; trust in Him; focus on how you can bring Him glory; lead others to Christ; and do good. *He will do what you can't do while you do what you can.* This is what we are instructed to do from the book of James:

> "Submit yourselves therefore to God. Resist the devil, and ***he will flee*** from you. Draw nigh to God, and he will draw nigh to you. Cleanse your hands, ye sinners; and purify your hearts, ye ***double minded***. Be afflicted, and mourn, and weep: let your laughter be turned to mourning, and your joy to heaviness. Humble yourselves in the sight of the Lord, and he shall lift you up" (James 4:7-10, KJV, emphasis added).

If you are double-minded, this means your words contradict what you believe. You need to always be cautious. Make sure you speak the proper words that will help you overcome the obstacles you are facing.

James is also telling you to receive Jesus so you "***cleanse your hands.***" This closes the door to the enemy's devices. It is Jesus that will help you get through the trials and bring you comfort and strength in times of trouble, which will increase your faith. When you do all that you can possibly do, and pour your heart out to Him; God promises you will have joy and be lifted up on the other side of your trial. This is what Jesus also taught His disciples when they were in the boat during a storm. *Jesus taught them to trust in Him as He calmed the storm.* They were then able to get to the other side of the sea without harm.

Jesus wants us to always trust Him because He will never fail us in any situation. He is our source for every single good thing in this life. When you find yourself in a difficult situation, edify yourself by remembering all the trials God has brought you through before. Remembering all the past times He delivered you really helps you let go of the fear of the current situation. I recently had someone speak a great deal of fear in my life. Some people love to feed off of fear because that is all they have ever known, and it becomes a way of life. It feels comfortable to them. That night when I went to bed, the fear climbed into the bed with me, so I remembered all the wonderful things God had done for me. I reviewed every single thing I could attribute to God's saving grace since childhood. Guess what? When I was finished, so was the fear. It had left the bed and my head. Thank you, Lord!

Please remember when you are in a trial, God is not trying to hurt you. He may not deliver you right away because the difficult situation is going to help you grow in some way and bring Him glory when He delivers you. When others see your blessing, they may be led to Christ. Stop and reflect on that for a moment. Your difficult situation has the ability to save people and glorify your Father in Heaven.

God wants you to remember He always has His hand on you: guiding, protecting, and providing for you. *He has you in His loving hand no matter what.* Remembering how much He loves you in the time of a trial, makes it more bearable. God tells us He has our names written in the palm of His hand: ***"Behold, I have engraved thee upon the palms of my hands…"*** (Isaiah 49:16, KJV, emphasis added). How precious is this? I am reminded of the puppy love of a schoolgirl crush: so in love with the boy in class all she does is constantly think of him. *Our Father loves us immensely—he is so enamored with us He writes our names on His hand!* Think of *that* next time you are going through a trial instead of the situation. Lift up your hands and praise your sweet Abba Father, and you *will* be delivered! *Remember when you praise Him, He shows up!* Remember this scripture during a trial: "Many are the afflictions of the righteous: but the LORD delivereth him out of them ***all***" (Psalms 34:19, KJV, emphasis added).

Please know God is not causing the heartache and suffering in your life; all of those bad things come from the enemy. God may not intervene right away because He will use many different avenues to achieve His purpose and plan for your life and those who you will touch. *He will take all the adversity in your life and somehow make it miraculously fit into the plan He created specifically for you.* I know because He took all of my sorrows and used it for good so I could be living proof of how God can take anyone and turn their life around to be a blessing to others: "***And we know that all things work together for good to them that love God, to them who are the called according to his purpose***" (Romans 8:28, KJV, emphasis added).

The Word also tell us, "Blessed is the man that endureth temptation: for when he is tried, he shall receive the crown of life, which the Lord hath promised to them that love him" (James 1:12, KJV). I know I have the crown of life because in my darkest hour, when I was tempted to fall apart, *I chose to praise God and there He was holding my hand.* When God shows up, the enemy has to flee:

> "***Because thou hast made the Lord, which is my refuge, even the most High, thy habitation; There shall no evil befall thee, neither shall any plague come nigh thy dwelling***" (Psalms 91: 9-10, KJV, emphasis added).

Throughout Scripture we are told God loves to be praised. This was the lifestyle of David. He actually instructed his soul and all that was within him to bless the Lord (Psalms 103:1). David also commissioned an entire praise team to worship the Lord around the clock (1 Chronicles 23:5-6). In contrast, I recently slid back into some old habits. My new habit of filling my home with praise and worship music had ceased due to the fact I had to "dogproof" my home when I brought a new pet. I had to move my speakers out of the living room, so all the worship music came to a grinding halt. I begin to experience some old patterns of terrible anxiety over nothing and everything. My mind was being totally tormented and the food addiction was trying to come back on me. It took a while for me to realize what was going on. The Holy Spirit kept prompting me to put on the music. Initially, I didn't even recognize His voice because I was submerged in negativity. The minute I put the music on and began to praise God, the anxiety left; the tormenting thoughts vanished; and the love of God overwhelmed me. I wept uncontrollably…tears of joy, gratitude, and awe due to my Father's immediate presence. This, in my mind, is definite proof that the spiritual realm exists. We can either co-exist with God through praise, or we can be surrounded by the rulers of darkness, who are under direct orders from the enemy to completely destroy us, which would give him great pleasure.

All of what you just read may seem like a contradiction to what I wrote under the section, entitled, "God is a Protector" in reference to the enemy's attacks increasing after you receive Salvation; but in fact, it actually supports the truth of what I wrote. If you *consistently and immediately use all of the spiritual warfare*, including saturating your environment with praise, then the enemy has no power over you. It is the praise that invites God into your life. This is the key to His presence. *Moreover, the enemy flees in the presence of God so he can no longer attack you because you have the Almighty Commander-in-Chief right by your side!*

When you find yourself in a trial, draw closer to God. He may be using your situation for this very reason. During the terrible trial I suffered after the loss of my husband, I drew extremely close to my Heavenly Father. I knew deep in my spirit He had a great purpose for me, and I trusted His plan would somehow come to pass and would be something extraordinary. I didn't know when or how it would happen, but I truly knew He loved me, and He knew what was best for me. *After all, He created me to love me, and He created you to love you!* It is the same when a parent brings a child into the world. They start planning and saving for his or her future to ensure he or she will be afforded every opportunity available to him or her. Adversity, while you are experiencing it, may not seem like an opportunity and certainly not a blessing, but in hindsight, you will have twenty/twenty vision and understand how God can turn it for good. God took the evil from all my bad experiences and drew me close to Him, all because of one simple prayer I prayed, which has brought me under God's perfect will.

I am truly grateful for the trials in my life, which have developed great faith and inner strength within me. But most of all I am grateful because the trials brought me into an intimate relationship with my Heavenly Father and helped me to see how much He truly loves all of His children. As difficult and painful as my past has been, I wouldn't exchange it for the love I now share with Him. What I have experienced through my trials is referenced by the Apostle James in the following scripture: "***Consider it pure joy***, my brothers, whenever you face trials of many kinds, because you know that the testing of your faith develops perseverance" (James 1:2-3, NIV, emphasis added).

Please know in times of trouble, God will send angels to guard you in all your ways (Psalms 91:11). *He will send angels to surround you, strengthen you, uplift you, and to minister to you! Thank the Lord for His divine intervention and believe your deliverance is on its way.* I recently was going through a trial and cried out to God. That night I dreamed there was a woman standing in a pulpit proclaiming, "The angels are coming!" This message was not just for me, but you as well. Take comfort God sends His army in times of trouble.

I will be forever grateful to my sweet Abba Father for pulling me out of that dark pit. He will pull you out, too—just don't give up, and keep praising and trusting in Him! Always remember what God has revealed to us: "***For I reckon that the sufferings of this present time are not worthy to be compared with the glory which shall be revealed in us***" (Romans 8:18, KJV, emphasis added). Many preachers interpret this to mean the glory will be revealed when you get to Heaven. However, *I can testify that glory is being revealed in me today. It is certainly not because of anything I have done, but because of my Lord and Savior who dwells in me and saved me in a multitude of ways.*

People have told me my face is lit up and they see God all over me. Recently I asked someone what she meant by that. She replied she could see peace all over my face. Now, I am not writing these things to boast, but to express a truth: *when you **fully** receive Christ, His glory is revealed in you.* It becomes an outward expression of peace, love, patience, and joy. *So, hold on to this truth, and have great expectations for Christ to be manifested in a very big way on the other side* *of that trial.* Trials teach you that you can do what you previously thought was impossible because "…with God *all things* are possible" (Matthew 19:26, KJV, emphasis added).

SOMETIMES WE GET DISCOURAGED

Throughout my life, I have prayed for death many times due to the emotional pain I have endured—but God had other plans for me. I thank Him from the bottom of my heart that He could look beyond my human frailty and know the plans He had for me were wonderful. He could see the person He created instead of the person I was allowing myself to be.

When I found myself in deep despair, He pulled me back out. In the book of Genesis, Joseph suffered great trials and tribulations. He became an Egyptian slave and ended up in a dungeon. He never took His focus off of God and in return, God greatly favored him (Genesis 39:21). Because God's favor was upon Joseph, he eventually became a great leader, only second to Pharaoh, all because of his faithfulness to his Heavenly Father. He went from a pit to having in his own palace.

We will all have trials and tribulations, but Jesus tells us to be of good cheer because He has overcome the world (John 16:33). I thank God for drawing me close to Him and making me the person I have become because of the adversity I have faced in my life. I now have great faith, which is the most wonderful gift. God truly worked everything out for good, just as He promised.

God instructs us to give him all of our troubles as noted in the following scripture: "Casting all your care upon Him for he careth for you" (1 Peter 5:7, KJV). *Pour your heart out to Him, and tell Him* everything. That includes your deepest feelings and secrets. Put all of your soul into it. Dig down to the depths and pull it out so you can cast it upon Him. Nothing will surprise or shock Him, and *nothing can ever separate you from His love:*

"For I am persuaded, that neither death, nor life, nor angels, nor principalities, nor powers, nor things present, nor things to come, nor height, nor depth, nor any other creature, shall be able to separate us from the love of God, which is in Christ Jesus our Lord" (Romans 8:38-39, KJV).

After you have poured your heart out, leave it there with Him; don't dwell on it anymore. When He says "cast," He means to throw it to Him. He didn't say to reel it back in! When you do this, you will be amazed at how light your load is.

IDOLS

God commands us not to have any other gods before Him. This commandment is significant, even today, as we have several gods that might distract us from Him. Just as any loving parent, God wants His love for us to be reciprocated. He wants our attention, love, and affection. He does not want to be placed on the back burner, as a mere afterthought reserved for Sundays, holidays, monthly devotionals, or times of trouble.

Idolatry is a strategy of the enemy. He will put things in your life to take your focus off of God and decrease your ability to be intimate with Him. When you aren't intimate with God, you can't hear His voice and you won't be able to discern His guidance. This prevents God's perfect will from being manifested in your life. If you continue in idolatry, you will leave this Earth without fulfilling your divine assignment. Just think how that will feel will you look into those beautiful loving eyes of your Savior.

If you ever had a loved one who only came around when he or she needed something, then you know how your Heavenly Father must feel: used, rejected, and unloved. You may be thinking, "Oh, come on. He is God. He doesn't feels like that." I perceive in my spirit He does. He made us in His image. We feel the same things He is capable of feeling. He gave His life for us in a way we can't even begin to comprehend, yet many people have turned away from Him. It is somewhat similar to loving parents who do every possible thing to love and care for their child. When the child grows up, he or she becomes so busy they don't have time for their parents. The parents become abandoned and live their elder years alone and forgotten. Don't forget about your Heavenly Father. Don't abandon Him. His greatest desire is to have an intimate relationship with you just as any loving father yearns to spend time with his child.

Don't let idols stand in the way of your relationship with your Heavenly Father. What is your idol? Is it food, television, a relationship, or some type of hobby? If so, try shifting more of your focus to Him and limiting these idols in your life. *Make Him the priority.* Pencil Him into your schedule every day. You *can* find time for Him. You can wake up fifteen minutes earlier or go to sleep fifteen minutes later so you have time to speak with Him. You can spend time with Him while you wait in traffic. That would be a lot better than feeling stressed over the frustration of wasted time as you creep along the highway. You can take your lunch to the park and talk to Him while out in nature, which is my favorite way to connect with Him. Go and sit in your car while on a work break, and talk with Him. *If you do these things, your entire perception of events will totally change and you will be amazed how your life will transform as your intimacy with Him grows.*

God tells us in the book of Isaiah how much more He can do for us than anything else in life that has become our god, which is found in the following passage:

> "Produce your cause, saith the Lord; bring forth your strong reasons, saith the King of Jacob. Let them bring them forth, and shew us what shall happen: let them shew the former things, what they be, that we may consider them, and know the latter end of them; or declare us things for to come. Shew the things that are to come hereafter, that we may know that ye are gods: yea, do good, or do evil, that we may be dismayed, and behold it together. ***Behold, ye are of nothing, and your work***

of nought: an abomination is he that chooseth you" (Isaiah 41:21-24, KJV, emphasis added).

The idols that fill our spare time are *utterly worthless* when compared to all the blessings you will receive when you spend time with the one and only true, living God and receive all of the good things He has planned for you. Do an inventory today and discard all of the useless distractions that keep you from your divine destiny and being intimate with your Heavenly Father.

ATTITUDE OF GRATITUDE

Being grateful is a wonderful way to overcome obstacles because it keeps our focus on God, who will deliver us from all things. The Bible tells us, "O give thanks unto the Lord; for he is good; for his mercy endureth for ever" (I Chronicles 16:34, KJV). A thankful heart plays a role in our maturing faith: "And he fell down on his face at his feet, giving him thanks…" (Luke 17:16, KJV). When we finally realize all of our provision comes from the Lord, our hearts become filled with gratitude. *An attitude of gratitude increases faith, and it brings favor into your life by allowing God's grace to flow freely.* This is evident in Paul's preaching: "As ye have therefore received Christ Jesus the Lord, so walk ye in him: Rooted and built up in him, and stablished in the faith, as ye have been taught, ***abounding*** therein with thanksgiving" (Colossians 2:6-7, KJV, emphasis added).

Just think how you feel when you are in a state of grumbling. You become angry and resentful, which increases the tension in your body. You may not even be aware of the muscles that are all knotted up around your neck and other parts of your body. The negative energy that encompasses you is dense and heavy. In a real physiological sense, you are blocked. How can anything flow through something that is closed off? It becomes a vicious cycle. The more you close yourself off with these negative thoughts and emotions, the more you close yourself off to the supernatural power of God's grace in your life.

Research indicates that sensitivity to energetic communication is related to the state of emotional and physiological coherence of an individual. Positive emotions are associated with the body's system, including the brain, heart, and other vital organs, which enable it to function in harmonic balance with each other. This harmonic balance, called coherence, results in "internal systems that are more stable, function more efficiently, and radiate electromagnetic fields containing a more coherent structure." Additionally, physiological coherence is indicative of a person's ability to be "more sensitive to information contained in the fields generated by others." Conversely, erratic and disordered heart rhythms, resulting in decreased synchronization of the nervous system caused by negativity, blocks our ability to receive.[17]

This research indicates that we are more than just flesh and bone. Our positive thoughts and emotions enable us to receive and send subtle information to and from others. The ability to receive energetic information, I believe, also, includes receiving from our Heavenly Father, who obviously has a vast amount of energy and power (Genesis 1, Job 26, Revelations 4:5, Hebrews 1:3). Don't allow negativity to block God's grace from flowing in your life by being angry, resentful, fearful, or anxious.

The Word tell us: "***Be anxious for nothing;*** but in everything by prayer and supplication with thanksgiving let your requests be made known unto God" (Philippians 4:6, NASB, emphasis added). *Let it go!* It doesn't matter. What matters is your ability to have God's power activated within you. Who are you? If you are saved, you are a child of God and have His power and glory within you: "***The Spirit of God, who raised Jesus from the dead, lives in you***..." (Romans 8:11, NLT, emphasis added). How awesome is that? *You* have the power to *overcome anything.* So, let it go! Don't let resentment keep you from tapping into the gifts which God has placed inside of you.

---

17 McCraty, R., *The Energetic Heart: Bioelectricmagnetic Communication Within People, in Bioelectric Medicine, P.J. Rosch and M.S. Markov, Editors. 2004, Marcel Dekker: New York. P. 541-562.*

Just picture yourself after you pass through the pearly gates. Jesus reveals to you all of His glory and power that was inside of you while living here on Earth, and you didn't use it. Maybe you didn't even know it was there before reading this book. You were too busy complaining and focusing on your *perceived* lack. Just think how that will feel. You wasted all that power, which you could have used to create good things in your life.

Gratitude is also important because it keeps your focus off of the negative: "For as he thinketh in his heart, so is he..." (Proverbs 23:7, KJV). You don't want to create a dense, heavy energy that stops the power of God from flowing through you. What you focus on becomes magnified. When you focus on God's blessing in your life, you receive more of His blessing, which will increase your expectations for more. It will flow freely like a river. Don't allow it to be dammed up by getting out of the love walk and into a path of pride, arrogance, hatred, anger, and any other negativity, which will prevent you from being grateful. Gratitude impacts the ability for God's grace to flow through you. Start your day with gratitude and see what a difference it makes.

You may be saying, "What do I have to be thankful for? My life is a disaster!" The truth is, however, you have received numerous blessings. Get a pad and pen and start writing. Here, I'll help you begin:

I have running water.

I can take a hot shower.

I have cold water to drink in the summer.

I have a roof over my head.

I have food to eat.

I have a God that loves me beyond measure.

I have a Savior who died for me and is now waiting for me.

Start writing and professing your blessings now, and see how it changes your life. God doesn't like complainers. Complainers can't enter into His rest. Beginning with the book of Exodus, we are told complaining is what kept the Israelites going around the same mountain for forty years:

> "...Why did you bring us out here to die in the wilderness? Weren't there enough graves for us in Egypt? What have you done to us? Why did you make us leave Egypt?" (Exodus 14:11, NLT).

Even though God delivered them from Egyptian bondage and showed them miraculous signs and wonders, *they still complained!* He had a great plan to bring them into the land of milk and honey, but they blocked the flow of grace with all their negativity. The original freed captives, with the exception of Joshua and Caleb, never entered into His rest or the Promised Land. Because they did not have an attitude of gratitude, they became stuck, which eventually led to their destruction.

The Holy Spirit revealed to me when we complain it opens the door to the enemy and his evil strategies. So, stop murmuring and complaining and focus on the positive. Magnify God's goodness and light and you will get more of the same. What would you rather have for the rest of your life—His blessing, from which all good things come, or the curse of the enemy, from which all bad things come? If you murmur and complain, whom do you think you are magnifying? It certainly isn't God.

Having an attitude of gratitude also increases your faith. You can feel a sense of lightness with this attitude, which will activate the peace and joy the Holy Spirit has placed within you. All the heaviness and denseness melt away as you begin to see God's blessing flow in your life. Favor shows up. You may not recognize it at first, but pay attention. It is there when the rain stops as you get out of your car or when you get a parking space in front of a crowded store. What a blessing it is to have the favor of God upon you!

There are several ways to show your gratitude to God. Telling Him through prayer is one way. You can also demonstrate your gratitude through worshiping Him with music, studying His word, and singing. You can give to others who are in need of your services or financial assistance. Giving to missions is another great way to honor God and express your gratitude for all He has done for you. We should always maintain a constant spirit of gratitude even in our trials, which will help us keep our focus on God instead of our problems. This will make us victorious and will allow us to overcome the adversity quickly. Paul instructs us to "...always be thankful" (Colossians 3:15, NLT). Don't let *anything* get in the way and prevent you from being thankful. Make a conscious effort to remove all barriers between you and God that would prevent an intimate relationship with Him. This was His reason for creating you.

YOU ARE NOT ALONE

Have you ever been in the presence of God? It defies description, but if I had to put it into words, it is like when you first fall in love, but magnified a hundredfold. Being in His presence is the most precious place to be.

How do you know when you are in His presence? Believe me, you will know it. It is unmistakable. It stops you in your tracks. It is overwhelming. I am sure the experience is different for all of us, but for me, it usually begins with a tingling sensation in my body. Sometimes I feel this warm feeling inside as though I am wrapped in a blanket of love. I am filled with joy and peace. Often, I am nearly brought to my knees in tears, but they're not tears of sorrow. It is difficult to explain. I am overwhelmed by love—it's like a floodgate that opens up and everything comes rushing forward. I am in total awe of His grace and His desire to fellowship with me. It is amazingly awesome when I stop and think the Maker of the Heavens, the Mighty One who is seated beyond our galaxy; the one who is declared King of the Universe; wants to spend time with *me*. He wants to spend time with the *me* that thought she was unworthy; the me that yearned for someone to express genuine care or concern; the me that suffered abuse; the me that never thought she was good enough or smart enough, or pretty enough or lovable, or even *likeable* enough; the me that avoided parties because she was afraid of people. Wow! This awesome God, Creator of the Universe, wants to spend time with *me!* No wonder I feel overwhelmed by His presence. I experience a deep sense of gratitude for His love and His desire to be with me! I can only begin to imagine what it will truly be like to stand before Him. I don't think I will be able to stand for very long.

So, if you think you are alone or you are feeling lonely, the cure is simple: just enter into His presence by praising Him with a sincere heart. You don't have to go to church to do it, although that is one way. You can be in His presence anywhere, anytime. That is one of His greatest promises to us: "...***I am with you always, even until the end of the world***" (Matthew 28:20, KJV, emphasis added). There are numerous scriptures throughout the Bible that reveal His promise never to leave or forsake us. "Be strong and of a good courage, fear not, nor be afraid of them: for the LORD your God, he it is that doth go with thee; he will not fail thee, nor forsake thee" (Deuteronomy 31:6, KJV).

When we accept Jesus as our Savior, He says He comes to live in us. My analytical mind has often pondered this mystery. I began to believe God's energy is so vast that it can encompass or fill anything and be anywhere and everywhere at once. This idea is also noted in Jesse Duplantis' video, *Close Encounters with the God Kind.* Duplantis describes how an angel took him to Heaven. Duplantis saw Jesus walk out and then down from the throne of God as though He were an extension of God's energy.[18] I believe Jesus alluded to this concept when He said: "I am the vine, ye are the branches" (John 15:5, KJV). Our spirits are sealed by Jesus' Holy Spirit, which become extensions of God's divine energy. We are all part of a composite divine connection. John Donne was extremely insightful when he wrote: " No man is an island unto himself." We are truly connected and our individual actions affect humanity.

---

18 *Close Encounters of the God Kind.* Jesse Duplantis. Jesse Duplantis Ministries, 2004.

We have God's divine energy in us because as Scripture tells us, He breathed His spirit in us when He brought us to life (Genesis 2:7). We have part of our earthly parents' DNA in us, right? Well, it is similar with our Heavenly Father. We have part of His spiritual "DNA" also. Moreover, when we accept Jesus as our Savior, He gives us His Holy Spirit and Jesus is then living inside us. As Scripture tells us, **"But he that is joined unto the Lord is one spirit"** (1 Corinthians 6:17, KJV, emphasis added). *Because we have the Creator's essence in us, we can do all things through Christ who strengthens us* (Philippians 4:13). When we get this revelation, we can overcome the sense of loneliness, rejection, and isolation.

Take hold of these truths and face your fears head-on because *you are more than a conqueror!* Go out in the world and make your life the way God intended you to live: abundantly! This is what I do to overcome my feelings of loneliness.

One thing that really helps me get into His presence is being in nature. I love to sit on the seawall and watch sea gulls drift above the wind's currents. It is as though my spirit is soaring with them. I can feel the awesomeness of God's creativity at those moments. I began to visualize Jesus with His arms wide open and He gives me a big hug. There are even times I can see myself dancing with Him. After all, we are His bride, and the groom will dance with His betrothed. We talk and laugh. Feelings of serenity, security, and love overwhelm me in those moments. There is nothing that can rob me of my peace when I am in His presence and it is the most wonderful place to be! His presence completely feels me with love and joy that transcends all things. The whole world just fades away. I believe this is what David was referring to when he wrote, **"He that dwelleth in the secret place of the most High shall abide under the shadow of the Almighty"** (Psalms 91:1, KJV, emphasis added). This is why God has told us to seek His face. Our *hearts* truly desire to be in His presence, even if our *minds* don't realize it: "When thou saidest, Seek ye my face; **my heart** said unto thee, Thy face, LORD, will I seek" (Psalm 27:8, KJV, emphasis added).

I have recently noticed when I praise God by repeating, "Blessed be the name of the Lord," I suddenly feel His presence. I am also able to enter into His presence whenever I meditate on His awesomeness and think about the wonder of who He is, including His power; His beautiful creations; His great sacrifice; and His incomprehensible love. I become overwhelmed with His love as He overpowers me with His beautiful energy. I am sure there are many ways to fellowship with Him. I believe it is not actually the technique, but the purity of heart during praise and your reverence for Him that matters. *Any father loves to be with a child who loves to be with and honors Him!*

I need to bring up another important point about God's presence. I believe you can experience His presence in degrees. *The more you spend time with Him, the stronger His presence becomes.* I think of it in the same way as a relationship between earthly parents and children. If a grown child doesn't want to spend time with his or her parents, then the parents may withdraw from the relationship because they feel like they are intruding into the child's life and the child may need some space. Perhaps the child needs some time to grow and figure out who he or she is and where he or she wants his or her life to be. It is the same thing with our Heavenly Father. He is a gentleman. *As much as He desires a relationship with you, He will not force it upon you. He will patiently wait for you to come to Him.* You won't usually feel His presence unless you deeply desire it and you invest time to spend with Him. When He knows you have a sincere desire to be with Him, He will reveal more of Himself to you. When we come back to Him, He lavishes more of His attention on us, and His presence grows stronger as our desire to be with Him also grows.

I came across the most beautiful scripture in Isaiah, in which God promises to make all things wonderful in our lives. He states what I am unable to fully describe when I am in His presence. This scripture describes the fullness of His blessing when we have an intimate relationship with Him:

> "When the poor and needy seek water, and there is none, and their tongue faileth for thirst, I the Lord will hear them, I the

God of Israel will not forsake them. I will open rivers in high places, and fountains in the midst of the valleys: I will make the wilderness a pool of water, and the dry land springs of water. I will plant in the wilderness the cedar, the shittah tree, and the myrtle, and the oil tree; I will set in the desert the fir tree, and the pine, and the box tree together: That they may see, and know, and consider, and understand together, that the hand of the Lord hath done this, and the Holy One of Israel hath created it (Isaiah 41:17-20, KJV).

It is God, *and only God*, who can truly fill you with all of those things that your heart longs for!

In addition to being in God's presence, you are not alone because you are surrounded by angels: "The angel of the LORD encampeth round about them that fear him, and delivereth them" (Psalms 34:7, KJV). There have been numerous accounts of angelic encounters throughout history. For example, there are reports of people being saved by strangers who suddenly appeared and then disappeared during tragic events. Jesse Duplantis speaks of visitations from angels in his church. He also writes about an angel that appeared to and commanded him to sleep when he was totally exhausted from his grueling schedule.[19] People near death often report seeing or talking to angels shortly before their deaths.

There have been several occasions when I needed supernatural help and asked God to send angels to come and assist me in times of trouble. I have frequently called out to God and asked Him to send Archangel Michael to help me in times of trouble. He is the angel that fought the enemy and kicked him out of Heaven.

I recently heard of an incident that included angelic assistance. A patient was on the operating table and her heart had stopped beating, but she was quickly revived. During the time she was clinically dead;

---

19 *Close Encounters of the God Kind.* Jesse Duplantis. Jesse Duplantis Ministries, 2004.

she floated above her body and could see an angel in the room who was guiding the physician's hand during the surgery.

There are numerous references in the Bible pertaining to angelic assistance. When the Apostle, Peter, was imprisoned, angels helped him safely escape (Acts 12:1-10). Jesus told His disciples, "Thinkest thou that I cannot now pray to my Father, and he shall presently give me more than twelve legions of angels?" (Matthew 26:53, KJV). Do you know how many angels are in a legion? This phrase was used as a familiar term in Jesus' time in reference to the Roman army. A legion meant at least six thousand soldiers. Jesus said more than twelve legions—that is more than seventy-two thousand angels. Now, keep in mind these are some big, powerful beings as noted in the following scripture: "That night the angel of the LORD went out to the Assyrian camp and killed 185,000 Assyrian soldiers. When the surviving Assyrians woke up the next morning, they found corpses everywhere" (2 Kings 19:35, NLT). That is one angel for an entire army! Always remember whatever God would do for Jesus, He would do for any of His children. Now, you probably wouldn't need seventy-two thousand angels to solve one of your problems—one would most likely suffice—but isn't comforting to know all you have to do is ask? I always ask God to surround me with an encampment of angels. They are here to rescue, comfort, and protect us. As demonic activity increases in these last days, so does angelic presence due to our Father's great concern for us and His protective nature. Know that you are not alone. As the Psalmist wrote, "For he shall give his angels charge over thee, to keep thee in all thy ways" (Psalms 91:11, KJV).

One day I was treating one of my patients. Her son entered the room. She told me he had been given a gift as a child and could see angels. He told me he saw a healing angel infusing energy into me as I worked with his mother. I was overwhelmed with gratitude and joy! A week prior to this incident, I had been praying for God to give me the gift of healing so I could help some of my patients who suffer from chronic pain. I felt like God had answered my prayer when this young man told me of the healing angel that was working with me.

I once had a patient slip off her shower chair to the bottom of the tub. Due to the fact she was overweight and the position she was in, I had no idea how I was going to get her up without assistance. However, when I squatted to lift her, she popped right up as though she was light as air. I truly believe I had angelic assistance. There was no possible way I could have done this on my own. I didn't even think about praying for help before I tried to lift her because I was so focused on the situation. God knew what we needed and supplied it before I even asked.

God will send His angels when we are in need of help. However, some people get so fascinated with the idea of angels they focus more on them than on God. Please don't ever do that! That is considered idolatry and it hurts God. He wants you to always come to Him first. He decides when and how to supply our needs. He knows best. His angels work for Him to carry out His divine will and purpose. They are here because He sent them here to do His work. He is their creator and they have no power or authority without Him.

We are told in Scripture, God meets our needs when we are in trouble. This truth is illustrated in the following biblical story. When Elisha and his servant awoke to find themselves surrounded by the Syrian army, Elisha prayed for God to open His servant's eyes and let him see God had *already* surrounded them with angels:

> "And Elisha prayed, and said, LORD, I pray thee, open his eyes, that he may see. And the LORD opened the eyes of the young man; and he saw: and, behold, the mountain was full of horses and chariots of fire round about Elisha" (2 Kings 6:17, KJV).

According to this scripture, we don't even have to ask to be surrounded by angels in times of need. God just does it: "...for your Father knoweth what things ye have need of, before ye ask him...." (Matthew 6:8, KJV). This includes relief from the *perception of being alone* or that sinking feeling of loneliness. *We are truly not alone.* Sometimes, we just think we are alone because we are unable to see with our spiritual eyes. Ask God to open them for you and allow you to see, just as Elisha's servant was able to see. You will then look upon all the love that surrounds you.

CHAPTER FOUR

WALKING IN FREEDOM

THE LETTER VERSUS THE SPIRIT OF THE LAW

If you look at all of the commandments, you may agree God created them because He wanted to protect us from physical, emotional, spiritual, and mental harm. It may even appear that the first two commandments concerning idolatry are for our own good as well, not solely for God's glorification. Making God the one and only God and priority in your life will bring you abundance in every single area of your life.   Even disobeying the third commandment by taking His name in vain can have detrimental effects because when we disrespect our Heavenly Father, we disrespect ourselves and offend others. Keeping the Sabbath day holy is not only about worshipping God, but it reminds us to rest in our relationship with Him because He has provided for us in every way. When we fully rest in Him, we become ever-increasingly blessed. Having respect for our parents teaches us how to respect ourselves and others. It also teaches us to respect our Heavenly Father, which will facilitate an intimate relationship with Him. The other commandments, which instruct us not to kill; commit adultery; steal; lie or covet; clearly show they were made for our own protection and self-preservation. Our Heavenly Father knows *sin is destructive to our entire being as it leads to condemnation by the enemy, our self, and others. Sin also opens the door to the enemy and all of his devices to completely destroy you.* I believe that is why God detests sin; he doesn't want the enemy to hurt His beloved children.

John Paul Jackson, an established authority on Christian spirituality, says this about sin:

> "Sin in its raw element is the most deteriorating thing, the most disorganizing thing, the most destructive thing that is entered into the creation that God created perfect. It's the entrance of that which decays; it's the entrance of that which disunifies; it's the entrance of that which destroys; it's the entrance of that which deteriorates. Sin in its simplistic form: that is exactly what it does."[20]

God created laws not only for our protection from the destructive force of sin, but as the Apostle Paul emphasized through his writing, God created them so men would come to the end of themselves (Romans 8:3). God's children would learn it was impossible to keep all of the commandments and ordinances and would, therefore, need a Savior. God had a magnificent plan. He would come down from His throne, save the world, and bring glory, as well as His children, back to Himself.

So, if God made these laws to protect us from ourselves and each other, and bring us back to Him, then we should not allow ourselves to be condemned when we make a mistake. If sin is a lifestyle for you, then that is a totally different thing, and that is not what I am writing about. However, when we have accepted Jesus Christ as our one and only Savior, we don't need to feel condemned when we make mistakes. We *will* make them because we are human. Now, don't misunderstand, that doesn't mean we should willfully or habitually sin. If you are truly saved, you don't want to sin, and it certainly won't be part of your lifestyle—that would go against your Christian nature—but when you make a mistake, thank Jesus for His cleansing blood and move on. Don't wallow in self-condemnation because, "There is therefore now no condemnation to them who are in Christ Jesus..." (Romans 8:1, KJV).

---

20 "What is Sin?" Joni Table Talk. Daystar. Dallas. 04 April 2013.

I nearly ran myself crazy trying to follow the letter of the law. For example, scriptures throughout the Bible teach us to be honest in all of our ways. Does that mean if I document my time sheet at work with a thirty second deviation from the actual time, I am a liar? Have I sinned? That would be the letter of the law. What God is more concerned with is the spirit of the law. If you lie about your neighbor's husband, which causes his wife to divorce him, then you would have committed a grave sin because you have harmed someone else. The law was written in the spirit of keeping us from harming others as well as ourselves.

God says the following about His laws:

> "For this is the covenant that I will make with the house of Israel after those days, saith the Lord; I will put my laws into their mind, and write them in their hearts..." (Hebrews 8:10, Jeremiah 31:33, KJV).

When God's Word is living in your heart, you will always want to do the right thing. You may not always succeed, but the desire will usually lead you in the right direction.

The Word tells us the law can't ever make us righteous, only our faith in the finished work of Jesus can bring us in right standing with God:

> "Knowing that a man is not justified by the works of the law, but by the faith of Jesus Christ, even we have believed in Jesus Christ, that we might *be justified by the faith of Christ*, and not by the works of the law: for by the works of the law shall no flesh be justified" (Galatians 2:16, KJV, emphasis added).

When we accept Jesus as our Savior, He sends the Holy Spirit to dwell within us, which is the Great Councilor who guides us, so we don't have to focus on the letter of the law:

> *"But if ye are led by the Spirit, ye are not under the law"* (Galatians 5:18, KJV, emphasis added).

Keep in mind God is concerned about souls and their eternal position. He is not obsessed with you dotting your 'i's and crossing your 't's. There is no way you can live the abundant life Jesus came here to give you and fully receive from Him when you are attempting to follow the letter of the law. That would be very stressful and would block His grace from flowing in you. Furthermore, Jesus wants us to have peace. How could we glorify our Father if we are robbed of our peace? The Apostle Paul, who was an expert on Jewish law, wrote the following:

> "For by grace are ye saved through faith; and that *not of yourselves*: *it is the gift of God. Not of works*, lest anyone should boast (Ephesians 2:8-9, KJV, emphasis added).

> "Therefore, as ye abound in every thing, in faith, and utterance, and knowledge, and in all diligence, and in your love to us, see that ye abound in this grace also" (2 Corinthians 8:7, KJV).

When Paul used the word "works," in the scripture in Ephesians, he was referring to *our efforts* to become righteous, which we can never do. Only Jesus living in us can accomplish righteousness for us. Notice how Paul defined salvation as a gift. A true gift comes without conditions. Since God is truth, *salvation is an absolute gift; it doesn't have to be earned.*

Paul also instructs us to abound in "this grace." We are to focus on the work of Jesus and let His grace fill our being as it washes us clean, destroys all illusions of unworthiness, frees us and opens our spiritual minds so that we know exactly who we are in Him: forgiven, protected, cherished, and loved eternally.

He further instructed we are righteous because of God's purity in our Savior. Note the word "Godhead," which means the divine essence of God:[21]

---

21 Online Strong's Concordance. EliYah.com. 2 Sept 2013. <eliyah.com>.

"For in him dwelleth all the fullness of the Godhead bodily. And ye are *complete* in him, which is the head of all principality and power" (Colossians 2:9-10, KJV, emphasis added).

In the book of Galatians, Paul wrote about sins that will prevent citizenship of Heaven (Galatians 5:19-21, NIV). This passage of scripture is not referring to those who occasionally make mistakes or have a weakness they are trying to overcome. These verses are in reference to those who practice a lifestyle of sin, who, therefore, aren't truly saved. There is only one way to the Father, and that is through His Son, Jesus Christ.

Under the Old Covenant in the Old Testament, people had to be ceremonially clean before they could enter into the temple to worship God. That was before they had a Savior to cleanse them from their sins. Now we have Jesus. Today, under the New Covenant, we still need to be pure when we come to worship: pure in thought and focused on Him. We need to leave worldly distractions outside the temple door. In this way, we honor Him and do not defile the altar.

If Jesus is your Savior, you are forgiven for past, present, and future sins (Romans 6:10, Hebrews 9:26, 10:10, 12-14), so don't drive yourself crazy with the letter of the law, but follow the spirit of the law. Take a few moments to contemplate the reason for these laws. They are for your benefit, for your self-preservation, to help you in your spiritual walk and in your spiritual growth. The laws are for your protection. The two commandments Jesus said are the most important are as follows: *that we will love God with everything that we are and love our neighbors as ourselves.* This is the *true* spirit of the law. Once you have mastered those, all the others will fall into place (Matthew 22:36-40). Don't obsess about following all of His laws to perfection—it is impossible. Paul refers to this in the following scriptures: "But if the *ministration of death, written and engraven in stones*, was glorious, so that the children of Israel could not steadfastly behold the face of Moses for the glory of his countenance; *which glory was to be done away*: How shall not the *ministration of the spirit* be rather glorious?" (2 Corinthians 3:7-8, KJV, emphasis added). Check out the bold phrases. Its meaning tells us focusing on the law, which leads to guilt and condemnation, will destroy you. The law can't make you glorify God, only Jesus' Holy Spirit living in you can do that. Therefore, just focus on His love for you. When you do this, you will automatically do your best to obey the commandments; it will come naturally. You won't have to focus on following the letter of the law. The Holy Spirit will be guiding you every step of the way. You will fall so in love with Jesus that you won't intentionally break His laws. You will do everything within your power to please Him because He loved you first. But when you slip, don't condemn yourself, and don't allow the enemy or anyone else to do so. Jesus' blood is continually cleansing you. *In His loving arms, you will find rest.* Just let Him embrace you. That is what He wants to do. Just relax right there. God has you in the palm of His hand. The real concern is not whether God is able to look upon sin or whether we can follow His laws without fail, but that we trust in His son's righteousness and we truly do find rest in His presence and receive His abounding grace.

GRACE

Due to the erroneous doctrine I learned as a child, I did not understand the concept of grace and the meaning of God's plan of salvation. Over the last few years, I recently began to understand God's grace through revelations in dreams, Scripture, and pastoral sermons. It is my prayer you will receive a revelation of the truth of God's Word and His New Covenant because of the work of our precious Lord and Savior, Jesus Christ.

Grace is a controversial issue in some religions. There are those who emphasize that the concept of grace gives you permission to do as you please. In essence, they are saying we have Jesus' permission to sin. *This is a spiritual travesty because Jesus Christ is grace:* "**For the law was given by Moses, but grace and truth came by Jesus Christ**" (John 1:17, KJV, emphasis added). He is the truth, and the truth *will set you free!* It is the enemy that creates the conflict and controversy around the work of our Lord and Savior. When we don't really understand the truth, the enemy has the power to destroy our lives.[22] When I received *a deep revelation of grace and what my Savior has actually done for me to makes me righteous, then the enemy had no power over me.* So, you can see why the enemy does every single thing he can to keep us from understanding the real truth of the gospel of Jesus Christ. When he loses his power over us, we can step boldly to the throne and claim our divine birthright.

Don't just take my word about the gospel of grace. Check out the verses in Hebrew that were written to newly converted Christians who were contemplating returning to the law of the Old Testament due to the persecution they suffered. This occurred after Jesus' resurrection and ascension. The Christian converts were being severely persecuted, socially and physically, by the Jews and Romans. The author of Hebrews emphasized the fact that the New Covenant was better because it secures our redemption forever through our High Priest, Jesus Christ. All we have to do is believe in His gift of righteousness and forgiveness and receive what He has done for us (Romans 1:5).

"Yes, the old requirement about the priesthood was set aside because it was weak and useless. *For the law never made anything perfect.* But now we have confidence in a *better hope*, through which we draw near to… Because of this oath, Jesus is the one who guarantees this *better covenant* with God…But because Jesus lives forever, his priesthood lasts forever. Therefore he is able, *once and forever, to save* those who come to God through him. He lives forever to intercede with God on their behalf" (Hebrews 7:18-19, 22, 24-25, NLT, emphasis added).

"But now Jesus, our High Priest, has been given a ministry that is *far superior* to the old priesthood, for he is the one who mediates for us a *far better covenant* with God, based on *better promises*" (Hebrews 8:6, NLT). "With his own blood—not the blood of goats and calves—he entered the Most Holy

22 Prince, Joseph. *Destined to Reign.* Tulsa, Ok: Harrison House Publishers; 2007:20, 24-25.

Place *once for all time and secured our redemption forever"* (Hebrews 9:12, NLT, emphasis added).

This is the total opposite of the Old Covenant, where the priest would make yearly animal sacrifices to cleanse sinners. However, with Jesus, we are eternally cleansed. *The work is finished once and for all because of grace—our Lord and Savior!*

Jesus has told us that we can't save ourselves through our own efforts:

> "When the disciples heard this, they were greatly astonished and asked, "Who then can be saved?" Jesus looked at them and said, *"With man this is impossible*, but with God all things are possible" (Matthew 19:25-26, NIV, emphasis added).

Read what the Apostle Paul says about the saving grace of Jesus: "...I no longer count on my own righteousness through obeying the law; rather, I become righteous through faith in Christ. For God's way of making us right with himself *depends on faith"* (Phillipians 3:9, NLT, emphasis added). If Paul had that much faith in Jesus as His Savior after He relentlessly hunted down Christians which led to their heinous murders (Acts 7:58, 8:3, 9:1), then we all should be able to let go of self-condemnation and trust that Jesus has paid the price for *all* of our bad deeds.

I must emphasize again this does not mean you have free will to do as you please. Once you have Christ living in you, you will always strive to please Him. When you fail, you will feel sorrow that you have not done the right thing for Him. That is what His powerful love does to you. *The love of Jesus will turn your heart to repentance.* Grace does not mean you don't have to repent; *grace is the power that makes it easy for you to repent.* It comes naturally when Jesus is living in your heart. If this is not where you are in your walk with Christ, invite Him into your heart and ask the Holy Spirit to fill you.

Unfortunately, the enemy will condemn you when you have sinned, which makes you think you are not worthy to receive God's grace. *When you are under the law, you continue to be sin-conscious, and guilt takes control.* The author of Hebrews 10:3 states the yearly sacrifices reminded God's people of their sins because it was an imperfect cleansing. *It is only the grace of Jesus that can completely and continually cleanse us.* This perpetual cleansing leads to freedom from sin and condemnation! I know from past experience being sin-conscious prevents His power from flowing in your life because it blocks you from receiving His love and grace. *You have to be Christ-conscious to lead the abundant life He came here to give us. When we magnify the power of His grace and love, sin will shrink from the macro to the micro.*

Please be aware condemnation from sin will cause all kinds of infirmities in your body. This is confirmed by Jesus when the paralyzed man was lowered down from the roof through the crowds so he could be healed: "When Jesus saw their faith, he said unto the sick of the palsy, Son, thy sins be forgiven thee" (Mark 2:5, KJV). Instead of saying he was healed, Jesus made the point to tell him he was forgiven so the man could let go of the condemnation and be made whole again. *Condemnation from sin will wreak havoc on your body and will ultimately lead to decay and destruction* if not resolved by God's saving grace.

Condemnation was one of the roots Jesus was talking about in the following scripture: "But he answered and said, Every plant, which my heavenly Father hath not planted, shall be rooted up" (Matthew 15:13, KJV). *When we know we are truly forgiven, we can then let go of condemnation and then we can live an abundant, healthy life. We will never be perfect. That is why we needed a Savior. However because of the vast love and grace of God, we become righteous when we accept Jesus as our Savior and receive His grace and love. Love covers a multitude of sins* (1 Peter 4:8).

The grace of God *teaches us to live holy and leads us into repentance and eternal life:*

"The steps of a good man are ordered by the Lord: and he delighteth in his way. ***Though he fall, he shall not be utterly cast down***: for the Lord upholdeth him with his hand" (Psalms 37:23-24, KJV, emphasis added).

It's also very important to remember when you are saved, you inherit what Jesus has, which includes a purified spirit and God's glory:

"And if children, then heirs: heirs of God, and joint-heirs with Christ: if so be that we suffer with Him, so that we may be also glorified together" (Romans 8:17, KJV).

According to God's Word, you are made righteous in God's sight:

"For he hath made him to be sin for us, who knew no sin; that we might be made the righteousness of God in him" (2 Corinthians 5:21, KJV).

We are also told through Scripture we are free from condemnation that stems from our inability to perfectly follow God's laws while we are in this flesh because of the work of our Savior:

"There is therefore now no condemnation to them which are in Christ Jesus, who walk not after the flesh, but after the Spirit. For the law of the Spirit of life in Christ Jesus hath made me free from the law of sin and death. For what the law could not do, in that it was weak through the flesh, God sending his own Son in the likeness of sinful flesh, and for sin, condemned sin in the flesh: That the righteousness of the law might be fulfilled in us, who walk not after the flesh, but after the Spirit" (Romans 8:1-4, KJV).

Another very important point that encompasses your salvation is the promise sin can't affect your spirit because it has been sealed, which is noted in the following scripture: "And grieve not the holy Spirit of God, whereby ye are sealed unto the day of redemption" (Ephesians 4:30, KJV). Sin can, however, affect your flesh if you allow yourself to be condemned by it. This is evident in people who are guilt-ridden, which leads to stress and anxiety resulting in destruction to the body.[23]

God isn't looking at our flesh when He sees us. He is looking at our spirit. God sees us as a spirit because He is a spirit being and we worship Him in the spirit (John 4:24, KJV). So when He looks at us, He is not looking at our flesh that has been contaminated with sin, He is looking at our spirit, which is married to Jesus' spirit. He, therefore, sees us as He sees his son: righteous, pure, and holy.

It is important you understand grace, not the law, teaches us to live holy. Grace does not give us a free pass to sin, as some opponents of grace would suggest. *If you don't believe in grace, then you don't truly understand who God is or what His redemptive plan is about.* Grace *is* what He is *all* about. Our Heavenly Father's wonderful plan of salvation is the result of grace. The following scriptures teach grace perpetuates holiness: "For the grace of God that bringeth salvation hath appeared to all men, ***Teaching us that***, denying ungodliness and worldly lusts, we should live soberly, righteously, and Godly, in this present world" (Titus 2:11-12, KJV, emphasis added). When we are saved by God's loving grace, we learn how to live according to His will. Because His love in us will "***... cover the multitude of sins***," (1 Peter 4:8, KJV), we will therefore want to always do what is right.

Since "God is love" (1 John 4:8, KJV), He does not keep track of our sins because love does not keep score:

> "Love is patient, love is kind. It does not envy, it does not boast, it is not proud. It does not dishonor others, it is not self-seeking, it is not easily angered, ***it keeps no record of wrongs***. Love does not delight in evil but rejoices with the truth. It always protects, always trusts, always hopes, always perseveres" (1 Corinthians 13:4-7, NIV, emphasis added).

---

23 Carnegie Mellon University. "How stress influences disease: Study reveals inflammation as the culprit." *Science Daily*, 9 Jun. 2013. <sciencedaily.com>

Nowhere does it say that love keeps a checklist of someone's sins, but it does say it keeps no records of wrongs. Neither does God because He *is* love. *You are forgiven through your Savior, Jesus Christ. Your sins have been erased and the record has been destroyed.*

Because God is love and love always perseveres, God's love for you is enduring. He waits patiently for you to come to Him through the saving grace of Jesus to live the life for which He created you. He doesn't simply give up on you because of the mistakes you make. Endurance and tolerance is what love is all about: it's what God is all about.

Because of God's enduring love, we need to think of the grace of our Lord and Savior, Jesus Christ, like a fountain that is *continually* covering, cleansing, and purifying us throughout our lives. This was prophesied by Zechariah prior to and fulfilled during Jesus' crucifixion:[24]

> "In that day there shall be a fountain opened to the house of David and to the inhabitants of Jerusalem for sin and for uncleanness" (Zechariah 13:1, KJV).

> "But one of the soldiers with a spear pierced his side, and forthwith came there out blood and water" (John 19:34, KJV).

When Jesus shed His precious blood for us, this fulfilled the New Covenant of God's promise for eternal salvation and an abundant life. The scripture in Zechariah includes all of us who are saved, including Gentiles. Our salvation results in being adopted into the family of Abraham.

Grace also teaches us that God wants us to rest in Him. His Word says, "Let us **labour therefore to enter into that rest**…" (Hebrews 4:11, KJV). *This scripture tells us to keep our focus on God—not on what we do, but on whom He is and what He has already done for us.* This requires effort because our flesh wants to dwell on the nega-

---

24 Henry, Matthew. "Matthew Henry's Concise Commentary." Bible Hub. Online Parallel Bible. 6 June 2013 <http://biblehub.com>.

tive. We are conditioned to think fearful thoughts when we are going through trials. When this happens, we need to remember God wants us to rest in Him. Like any good father, He modeled the appropriate behavior for us. He rested from His work after His creation was complete, just as we need to rest from our work, which includes our fears and worries. He wants us to simply rest in Him. Paul tells us resting on the Sabbath was a shadow of the coming of Christ (Colossians 2:14-17). Jesus is our Savior in all things and we are to rest in His grace and mercy, which includes knowing we are forgiven. He supplied every single thing we would need on Earth and gave us dominion over it (Genesis 1:26). We can reach out through faith and obtain everything we need because of His wonderful grace and love for us.

The Apostle Paul tells us to fight the good fight of faith. Paul is telling us to trust in our Savior who has taken everything to the cross for us. Because of His great sacrifice, we can receive salvation not only for eternity, but for the here and now. This means salvation from all of life's trials. So have faith everything will turn out for good and receive Jesus' precious gift of grace. When you can fully receive from your precious Lord and Savior, you *will* find rest. You need to receive Him daily. In this way you will follow Paul's instructions to "Fight the good fight of faith…" (1Timothy 6:12, KJV).

The concept of fighting the good fight of faith really resonates within me because *it is a fight.* Hold up your shield of faith and always guard your heart and mind so you don't allow anything to enter except God's love for you. Only then will His grace flow through you like a refreshing stream of never ending goodness.

YOU ARE FORGIVEN

Since I was a child, I believed I *had* to ask forgiveness for all of my sins so I would inherit eternal life in God's kingdom. After I truly received Jesus as my Lord and Savior and drew closer to God, I began to feel uneasy when I reviewed and asked for forgiveness for each of my sins. Whenever I did this, I felt strongly that I was negating the great sacrifice of my Savior. Please don't stop reading. I am in no way saying it is okay to practice a lifestyle of sin. I know what you are about to read may go against every religious belief you have, but it is my prayer that you will reflect upon these truths as God has showed me His plan of salvation has frequently been misinterpreted.

When I was visiting a church on New Year's Day, the pastor had us hold Communion. He asked us to focus on any sin for which we needed forgiveness, even if we had already asked for forgiveness. *Deep in my spirit I knew that was absolutely wrong.* So I just thanked God for His Son and His gracious gift of forgiveness because I had a *strong revelation this had already been done for me on the cross.*

That same afternoon, I asked God about the concept. I told Him it didn't make any sense to me. He already gave us our Savior, Jesus, who died on the cross and took all of our sins for us. In all His right-eousness, He became sin, and we became righteous (Romans 8:1-4, KJV). The very last words Jesus uttered were, "*...It is finished!...*" (John 19:30, NLT, emphasis added). So why on earth would we still have to ask Him for forgiveness? *Why would He have gone through such unimaginable agony, if He expected us to continue to offer a sac-rifice for our sins? If this is necessary for our salvation, then Jesus was tortured and died in vain.*

Right after I asked God for clarification on asking for forgiveness, I turned on the television, and there was Pastor Joseph Prince, a world-renowned evangelist, confirming my belief that forgiveness is a done deal. I knew God had answered my prayer because I had randomly selected a show when I turned on the television; Prince's broadcast was not one that I routinely watched. God led me to the truth of His gospel through Prince's sermon.

That same night, I had a dream about the teaching on the concept of grace. God even gave me a scripture in the dream from the book of Habakkuk confirming He wanted me to write about this: "Then the LORD replied: 'Write down the revelation and make it plain on tab-lets so that a herald may run with it" (Habakkuk 2:2, NIV). I was not familiar with this scripture so I knew that this was a message from God and was not coming from my subconscious.

Several months later when I was reading Prince's book, *Destined to Reign*, I came across a chapter in which he was making an analogy about being cleansed from sins by comparing them to dirty laundry. The dream I had that night after first hearing his sermon also had the same symbolism of comparing dirty laundry to our sins. I kept trying to wash my clothes, but they would not get clean. We can never clean sin ourselves no matter how hard we try, but Jesus does: "For he hath made him to be sin for us, who knew no sin; that we might be made the righteousness of God in him" (2 Corinthians 5:21, KJV).

I learned the misinterpretation of the confession of sins comes from the scripture 1 John 1:9, where the Apostle John states, "*If we confess our sins, he is faithful and just to forgive us our sins, and to cleanse us from all unrighteousness.*"[25] First of all, the word "confession" translated from the original Greek language in the New Testament is "*homologeo,*" *which* means "to assent, i.e. covenant, acknowledge:— con- (pro-)fess, confession is made, give thanks, promise."[26] Notice the root meaning is to assent, which means to agree. *One of the ways* you can agree is by verbalizing your position, but you can also agree in your heart. God knows your heart and *He wants you to agree with Him what you have done is not in alignment with His will. It's not necessary to tell Him what you have done; He already knows that.* You just need to agree in your heart it is wrong. When you agree with God and His Word, you are in the Spirit. Anything that contradicts His Word means you are operating in the flesh, which is sinful. Moreover, when Jesus is living in you, agreement with God's will comes naturally, so reviewing and verbalizing your sins isn't necessary.

Second of all, you need to be aware, when you dwell on something, it is given power. Therefore, when you focus on your sins they will become magnified. *Verbalizng your sins makes you sin-conscious*

---

25 Prince, Joseph. *Destined to Reign.* Tulsa, Ok: Harrison House Publishers; 2007:106-107.
26 Online Strong's Concordance. EliYah.com. 26 June 2013. <eliyah.com>.

instead of Christ-conscious: As we are told: "***Death and life are in the power of the tongue***..." (Proverbs 18:21, KJV, emphasis added).

It is God's grace that leads you to repentance, not your effort to change your behavior; that's not possible without the power of Jesus' saving grace activated within you. Thank Him for His power and His saving grace that is changing you into the person He created you to be. It is His forgiveness that allows love to flow in your life: "Wherefore I say unto thee, Her sins, which are many, are forgiven; for she loved much: but to whom little is forgiven, the same loveth little" (Luke 7:47).

If you are out of His will by not loving yourself, others and Him; thank Jesus for helping you to be more like Him and then expect it to happen. *Jesus does not want us focusing on our sins. He wants us to focus on His finished work. When you do this, you will receive a deep revelation of His love, and be empowered to turn from sin, which is what He instructs you to do.* You will then be able to live the abundant life He came here to give you. Don't continue to dwell on and talk about sin, which will cause self-condemnation and condemnation from the enemy. You don't have to speak your confession, but your thoughts and actions have to be reversed so they line up with God's will. This will come naturally when you fully receive Jesus and a deep revelation of His love for you.

Let's examine further what has led us to believe confession of sins is necessary for forgiveness. When studying Scripture, it is imperative to divide the Word correctly. All the letters John, Paul, Peter, and James wrote also addressed nonbelievers just as today's preachers will frequently do in their sermons. We have to understand who the author is speaking to and if it is under the Old or New Covenant. *When verses are taken out of context, they become non-scriptural, and the enemy can use them as a tool to condemn us.*[27]

If you look closely at the scriptures concerning forgiveness of sins and purification in the first and second chapter of the first book of

27 Prince, Joseph. *Destined to Reign.* Tulsa, Ok: Harrison House Publishers; 2007:92, 106-108.

John, there appears to be a contradiction. This can be a source of confusion for the reader. John was addressing nonbelievers in the first chapter, when he referred to confession and the forgiveness of sins. In 1 John 2:12, he was addressing believers as he writes, "I write to you, little children, Because your sins *are* forgiven you for His name's sake" (emphasis added). John is actually emphasizing what God has already told believers: "For I will be merciful to their unrighteousness, and their sins and their iniquities will *I remember no more*" (Hebrews 8:10, KJV, emphasis added). This promise is repeated in Jeremiah 31:34, Isaiah 43:25, Hebrews 8:12 and 10:17. The Lord must really want us to know we are forgiven. He said it four times throughout the Old and New Testaments. In contrast, confession of sins to God is only mentioned once in the New Testament by the Apostle John. The Apostle Paul never instructed on it and he wrote approximately two-thirds of the New Testament.[28]

For the sinner who has not been saved, God will forgive each of your sins, when and if you confess them (1 John 1:9), but that does not get you into Heaven. *There is only one way to Heaven, and that is by accepting Jesus as your Savior.* Confession will enable you to be for-given for only some of your sins. It is impossible to confess them all as you don't even realize some of the sins you commit. Forgiveness, exclusive of Jesus, does not qualify you for citizenship of Heaven. Believing in Jesus (John 3:16) and confessing Him as your Lord (Romans 10:9), not confession of sins, is the criteria that registers your name for entrance into those pearly gates.

You may be thinking, as I once did, "Well, what about the sins I have committed after I was saved?" *All sins are forgiven: past, present, and future.* This is stated throughout Hebrews and Romans. *Furthermore, there is no time in the eternal. There is only now. God operates out-side the constraints of time. So, ALL your sins are forgiven.* If your sins weren't completely forgiven, Jesus would have to go to the cross every year, just like the Israelites had to bring a lamb to the altar every year. But Jesus sat down at His Father's right hand when He ascended.

---

28 Macleod, Hector, C. "Thoughts on 1 John Chapters 1 and 2." Grace Station. 11 July 2013. <gracestation.net>

He sat down because His work was finished,[29] just as God rested on the seventh day. He didn't rest because He was exhausted, he rested because His work was finished.

Moreover, we are told that: "Now when sins have been forgiven, there is no need to offer any more sacrifices" (Hebrews 10:18, NLT). The word "sacrifice" from the original Greek language is defined as an offering.[30] The scripture is clearly instructing us that Jesus has already taken care of our sins and there is no need to offer a confession.

Forgiveness is a done deal because of Jesus' precious saving blood. It is like an eternal, perpetual river that flows through you and washes you clean. As fast as you may sin, many times without being aware of it, His blood washes it away just as quickly. We are told that Jesus *takes* away our sins (1 John 2:2, NLT). The word "takes" means that it is a continual process. That is the power of His blood: "But if we walk *in* the light, as he is *in* the light, we have fellowship with one another, and the blood of Jesus, his Son, *purifies* us from *all* sin" (1 John 1:7, NKJV, emphasis added). The first part of this scripture has been misinterpreted to mean "walking in the light" refers to our behavior, but in essence, it refers to *where we are in the kingdom* when we receive Jesus' right-eousness after accepting Him as our Savior. Jesus *is* the light (John 8:12) and we are *in* Him (Ephesians 2:13). *This scriptural phrase is actually defining who we are as God's children: holy, which means we are set apart because of the great sacrifice of our Lord.* It describes our eternal *relationship* with Our Heavenly Father and our eternal, as well as present, *position* in His kingdom: we are *in* good standing with Our Heavenly Father and are *in* line to be co-heirs with Christ.

If this phrase did refer to our behavior, then we would be jumping back and forth from light to dark constantly as we sin and are then cleansed by Jesus' blood. The Almighty God wouldn't have created such an imperfect plan. His plan is perfect and includes eternal and perpetual cleansing. It is also important to note that the scripture is in

---

29 Prince, Joseph. *Destined to Reign*. Tulsa, Ok: Harrison House Publishers; 2007:175-177.

30 Online Strong's Concordance. EliYah.com. 11 July 2013. <eliyah.com>.

the present tense—"purifies" and not "purified"—which means this is happening right now! God isn't waiting for us to confess before He cleanses us from all sin—He does it as soon as we begin to sin! His blood, not confession of sins, cleanses us.[31] Furthermore, the Word tells us we are not saved by our works, which includes confessing sin. Salvation is a *gift* of God (Ephesians 2:8-9).

Moreover, if you *thoroughly* examine the context of this scripture in the preceding verse, 1 John 1:7, you could conclude that John was talking to non-believers: "So we are lying if we say we have fellowship with God but go on living in spiritual darkness;…" (1 John 1:6, NLT). Living in spiritual darkness is rejection of Jesus since He is the *light* (John 8:12). John then starts the next verse, concerning walking in the light and being purified, with the word "but." The word "but" was used to emphasize a contrast between two spiritual truths. The first truth he emphasized in 1 John 1:6 was in reference to non-believers who reject Jesus, which will prevent them from receiving salvation. The second truth he wrote about in 1 John 1:7 included believers who receive Jesus' grace, which places them in His light, cleanses them, and empowers them to have a repentant heart, which positions them in good standing with their Heavenly Father.

If you look closely at the next verse, it becomes clearly evident, John was talking to non-believers: "If we claim we have no sin, we are only fooling ourselves and not living in the truth" (1 John 1:8, NLT). John is once again making reference to those who reject Jesus, since *Jesus is the truth* (John 14:6). John then makes another contrast using the word "but" in the following verse. I believe he was emphasizing the forgiving nature of our Heavenly Father in reference to his faithfulness *even toward the nonbelievers who rejected His beloved son after he was tortured and died a horrendous death for them*: "***But*** if we confess our sins to him, **he is faithful and just to forgive** us our sins and to cleanse us from all wickedness" (1 John 1:9, NLT, emphasis added). God's faithful and forgiving nature isn't contingent on our actions. He freely forgives; that's what love does, no matter whom we are or what

---

31 Prince, Joseph. *Destined to Reign.* Tulsa, Ok: Harrison House Publishers; 2007:92, 108.

we believe. The non-believer, however, can confess until the end of time and God *will* forgive them, but without Jesus, there is no eternal life (Acts 4:10-12).

Additionally, the New Living Translation of the Bible in the introduction to the first book of John states that John was writing to encourage believers due to the false teachers and non-believers who rejected Christ and had filled the Church. Their rationale centered on the belief since flesh was evil, there was no way that the Messiah they waited for could come in the flesh. This caused doubt and confusion for Christians. John's purpose to encourage believers makes it evident that he was clarifying the truth concerning the forgiveness process between believers and non-believers. John wanted believers, his "dear children" to know they *were already* forgiven (1 John 2:12). This knowledge would free them from ever being burdened again by sin-cleansing rituals.

This understanding of Scripture has freed me from focusing on each of my sins as I did for most of my life. Now when I pray, and when I am aware of sin, I thank God's precious Son for forgiving and cleansing me. However, I never review each of my sins to ask for forgiveness; I am *already* forgiven. *I want to exalt my Savior, not my sin. He is more powerful than my sin, and His blood cleanses me from all sin!*

I am now trying to practice Christ-consciousness, not sin-consciousness. I ask God to make me just like Jesus. I try not to focus on the sin and give power to it, but rather focus on my Savior, who renews me. I pray to be in God's perfect will. When you do these things, sin will lose its power over you. Repentance will then come naturally. *Repentance is not confession.* They are two different things. The word, "repentance," is translated from the original Greek text's "*metanoeo*", which means reversal of decision.[32] Repentance, therefore, means to change your thinking; it means to renew your mind with God's Word so you think like Him and develop His loving attributes.

---

32 Online Strong's Concordance. EliYah.com. 7 June 2013. <eliyah.com>.

When I am aware of some *pattern* I can't seem to break, I will look at the motives for my actions and the thoughts I allow myself to dwell upon. If anything doesn't line up with the will of God, and if I feel like some area is a real weakness for me, I thank Him for helping me to overcome it and making my heart like my Savior's. I profess in my weakness, He is strong, but I don't continue to verbalize or dwell upon my weakness. I thank Him for His power that will weaken my weaknesses. I know I am praying according to His will so I have great expectations my prayer will be answered and He will change me into the person He created me to be.

Instead of verbalizing your sins, you should say: "I am the righteousness of God through the blood of Jesus Christ. Therefore, there is now no condemnation in me because I belong to Jesus Christ."[33]   It took a while for my head to come into alignment with what I knew in my heart. I had believed all of my life I had to confess all my sins or I would burn in hell. I now have a deep conviction that can't be shaken: I am forgiven for past, present, and future sins; I am righteous because of who Jesus is, not anything I have done or haven't done.

The Word actually tells us to confess we are righteous: "For with the heart a person believes (adheres to, trusts in, and *relies on Christ*) and so is justified (*declared righteous*, acceptable to God), and with the mouth he confesses (declares openly and *speaks out freely his faith) and confirms [his] salvation*" (Romans 10:10, AMP, emphasis added). Confess *this truth*, not sin, and one day you will know without a doubt it is *the absolute truth.*

It is your *faith in the work of your Savior, Jesus,* who makes you righteous, just as it was *faith in God,* not the law, that made Abraham righteous (Galatians 3:6). Abraham wasn't under a legalistic doctrine. The Ten Commandments weren't written by God for several more generations following Abraham's death. Moses carried those tablets down the mountain after the Israelites boasted in their own efforts following their deliverance from the Egyptians. God then was obliged to

---

33 Prince, Joseph. *Destined to Reign.* Tulsa, Ok: Harrison House Publishers; 2007:140.

institute the law to mirror their shortcomings and the subsequent need for grace.[34]

Scripture states you *will* "come short of the glory of God" (Romans 3:23, KJV), but you can allow the grace of Jesus to cleanse you. Instead of focusing on your sins and allowing them to grow into a bitter root of condemnation, allow yourself to be washed clean by the fountain of Jesus' precious blood. You don't have to dwell upon on each and every sin, which will magnify sin-consciousness—just believe and be grateful you are being cleansed. Allow the grace of Jesus to lead you into repentance. Jesus took all your sins to the cross. He bore them so you wouldn't have to. Refuse to bear them and refuse to be condemned. If you condemn yourself for your actions, then Jesus died in vain.

I understand these biblical principles have been misinterpreted and have caused confusion. I have lived in confusion most of my life over these misunderstandings. *However, when you truly understand the Word, you will then know you don't need to review and verbalize each and every sin to be forgiven if Jesus is your Savior.*

If you really think about it, it is truly impossible to confess and ask forgiveness for each and every single sin. I think this is reflected in Paul's preaching in Galatians 5:1, when he said, *"It is for freedom that Christ has set us free. Stand firm, then, and do not let yourselves be burdened again by a yoke of slavery"* (Galatians 5:1, NIV, emphasis added). At that time, Paul was referring to Jewish rituals of sacrifice for the cleansing of sins. I believe that yoke can be applied to Christians today. You can drive yourself crazy worrying about every single thing you do when you don't have a deep revelation of God's saving grace.

I was going down that road when I was first saved. It became an obsession of purity. Prince said he almost lost his mind trying to follow 1 John 1:9. Every time he would commit a sin, he would stop what he was doing to ask for forgiveness, as his primary desire in life was

---

34 Henry, Greg. "Why God Gave the Ten Commandments." Gospel Revolution Church. 7 June 2013.<gospelrevolutionchurch.com>.

to be holy. His point is if you are going to believe this scripture was written for the saved, then you have to believe it all the way.[35] You would have to confess every single time you did not follow Scripture: when you are afraid; when you don't love your neighbor as yourself; when you don't love God with every part of your being; when you don't trust God for every single thing in your life; when you have put someone or something else before God; when you run to someone else to tell them your problems instead of God; when you listen to someone else's advice instead of God's, when you don't reverence your spouse as you reverence Jesus, etc. Furthermore, being sin-conscious and asking forgiveness for every single thing we do wrong would negate the Lord's instructions about not being anxious and keeping ourselves in perfect peace by focusing on Him. That would be impossible to do if we focused on the sin in our life. I know when I dwell on the things I have done wrong, it sends me to the pit of condemnation, sadness, guilt, and anxiety. The enemy wants us in the pit, not Jesus! Jesus came here to set us free. That surely doesn't involve living in a pit of self-condemnation. I keep my focus on my Savior, who helps me to avoid sin in the first place.

Moreover, you really wouldn't have time for anything else if you confessed every single sin! You certainly wouldn't have time to focus on God or advance His kingdom. He knew this. That is why He sent a Savior. Jesus came and fulfilled the law. *He took all of our sins and the great sacrifice became greater than our sin.*[36] *He overcame it for us, so we wouldn't have to.*

"Herein is our love made perfect, that we may have boldness in the day of judgment: because *as he is, so are we in this world*" (1 John 4:17, KJV, emphasis added). This scripture tells us because love is perfected within us, we don't have to fear on judgment day. Christ already judged our sins on the cross. *The only judgment saved Christians have to face is judgment for our works so God can determine what rewards*

35 Prince, Joseph. *Destined to Reign.* Tulsa, Ok: Harrison House Publishers; 2007:106.
36 Prince, Joseph. *Destined to Reign.* Tulsa, Ok: Harrison House Publishers; 2007: 95.

we deserve. This is a source of confusion for many people. They believe they will be judged for every bad thing they ever did. *God showed me this is why many people reject Jesus and His message of love.* They know they will never be able to follow the laws—they will never be holy enough, worthy enough, or measure up in any way. *God wants you to know some religions have it wrong! Christ's last three words were, "…It is finished!"* (John 19:30, NLT*). He wants you to know you are forgiven for all sins: past, present, and future. What a wonderful God we serve.*

In Prince's sermons, he drives home the point *the law doesn't teach us to love, but Jesus and His finished work does.* This is analogous to living with very strict parents. Children usually rebel against overly strict parents because the children can't live up to all the excessive rules and regulations. However, children feel loved, safe, and secure when they have parents who balance discipline with love and understanding. They then grow into loving, well-balanced adults who function appropriately in society.

Because God sees us as He sees His son, He isn't looking at our sins. It is the same when *loving*, earthly parents look at their children. They don't focus on their children's mistakes, but on how much they love their children. *Now you can be confident that no matter what your past sins were they are forgiven, if Jesus lives in you, and you are deeply loved regardless of your mistakes!*

I believe those who argue grace perpetuates sin do not have a deep revelation of the Father's love. *When I fully received Christ, I understood how much God really loved me. I certainly didn't want to do anything to displease Him, so I avoided sin. When I understood just how much He loved me, it made me love Him and others more. Love is perfect, and it magnifies everything within it. It is the most powerful force in the universe. Love is God!* Although we are not perfect and never will be, we strive to please God because He loved us first. Grace certainly doesn't perpetuate sin, but it *covers a multitude of sins!* Just remember that *God isn't looking at our flesh. He looks at our spirit, and our spirit is sealed when we accept Jesus as our Savior. Sin can't contaminate it* (John 4:24, Ephesians 4:30).

I truly believe that understanding and *fully* receiving God's grace through our precious Lord and Savior is what Jesus meant when He said:

> *"And ye shall know the truth, and the truth shall make you free...*If the Son therefore shall make you free, ye shall be free indeed. I know that ye are Abraham's seed; but *ye seek to kill me because my word hath no place in you"* (John 8:32, 36-7, KJV, emphasis added).

In that last scripture, it appears Jesus was talking about His death on the cross. *However, on a deeper level, I believe He was actually saying there are those who are not able to fully receive God's gift of grace due to their belief they have to perfect themselves by their own works, including confession of sins. Their lack of faith in Jesus' finished work will perpetuate self-condemnation and they will continue to live in uncertainty about their eternal salvation. This lack of faith blocks His blessing, which includes the power of the Holy Spirit, from freely flowing in their lives. They will continue to live in bondage and, therefore, will never be free.* How tragic is that? All you have to do is reach up and grab what has already been done for you. It is yours for the taking! *Don't let this precious gift pass you by. It is the most awesome thing you will **ever** receive.*

I know when I became Christ-conscious instead of sin and law-conscious, His grace; power; mercy; and love came rushing forth. My intimacy and ability to hear God grew stronger. When you condemn yourself, you are blocked, and you can't receive the blessing from our sweet Abba Father and precious Lord and Savior, Jesus Christ. You will miss out on the most wonderful thing you could ever experience and will never have the abundant life Jesus came here to give you. Don't reject His precious gift of grace. It will break His heart. *It hurts Him to see you hurting. He's not focusing on your sin. He's focusing on your inability to receive from Him on a daily basis.*

I recently asked Jesus what He was writing in the biblical story (John 8) when He bent down near the ground as a hoard of people were going to stone the woman who had committed adultery. He said He was writing, "You are forgiven." He also revealed He wrote it on the ground because forgiveness is the foundation of Christianity. When you know you are forgiven and loved, you can then love and forgive others, which will empower them to do the same for the next person.

Now, you may be wondering the following: if God is the Creator of the Universe and knows everything, He, therefore, knew no human could follow all of His laws, so why did He create them as well as the redemptive covenant carried out by Jesus Christ? I pondered this mystery. Why *would* He do all of this? Scripture tells us He wanted to bring man to the end of Himself so we would see the need for a Savior (Romans 8:3). Still, I felt there was something more that I needed to understand.

After pondering this for a few days, I woke up one morning and I heard the song "For the Glory of God" playing in my head. He had also given me a dream that night. I knew God had answered my questions.

He was telling me He did all of this for His glory. He wanted man to see it was virtually impossible to follow all of those laws, and *man couldn't save himself by his own works.* He then came down in the flesh to save us so we could love, worship, fellowship with, and glorify Him. He wanted to show His love, mercy, kindness, compassion, and *the extent of what He would do for those that love Him. He wanted us to know who He **truly** is: Our Father, who loves us beyond what we could ever imagine, hope, ask or dream of!*

What better way to prove Himself than to become a Savior of the world? Just think about this for a moment. He made us in His image. We like getting compliments, rewards, affection, attention, and love, right? God likes the same things. He loves to be praised. He had to do something on a grandiose level to capture the attention of the world for all time and bring His beloved children back to Him. That is exactly what He has done. It's been two thousand years since Christ died. He has not been forgotten. He is loved by millions all over the world. His

Word still rings true today and the Bible is the best-selling book of all time.[37] God certainly accomplished His goal through His magnificent plan. The means justified, not a conclusion, but an eternal state of grace. *He deserves all of the glory, honor, and praise!*

FORGIVE YOURSELF

As mentioned in the previous chapter, Jesus alludes to the fact it is self-condemnation that brings disease when He tells the paralyzed man he is forgiven instead of emphasizing he is healed:

> "For whether is easier, to say, Thy sins be forgiven thee; or to say, Arise, and walk? But that ye may know that the Son of man hath power on earth to forgive sins, (then saith he to the sick of the palsy,) Arise, take up thy bed, and go unto thine house" (Matthew 9:5-6, KJV).

Self-condemnation *will* destroy you. I witness this frequently in the lives of others. Those who focus on their sins appear to have more illness, pain, and other types of infirmities. *Condemnation keeps God's grace, love, and power from flowing in your life.* When you yield to sin and focus on it, instead of the forgiveness of your Savior, your body and soul will become defiled. This opens the door for the enemy to bring sickness, discouragement, depression and destruction upon you (1 Peter 5:8-9, KJV). When we are sin-conscious, a root of condemnation is planted deep within our soul, *which will lead to fear and stress.* A root of condemnation can grow into bitter fruit that may include anger, resentment, and insecurity, which ultimately leads to disease.[38] *If you are saved, then God has forgiven you. It is imperative, however, you also forgive yourself.* Think of it this way. If Almighty God has forgiven you, then you need to forgive yourself or you won't be operating in His will.

---

37 Guiness World Records. <guinnessworldrecords.com>. 26 June 2013.
38 Prince, Joseph. *Destined to Reign.* Tulsa, Ok: Harrison House Publishers; 2007: 130-131.

You have to receive forgiveness by forgiving yourself. This includes letting go of self-condemnation and not allowing the enemy to condemn you, which He will do if you dwell upon and continue to verbalize your mistakes. Condemning yourself for your mistakes is one of his most powerful tools to destroy you. Don't let Him! You tell Him to get behind you because you are the righteousness of God through Jesus' powerful blood. Keep declaring God is making you brand new and you are progressing into the person He created you to be. You are fulfilling His divine plan to advance His kingdom and bring Him glory as you win souls to Him. Focus on that instead of your past failures. Profess it so the enemy can hear you make these declarations of spiritual warfare. He will be defeated!

You are most likely aware research has proven stress is a major cause for a multitude of diseases and conditions. If you take apart the word "disease," you can see it is dis-ease: you become at dis-ease or uneasy with yourself. Stress leads to an imbalance of the central nervous system, which then causes the endocrine system to become hyperactive, and the body receives abnormal amounts of hormones. *Stress greatly affects the mind and body.*[39] Stress can cause heart palpitations and lead to heart attacks.

When I experience stress, I can actually feel a dramatic change in my physical well-being. I become light-headed, cannot focus, and experience extreme fatigue. I have noticed since I was transformed by the grace of Jesus and now have joy and peace in my life, when I do allow stress to creep in, it totally wrecks my body for the entire day. The symptoms that come with stress are now much worse. Before I was saved, it would take a great deal of stress to cause symptoms that impeded my ability to function. Now it only takes minor stress to achieve the same effect. Perhaps it is difficult for the body to manage episodes of negativity when it usually functions in a medium of positive energy. We are mind, body, and spirit. When one component gets out of alignment, the other parts then become imbalanced. Research indicates that a coherent heart rhythm and the electromagnetic field it

---

39 Porth, Carol M. "Stress and Adaptation." *Pathophysiology.* 2nd ed. Philadelphia, Penn: J.B. Lippincott, 1986:86-88.

produces is the key to the healing process by "regenerating and stabilizing the basic autonomic rhythm of the organism." The results found that exposure to a coherent electrocardiogram signal resulted in the inhibition of the growth of cancer cells and stimulation of the growth of healthy cells.[40] From this information, it is clear that your heart needs to be free of all negative influences. Let the grace of God transform your heart so you can begin the healing process. Don't allow condemnation, which leads to guilt and causes stress, to remain rooted in your heart. God repeatedly instructs us through His Word to avoid stress. Pray you will receive the revelation you are forgiven so you can let go of all condemnation that may come from yourself, others and the enemy. Meditate upon this scripture:

> *"There is therefore now no condemnation to them which are in Christ Jesus, who walk not after the flesh, but after the Spirit. For the law of the Spirit of life in Christ Jesus hath made me free from the law of sin and death"* (Romans 8:1-2, KJV, emphasis added).

YOU WILL FORGIVE

If you have truly been saved, you will eventually forgive others. If you are in a state of pride and continue to think vengeful thoughts against a person who has hurt you, and you have no intention or desire to forgive that person, then you need to ask Jesus to come live in your heart and save you. The Bible states if we don't forgive others then God can't forgive us. I believe this scripture points to two circumstances: to those who haven't yet been saved; and to those who have received *eternal* salvation but have not *fully* received the grace of Jesus for *comprehensive* salvation. Those who haven't fully received Jesus are likely to have hardened hearts due to life's circumstances, which has blocked the saving grace of Jesus' blood from cleansing them due to the resentment they are harboring. However, when you do have a

---

40 McCraty, R., *The Energetic Heart: Bioelectricmagnetic Communication Within People*, in *Bioelectric Medicine*, P.J. Rosch and M.S. Markov, Editors. 2004, Marcel Dekker: New York. P. 541-562.

forgiving heart, then God's grace will flow through you. This truth is supported in the prophecy of Isaiah:

> "For thus saith the high and lofty One that inhabiteth eternity, whose name is Holy; I dwell in the high and holy place, **with him also that is of a contrite and humble spirit**, to revive the spirit of the humble, and to revive the heart of the contrite ones" (Isaiah 57:15, KJV, emphasis added).

In the forgiveness process, it's important you distinguish your feelings from your heart's desire. You may not *feel* like forgiving someone because of the pain, but you *want* to forgive that person because, in your heart, you know God instructs you to do so for your own self-preservation. All of those negative thoughts focused on that other person will totally zap your energy, dampen your spirit, and create destruction in your life (Hebrews 12:15). During the forgiveness process, don't dwell on the emotion attached to the hurtful event. Cast it down and take authority over it. Meditate upon this verse to help you release the pain while you are in the forgiveness process: "No weapon that is formed against thee shall prosper" (Isaiah 54:17, KJV).

More importantly, when you focus on the pain, you are focusing on the wrong thing. The only thing we should magnify is God. When we keep our eyes on Him, His power will flow into us, and His great plans for us will then easily manifest in our lives. If we focus on negative thoughts stemming from negative emotions, then we will produce and attract[41] some rotten things in our lives. If we dwell on the hurtful event and the pain, we will become resentful. In essence, we are giving our power to the person that hurt us. Forgiveness means we don't focus on the hurt and the behavior behind it. We have to release the person and focus on God's power and plan for our lives. God will turn it around for good when we walk with Him (Romans 8:28). He *always* does.

---

41 McCraty, R., *The Energetic Heart: Bioelectricmagnetic Communication Within People, in Bioelectric Medicine, P.J. Rosch and M.S. Markov, Editors. 2004, Marcel Dekker: New York. P. 541-562.*

God turned it for good for Joseph after he forgave His brothers who sold him into slavery: "But as for you, ye thought evil against me; *but God* meant it unto good, to bring to pass, as it is this day, to save much people alive" (Genesis 50:20, emphasis added). "Joseph is able to forgive because he sees his situation from an eternal perspective. He realizes that even though his brothers intended to harm him . . . . God was working through even those sinful intentions." [42] God *will* make it all work out when you forgive and believe in:

His plan
His power
His restoration
His redemption
His undying love for you
His faithfulness
His favor
His righteousness
His justice
His unending mercy
His forgiveness
His peace
His joy
His patience
His wisdom
His knowledge
His grace

There is an amazing story of forgiveness concerning a man, Robert Cotton, who was wrongfully imprisoned for several years after being convicted of rape. When his sentence was finally overturned, his accuser, Jennifer Thompson, mustered up enough courage to ask him to forgive her. She had been overwhelmed with shame and guilt. Cotton forgave her and Thompson became a crusader to create legislation to compensate those who are wrongfully convicted. Cotton later received one hundred and ten thousand dollars due to the new legisla-

---

42 Goettche, Bruce. Lessons on Forgiveness. Union Church. 28 June 2013. <union-church.com>

tion. His ability to forgive brought him restitution. He and Thompson now work together as a team to reform laws for innocent prisoners. Because of Cotton's forgiving heart, there will be many people who will benefit, lives will be restored, and healing will take place.[43]

Cotton and Thompson's story demonstrate how God works it all out for good (Romans 8:28). He can take your pain and do the same thing. I know because He did that for me. I was able to forgive those who have hurt me and keep my focus on God. His blessing flows in my life and allows me to bless others. He will also turn around your pain if you allow Him to do so and create great things for His kingdom. Your pain may be the flame that ignites healing, restoration, and provision for many people.

In order to initiate the forgiveness process you need to declare forgiveness. Let's say your hypothetical friend, Karen, did some terrible thing that really hurt you and you are having difficulty forgiving her. Just keep declaring you freely forgive her. Also ask God to help you to forgive her. Treat Karen as though you have forgiven her. That doesn't necessarily mean you have to go out of your way to spend time with her, but treat her with love and respect if and when you are together. Above all, pray for God to bless and forgive this person. *Remember, the enemy influenced her to hurt you. She didn't do it **totally** alone:* "For we **wrestle not against flesh and blood**, but against principalities, against powers, against the rulers of the darkness of this world, against spiritual wickedness in high places" (Ephesians 6:12, KJV, emphasis added). This spiritual truth always helps me in the forgiveness process. I strongly believe it will help you too, if you receive a revelation of it.

You have probably heard forgiveness is actually for you so you can free yourself from the bondage of the negative emotions attached with the infraction. These hurtful feelings, in essence, attach you to the perpetrator. But I believe it goes deeper than that. *You are blaming the wrong person.* The one who hurt you was simply a pawn on the chess-

---

43 "An Incredible True Story of Forgiveness." Willson, Elizabeth Moss. Blue Ridge Now. 10 June 2013. Published 06 June 10. <blueridgenow.com>.

board of evil. The enemy is the culprit. He is the one that influenced the person to behave in ungodly ways that caused the hurtful behavior as emphasized in the following scripture: "Then entered Satan into Judas..." (Luke 22:3, KJV). This occurred prior to Judas betraying Jesus, which led to His crucifixion. This speaks volumes. Just think about this for a moment. This man walked with Jesus and experienced not only His miracles, but also His beautiful countenance and magnificent love. There is no way this ultimate betrayal could have happened without the power of the enemy driving such an event. This is how the rulers of darkness operate in the world in which we live.

This operation from the darkness is perhaps what Jesus meant when He said on the cross, "*...forgive them for they know not what they do*" (Luke 23:34, KJV, emphasis added). The enemy's power works in those who have not been saved and encourages them to do evil, just as Christ's power is in Christians and enables us to do good works. *So you need to forgive your enemies and bless them because on a deep spiritual level they do not fully understand what, or, more importantly, why they do it.* I am not by any means saying they are completely blameless in their actions, but I have to emphasize that the hurtful behavior is influenced from the rulers of darkness and spiritual wickedness in *high places* (Ephesians 6:12). This dark influence has a significant role in initiating and executing the process of the perpetrator's behavior.

The forgiveness process includes speaking blessings over your enemies. Ask God to open their hearts so they will run to Him and become new creatures in Christ. Pray they will never be influenced by the enemy to hurt others again. This is how we should all pray for those who have hurt us. Just reflect on this for a moment. If we all prayed this way, God would intervene because He doesn't want people hurting each other. I know these prayers would be extremely powerful because there would be millions of them at any given moment in time going up to Heaven. When prayers go up, blessings come down (Genesis 28:12). That would be the ultimate revenge on the adversary—he would not be able to influence anyone ever again to do his dirty, rotten work. Then there would be no more pain and suffering in the world. I truly believe that is why God tells us to pray for our enemies.

Keep in mind forgiveness may not happen overnight, but you will eventually get there. It does take a while to process all of those feelings and let go of them. Over time, God's love, mercy, and power of His cleansing blood will completely wash away all those hurt feelings of anger, bitterness, and resentment.

However, if you are in state of pride and your heart is hardened, you won't be able to forgive because you haven't fully received Jesus and been transformed by His grace. A hardened heart is like a dam that holds everything in and keeps everything out. It blocks God's power, His grace, and His tender mercy from freely flowing through you like the river of life that it truly is. If you think you are saved and have been through all of the motions—the prayer of salvation and baptism—but your fruit is still rotten to the core, then ask God to help you to fully receive Jesus into your heart. This is what I experienced because I had blocked the love of Jesus out of my hardened heart due to the abuse and pain I had endured. It took the death of my husband to truly desire Jesus to come and live in my heart. I finally realized Jesus was my only hope. Many times, unfortunately, that's what it takes for most of us: a tragedy to open our eyes and our hearts to Jesus' saving grace. Pray ahead of time. *Ask Jesus to soften your heart and invite Him in, so He doesn't have to hit you over the head to get your attention.*

I frequently say aloud, "I freely forgive everyone that has every hurt me and I speak blessings over their lives. I release all persons that may have hurt me to you, Father. They are yours and I know you will take care of them." I feel this will cover any resentment I may be unconsciously harboring and release all attachments that I may have to any individual who has caused some type of problem in my life.

I know from experience it is imperative to make the first move during the forgiveness process. The perpetrator may be experiencing feelings of guilt or shame. He or she may be fearful of approaching you due to the uncertainty of your reaction. When you show them kindness and love, it often brings relief from their own pain; and the healing process for both of you will begin.

Forgiveness is like a chain reaction. When Christ forgives us, it enables us to be loving and forgiving. When we forgive others, it softens their hearts to receive the love of Jesus as they are able to let go of the shame, guilt, regret, and pain that resulted from the hurtful event. They are then empowered to initiate the forgiveness process and bestow the same gift upon the next person.

If you are having difficulty with forgiving someone, focus on the forgiveness of Jesus. As He hung on that cross in agony, He said, "… Father, forgive them; for they know not what they do" (Luke 23:34, KJV). If He could forgive after all that was done to Him, we should also be able to forgive those who have hurt us.

CHAPTER FIVE

KNOW YOUR DIVINE
BIRTHRIGHT AND CLAIM IT

HE DOES RESTORE

The Holy Bible is, in essence, the will of Almighty God. Within the Bible are numerous promises of restoration. The Holy Spirit revealed to me one of the reasons God wants to restore His children is because He is just and He knows the enemy *influences* us to make bad choices, which ultimately leads to destruction in our lives. It is imperative I point out the enemy can't *make* you do anything, but he can, however, definitely influence and initiate the action if the desire to do something sinful in your life is already present. Scripture tells us that in James 1:14, but I believe the majority of Christians, and perhaps non-believers as well, wouldn't have committed those acts if we hadn't been prodded to do so. The enemy will play on your weaknesses with every strategy he has to get you off track by taking your eyes off of God.

I am repeating this scripture because I want you to be aware of what you are dealing with: "For we *wrestle not against flesh and blood*, but against principalities, against powers, against the rulers of the darkness of this world, against spiritual wickedness in high places"

(Ephesians 6:12, KJV, emphasis added). I know there are many people who think this is false, but I can testify to this truth as I have had a few visions that have given me a glimpse of the darkness in this world and some of the evil people in it.

Ultimately before we were saved, we didn't have any authority over the strategy of the enemy, who influenced us to be out of God's perfect will. Keep in mind the enemy comes only to kill, steal, and destroy. That is his one and only mission (John 10:10). However, when we come to God and give our lives to Him, then we are under His saving power of grace, and we have then chosen the right path. Therefore because God is just, He wants to restore us. More importantly, He is our sweet Abba Father who wants all good things for His children. He understands what we have been through and why we have been through it.

I recently reminded God, in one of my morning prayers, of His great promise of restoration. I told Him I was angry at the enemy for trying to destroy me, but I wasn't angry with the people that he'd used to hurt me. I wanted *every single thing* the enemy had stolen from me: relationships; including my intimacy with my Heavenly Father, finances; my health; my emotional stability; and my self-confidence. How dare he keep what belonged to me! I now belonged to God and I demanded the enemy take his hands off of me. I heard God say, "Have no fear, little child." Now I knew this was God speaking to me because I don't talk that way, and He was saying it at the same time I was praying. I know He wanted to make sure I received the message, and I did. I knew it was Him because it's impossible to have two conversations going on in my head at one time, unless He was also speaking. *He was reminding me just to trust and rest in Him because He is in control and is handling every single thing.* I can be assured He is taking care of me, just as He always has and always will.

Later that day, He directed me to the following scripture, which confirmed what He had spoken to me: "Now unto him that is able to do **exceeding abundantly above all** that we ask or think, according to the power that **works** in us," (Ephesians 3:20, NKJV, emphasis added).

Look at the adjectives in the scripture. God is telling us He will greatly exceed our expectations when we approach Him for assistance. He can and *will* blow our minds. Our brains will be short circuited: "does not compute, does not compute!" He will continue to amaze us with divine intervention. Notice the verb tense of the word "work" in the scripture. It is in the present tense, which means His power is in you right now. That power is the Holy Spirit *working* in you. He is your partner in your spiritual walk with God and will ensure God's promises will be fulfilled. The Holy Spirit has placed great faith in me, which is one of His gifts. I have great faith in a complete restoration for my life. Pray the Holy Spirit will activate the faith He has placed within you. It is one of the most wonderful gifts you will ever receive.

Restoration is not only one of His promises, but it is a biblical pattern. As previously mentioned, Job lost everything. In the book of Job, we learn God wanted Job to be fully restored. He restored him sevenfold. Remember, the Word tells us God is not a respecter of persons. What He has done for one person, He will do for all, and that includes you. *You are His child, His own special treasure. He holds you in the palm of His hand, and He wants to restore you. You are more precious to Him than gold, silver, or jewels and His greatest desire is to restore your life because He truly loves you.*

There are numerous passages in the Bible that tell of destruction and restoration. Throughout the Old Testament there are numerous stories of restoration from God's people being oppressed and robbed. Throughout the New Testament, Jesus restored physical health to numerous people. In fact, Jesus' purpose was restoration. He restored us to our former relationship with God and paved the way for us to receive eternal life and our divine inheritance. His last words on the cross were, "...***It is finished***!..." (John 19:30, KJV). He only said three words, but in my opinion, those last three words were the most powerful words He ever said. *He dissolved all the power of the destructive evil forces for those who would claim Him as their Savior and receive the fullness of who He truly is: the son of God who wants every good thing that our Heavenly Father planned for us. When we keep our focus totally on our Lord and Savior and fully receive His grace, we* *will receive comprehensive salvation and have kingdom living on this Earth here and now!*

The enemy's sole purpose is to destroy us, but w*hen we identify the thief and demand restoration, he has to return everything he took from us sevenfold* (Proverbs 6:31). Since the rulers of darkness create the evil in your life, you have to demand restoration from them. They are the thieves that have robbed you of the abundant life Jesus came to give you. Let's say you have a problem with rejection. You need to specifically identify the perpetrator, the spirit of rejection, and demand it restore you sevenfold so you can develop and maintain healthy relationships.

In Luke, chapter 18, Jesus tells a parable about the persistent widow who repeatedly approached a judge who did not fear God or man. She was demanding justice for some wrong done to her and the judge repeatedly denied her. Because she was insistent and demanded her rights, he finally gave in and granted the justice she had insisted was her due. *Jesus goes on to say if an ungodly judge will grant justice to someone, a righteous God will surely do the same.* From the story, *it is apparent we need to be persistent and demand restoration. If an enemy has stolen from you, whether it is material or spiritual treasures, demand it be restored to you sevenfold as your Heavenly Father has promised. Keep God in remembrance as He instructs us to do.*

He will not just restore you, but everything taken *from your ancestors* as well. This is emphasized when God instructed Abraham to leave his homeland and family, which resulted in God's promise of restoration through Abraham's descendants:

> "And Abram passed through the land unto the place of Sichem, unto the plain of Moreh. And the Canaanite was then in the land. And the Lord appeared unto Abram, and said, **Unto thy seed** will I give this land: and there built he an altar unto the Lord, who appeared unto him" (Genesis 12:6-7, KJV, emphasis added).

The promise to Abraham's descendants is repeated throughout the Old Testament:

> "And, behold, I *am* with thee, and will keep thee in all *places* whither thou goest, and will bring thee again into this land; for I will not leave thee, until I have done *that* which I have spoken to thee of" (Genesis 28:15, KJV).

> "And Joseph said to his brethren, I die: and God will surely visit you, and bring you out of this land unto the land which he sware to Abraham, to Isaac, and to Jacob" (Genesis 50:24, KJV).

> "Then the Lord (Adonai) said to Moses "And I will bring you in unto the land, concerning the which I did swear to give it to Abraham, to Isaac, and to Jacob; and I will give it you for an heritage: I am the Lord" (Exodus 6:8, KJV).

> "And the LORD thy God will bring thee into the land which thy fathers possessed, and thou shalt possess it; and he will do thee good, and multiply" (Deuteronomy 30:5, KJV).

God is a restorer today as well as yesterday. He revealed His promise of restoration to me in the following dream, which I would like to share with you. God does not play favorites among His children, which means *this dream is for all who are reading right now!* When He gives one of us a message about His promises, He wants all of us to hear it because His promises are for all His children.

The dream I had occurred the night before a guest speaker delivered a sermon at the church I was attending. The message in the dream was confirmed when the reverend spoke of God's promise of restoration several times during his sermon.

I dreamed I was in church where there was a rabbi in the pulpit. He later changed into an Egyptian robe. I praised him by telling him how good he looked in his robe, and it was obvious how much pleasure my praise gave him. He then handed me three trays of very beautiful gemstones and jewelry and then walked away. I thought to myself the jewels must not be real. How could he trust a stranger with such precious valuables?

Prior to this dream, I had three related dreams over a period of about three weeks. Two of the dreams came to me in one night. All three were all about going to Ireland. This was a place I had always wanted to visit because of its incredible beauty and the fact my *ancestors* came from there. In one of the dreams about Ireland, I was standing in a valley, and I could see on a hilltop in the distance a big sign that read Edinburgh. (I realize Edinburgh is in Scotland, but my dream took place in Ireland, and God was trying to make His point as my ancestors came from Ireland.) I thought maybe God was telling me to move to Ireland, so I kept asking Him what He was trying to tell me.

After some pondering on the dreams' symbolism, I then realized my dreams about Ireland were connected to my dream about the rabbi. God was telling me to be patient and trust Him. Because of my ability to trust in and receive from Him, He was going to restore everything the enemy had stolen, not just from me, but from other generations as well.

I surrendered to God in my darkest hour through one simple prayer during my husband's illness, which was totally devastating, as he had been everything to me. God heard me and answered my prayer. I trusted Him to turn my life around. *Because of this one touch from God*, He is now bringing me into the Promised Land, just as He took the Israelites out of bondage in Egypt to bring them there. Now, if you know your Bible history, you may be thinking only two were brought into the Promised Land, but those two had praised and trusted God. The remaining Israelites, who were originally freed from Egypt, never received the blessing because of their complaining and distrust of God, despite all the miracles and amazing love He had showed them.

Also in the Bible, we are told God made the Egyptians give His chosen people precious jewels and metals to build a tabernacle in the wilderness. He is doing the same for me and will for you as well. He has taken me out of the wilderness, as I was a lost soul, and has given me the resources to create a wonderful temple within me where I worship Him. It has become a lifestyle, not just something I do on Sunday.

A few years ago, I would have never seen myself doing this, but He had other plans for me. This is *why* He created us—to bring Him great pleasure and to love us. He, therefore, wants the best for us. Doesn't that make sense? How could we bring Him pleasure if we live in misery and poverty? This is not His will for us; instead, we are to have the abundant life for which Christ came to give us (John 10:10, KJV).

He has shown me through this dream He has given all of us precious gifts to create an Eden, which was symbolized in my dream by the Edinburgh sign on the hilltop. *He has given all of us the ability to overcome any situation, wherever we may be, whatever our circumstances are,* just as I have now created an Eden following the devastating death of my beloved husband. I can truly say this because I have unspeakable joy and peace, which surpasses all understanding. The life I now have is totally beyond my comprehension after losing my Johnny. He was my entire life and I wanted to die with him. In essence, I was dead. I was a walking corpse just going through the motions of the daily grind of life, hoping it would one day end soon. ***But God! That says it all! But, God! I have to pause again and say, "Thank you, my precious Lord and Savior for making me new!"*** I know He will also make you new. That is His promise, which is what He specializes in!

> "And he that sat upon the throne said, Behold, I make ***all*** things new" (Revelations 21:5, KJV, emphasis added).

God loves us, and He loves it when we sincerely worship Him. This was symbolized in the dream when I told the rabbi how good he looked in his robe and by the pleasure my praise gave him. God is now blessing me because I did not complain, but turned to and praised Him during the worse trial of my life. When we worship God with our *whole* heart, especially in our trials which demonstrate our faith and trust in Him, intimacy with Him grows. He then lavishes us with great rewards, which was symbolized by the jewels in the dream. He has rewarded me in every area of my life simply because I chose Him instead of focusing on the evil that surrounded the tragedy of my husband's death.

After I had these dreams, I felt a great excitement within me began to stir and rise up. I felt like great and wonderful things were coming my way. Just two months later, I began writing this book for my Heavenly Father. *He does restore!* I know this is true because I have experienced restoration in all areas of my life since these dreams.

He is faithful to His promises. You may be in the valley right now, but if you hold on; trust in Him; and continue to renew your mind in the Word, you will soon be on the mountaintop. Whatever happens, no matter how you feel, don't stop praising Him! *Part of the reason God is faithful is because He is truth:* **"God is not a man that he should lie"** (Numbers 23:19, KJV, emphasis added). God always tells the truth—He can't help himself. A lie cannot fall from His lips. *So, it stands to reason He will fulfill all of His promises—not only the ones in the Bible, but any that He has made directly to you.* When we begin to understand His truthfulness and faithfulness, our faith in Him grows. In reality, it becomes a divine cycle of faith and trust.

Are there things in your life that need to be restored? Well, have no fear, little child. His promise is for you, too. God has promised, "… even to day do I declare that I will render double unto thee;" (Zechariah 9:12, KJV). One of the most beautiful promises of restoration is found in Isaiah, which prophecies the purpose of the first coming of our Lord and Savior, Jesus Christ:

> "The Spirit of the Sovereign Lord is on me, because the Lord has anointed me to proclaim good news to the poor. He has sent me to bind up the brokenhearted, to proclaim freedom for the captives and release from darkness for the prisoners, to

proclaim the year of the ***Lord's favor*** and the day of vengeance of our God, to comfort all who mourn, and provide for those who grieve in Zion—to bestow on them a crown of beauty instead of ashes, the oil of joy instead of mourning, and a garment of praise instead of a spirit of despair. They will be called oaks of righteousness, a planting of the Lord for the display of his splendor." (Isaiah 61:1-3, NIV, emphasis added).

Look at the phrase in bold. God tells us He will favor us. This means He will shift events for us so His plan for our lives will be fulfilled. You can't help but glorify the Lord when He has restored you from a bottomless pit to a Garden of Eden!

There are several other places in the Bible where God promises restoration:

"He restoreth my soul…" (Psalms 23:3, KJV).

"Return, ye backsliding children, And I will heal your backslidings" (Jeremiah 3:22, KJV).

"For whatsoever is born of God overcometh the world: and this is the victory that overcometh the world, even our faith" (1 John 5:4, KJV).

"For I will restore health unto thee, and I will heal thee of thy wounds, saith the LORD; because they called thee an Outcast, saying, This is Zion, whom no man seeketh after" (Jeremiah 30:17, KJV).

"Verily, verily, I say unto you, He that heareth my word, and believeth on him that sent me, hath everlasting life, and shall not come into condemnation; but is passed from death unto life" (John 5:24, KJV).

Let's take a look at the definition of restore translated from the original Hebrew language of the Old Testament. The Hebrew word, "chayah khaw-yaw" means to revive, give life, live, nourish up, preserve, quicken, recover, repair, restore (to life), save, and be whole.[44] This definition suggests *every facet of your life will be restored* under God's promise. God promises not only to give it back to you, but give you more than you originally had:

> "For your shame ye shall have double; and for confusion they shall rejoice in their portion: therefore in their land they shall possess the double: everlasting joy shall be unto them" (Isaiah 61:7, KJV).

I can really relate to the scripture in Isaiah, as many of us can who have dealt with some type of dysfunction in our lives. There were things I had to deal with when I was growing up that were really embarrassing to me. People can be very cruel, especially to someone who is obese. So I have great expectations God will give me that twofold recompense because of everything I had to endure. He has already begun and continues to perform a great restoration in my life. *God loves us so much He wants to restore us so He can make up for all the pain we have endured.*

I have so many wonderful blessings because of God. He delivered me on all levels—physical, emotional, spiritual, mental, relational, and financial. God promises us:

> "Because he hath set his love upon me, ***therefore will I deliver him:*** I will set him on high because he hath known my name. He shall call upon me, and I will answer him: I will be with him in trouble; I will deliver him, and honour him" (Psalms 91:14-15, KJV, emphasis added).

I know right now, as I type these very words, God is doing a mighty work in my life and He will do the same for you. All you have to do is rest in Him and *receive* what has already been done for you. *Ask God to help you to receive* all of His wonderful blessings that are awaiting you and

---

44 Online Strong's Concordance. EliYah.com. 7 June 2013. <eliyah.com>.

then just sit back and see how your life will change. But first you have to submit yourself to God. Putting Him first, by developing a relationship with and resting in Him, will help to fix your "receiver." As Matthew tells us, "But seek ye first the kingdom of God and his righteousness, and all these things shall be added unto you" (Matthew 6:33, KJV).

If you received salvation later in life, God will restore all the years you lost due to the enemy's control over you. He is a redeemer of time. This is what God meant when He said, "And I will restore to you *the years* that the locust hath eaten" (Joel 2:25, KJV, emphasis added). "Through repentance all which has been lost by sin is restored."[45] He restored me after I turned back to Him. I had rejected Him and my life was nearly destroyed. But like any loving father, He wants His children to have all of those wonderful things He planned for us before we were created. He restored me to who He created me to be: a child of a King, whole, healthy, prosperous and blessed to be a blessing! *I know deep in my heart, it is His will to restore you also.* Because of all of those years you couldn't receive His blessing; He is going to make sure you obtain what is rightfully yours. The enemy is a thief, and *God will make him pay you back if you are His child, not because of who you are or what you have or haven't done; but because of who God is. He is the God of justice, righteousness, mercy, wisdom, faithfulness and enduring love. He can't bear to see you abused, neglected, mistreated, robbed, or cheated (Isaiah 61:8). Rest assured, when you bring the enemy before the Supreme Justice, He will execute the order for restitution!*

Since God is a redeemer of time, He is able to make regrets vanish. You may have a sense of loss over a relationship that you put to the side or didn't develop because of past hurts. Perhaps you have been estranged from someone for decades. Now that God has mended things, you may wonder why you allowed there to be a barrier between you and the other person all those years. Don't worry. God can and will fix that too. *It will be like you never lost the time.* As your relationship grows stronger and deeper, those lost years won't even matter anymore. All that will be important is the depth of what you now have. *God will draw you*

---

45 "Barnes notes on Joel 2:25." Godvine. 09 June 2013. <godvine.com>.

extremely close to that other person and Himself. The spiritual bond you will share will make everything else irrelevant. God is the restorer of all things. Nothing is too big or impossible for Him, "…but with God all things are possible" (Matthew 19:26, KJV, emphasis added).

My turnaround during the restoration process was actually fairly quick. It didn't drag out over years, but took only a few short months. God will do that for you also if you put your whole heart into Him. *All the time you lost doesn't matter because you will be living an abundant life and God's great restoration will make up for what the enemy stole from you.* More importantly, when you know you will live in eternity with *the most loving being in the universe, your sweet Abba Father,* then the past doesn't matter any longer. It becomes like dust in the wind. *Thank you, Lord!*

God has fully made my relationship with my earthly family new. That is a true miracle. We were never close and had been estranged for several years. As an adult, I became full of bitterness, resentment, anger, and sadness over not having a loving relationship with my family. After I rededicated myself to the Lord, I reminded God of His wonderful promise to restore my relationships. He did exactly that, so wonderfully and beyond my wildest imagination. Now, I truly love them. They mean the world to me. I really enjoy being with them. I never thought this would ever be possible, but *God is the great restorer!*

God also promises, "And he shall be unto thee a ***restorer of thy life***" (Ruth 4:15, KJV, emphasis added). If you have suffered because of anything not created by your Heavenly Father, including poverty, illness, loneliness, depression or rejection, ***God wants to and will give you back your life.*** *He does not want you sitting in a corner somewhere wasting your precious time. He created you to plant the Heavens and the Earth* (Isaiah 51:16) *and He wants to see His plan carried out to completion.* It is His will to *completely* restore you.

So, how do you begin the process of restoration? All you need to do is demand restoration from the enemy and remind God of His promises, which He instructs us to do (Isaiah 43:26, 62:6-7). You have a divine inheritance from your Heavenly Father. When an heir has been robbed of what is rightfully theirs, they stand up and demand their birthright be returned to them. This is what you have to do. Demand the enemy restore all of those things He stole from you.

If you are now walking with God, remind Him of His promise to restore. *He tells us to "**put me in remembrance…**"* (Isaiah 43:26, KJV, emphasis added). I have wondered why God would say this. Does He have a memory problem? Does He have so many things to do it is hard for Him to get to everything? Is His list so long it impedes His concentration? Of course not. God is almighty and knows everything. He has given us free will and He is a gentleman. He is just waiting for you to demand the enemy give back *everything* he took from you!

I also believe He wants us to remind Him because it's possible the timing isn't right for restoration when the enemy first steals something from us. Perhaps God wants us to consider the situation and learn something from it. Maybe it is going to strengthen us in some kind of way. Maybe the waiting period will help us develop some amazing testimony for God. It may be He is waiting for your faith in the saving grace of Jesus to develop further. Whatever the reason, the Bible tells us, "To every thing there is a *season*, and a *time* to every purpose under the heaven" (Ecclesiastes 3:1, KJV, emphasis added).

It might be He is waiting for you to accept Jesus as your Savior. This was the case for me. He began to restore me in many ways soon after I rededicated myself to Him. Even though I had turned away from God, he *never* turned away from me. So, when God says to keep Him in remembrance, perhaps He is saying, "I'm not going to restore you at the exact moment of the incident, but I am going to do it later, so remind me." *I frequently remind God of His promises.*

Now that you are aware of God's great promise, tell Him you have great expectations for a full restitution. This is working your faith. You believe He will restore everything taken from you as He promised, and now you are acting on it. Make specific demands on the enemy for recovering your stolen treasures whether it is relationships, finances or your health. Be clear, concise, and authoritative. Remember, you have power over him, so be demanding!

Now here comes the part that may seem difficult, or at least perplexing. *Tell God you freely forgive* all those people who have hurt you in some way *and ask Him to bless them.* Then, speak blessings over their lives. If you have resentment, it will block His blessing from flowing. You can't receive, when you can't forgive. When you forgive, it opens the flood gate of God's love, which heals the hurt and melts the resentment buried under the pain.

Now that you have kept God in remembrance of restoration and forgiven your enemies, you need to speak God's promises to restore. Then you need to visualize what restoration looks like in your life. This puts your faith into action, which is necessary because "…faith without works is dead" (James 2:20, KJV). For example, I visualize myself surrounded by loving people. I even visualize having interactions with them. Remember what the scripture says: "Now faith is the **substance** of things **hoped** for, the **evidence** of things not seen" (Hebrews 11:1, KJV, emphasis added). The word "substance" implies faith has energy. Faith begins with a thought, develops into a belief, and results in some type of action as noted in the book of Mark: "Since they could not get him to Jesus because of the crowd, they made an opening in the roof above Jesus by digging through it and then lowered the mat the man was lying on. When Jesus *saw* their faith, he said to the paralyzed man, "Son, your sins are forgiven" (Mark 2:4-5, NIV, emphasis added). Put that energy (belief) into motion, which will allow your Heavenly Father to *see* your faith. *When he sees your faith, He will release the blessing to create your divine destiny that He planned for you.*

God's promise to restore, in my opinion, is His greatest promise because restoration not only includes salvation, but encompasses prosperity. Many people think of money when they hear this word, but it is so much more than that. The biblical definition of prosperity from the New Testament original Greek language is to be blessed.[46] Being

---

46 Online Strong"s Concordance. EliYah.com. 15 June 2013. <www.eliyah.com>.

blessed gives you the ability to accomplish God's will. *Therefore, to be prosperous means the fruit and one or more of the gifts of the Holy Spirit is manifesting in your life to glorify God.* This includes the characteristics of love, joy, peace, forbearance, kindness, goodness, faithfulness, gentleness, and self-control. It also may include extraordinary faith, wisdom, healing power, knowledge or prophetic ability. These attributes of the Holy Spirit may be lying dormant even after we are saved; therefore, we need to remind God of His promise to restore and ask the Holy Spirit to help us access it. We will then be empowered to wins souls to Jesus, advance God's kingdom, and bring Him great pleasure. This is the purpose for which He created us.

POWER IN THE BLOOD

It is our divine birthright as co-heirs with Jesus to call on the power of His blood. There *is* power in the blood of Jesus Christ. Thank God daily for covering you with the blood before you get out of and into the bed. Always plead the blood over you, your loved ones, your pets, and your property for protection against the enemy.

God speaks about blood throughout the Bible. He instructed the Israelites not to consume the blood of animals. God also instructed the Israelites to mark their doorposts with blood, which identified them as His people. Subsequently, their lives were spared as He executed judgment against the Egyptians before He delivered His people from bondage:

> "And they shall take of the blood, and strike it on the two side posts and on the upper door post of the houses...For I will pass through the land of Egypt this night, and will smite all the first-born in the land of Egypt, both man and beast; and against all the gods of Egypt I will execute judgment: I am the Lord. And the blood shall be to you for a token upon the houses where ye are: and when I see the blood, I will pass over you, and the plague shall not be upon you to destroy you, when I smite the land of Egypt. And this day shall be unto you for a memorial; and ye shall keep it a feast to the Lord throughout your

generations; ye shall keep it a feast by an ordinance for ever" (Exodus 12:7, 12-14, KJV).

God's blood is cleansing, purifying, healing, and protective. Blood is the life force of every living creature, and the blood of Jesus Christ is God's divine energy that was transferred into human composition. His precious blood must be more powerful beyond what we can ever comprehend.

God set the guidelines that blood was to be used to cleanse sins. "For the life of the flesh is in the blood: and I have given it to you upon the altar to make an atonement for your souls: for it is the blood that maketh an atonement for the soul" (Leviticus 17:11, KJV). God also gave Moses the following instruction on how to use the blood of animals during sacrificial offerings for the forgiveness of sins:

> "And the priest shall dip his finger in the blood, and sprinkle of the blood seven times before the Lord, before the vail of the sanctuary. And the priest shall put some of the blood upon the horns of the altar of sweet incense before the Lord, which is in the tabernacle of the congregation; and shall pour all the blood of the bullock at the bottom of the altar of the burnt of-fering, which is at the door of the tabernacle of the congrega-tion" (Leviticus 4: 6-7, KJV).

These animal sacrifices foreshadowed the precious sacrifice of our Lord and Savior's blood (Hebrews 10, KJV). Jesus' precious and powerful blood was spilled from all over His body. He was scourged beyond recognition prior to His crucifixion. *The stripes on His back, from the torture He endured for us, provide our heal-ing. He identified with **all** of our physical suffering, which enables us to identify with His glorified, strong, healthy body. This is the great exchange that took place due to the New Covenant. "...with His stripes ,we **are** healed"* (Isaiah 53:5, KJV, emphasis added). We need to step boldly to the throne and claim healing and *have great expectations for receiving it.* Whatever may be blocking this great reception—whether it is guilt, condemnation, bitterness, etc.—cast it out now and keep casting. Ask God to refill you with His Holy Spirit until you receive His great work that has already been done for you. Otherwise, Jesus has died in vain for you! *Furthermore, don't just cast out without replacing those empty places with the Holy Spirit!* There is a biblical story where seven demons returned when one was cast out (Luke 11: 22-26). You should ask to be refilled with the Holy Spirit every day. If you have empty places something is going to fill it. It is the Holy Spirit that needs to be in those spaces to bring you abundance!

Whenever I feel illness trying to come upon me, I *immediately* demand the spirit of infirmity and illness leave. I take authority over it and declare the blood of Jesus over me. I profess I am healed by His stripes and my leaf shall never wither. I then thank Jesus for His healing and ask the Holy Spirit to fill me up from the top of my head to the bottom of my feet. By the next day, the symptoms are gone.

Jesus' blood not only provides for our physical health, but our mental health as well. After Jesus was scourged, they placed a crown of thorns on His head to mock our precious Savior. His blood spilled out and ran down His beautiful face. He also perspired blood in the Garden of Gethsemane when He prayed while He was under unimaginable stress to our Heavenly Father: "And he said, Abba, Father, all things are possible unto thee; take away this cup from me: nevertheless not what I will, but what thou wilt" (Mark 14:36, KJV).

Do you have thoughts that torment you? Do you let stress rob you of your peace? *God does not want us to experience doubt, fear, anxiety, paranoia, depression, or poor self-esteem. This is not His will for you. His Word instructs against it. He wants your mind to be focused upon Him and His love for you.* Claim His healing power for your mind and let His blood cleanse everything from it that contradicts your Heavenly Father's will for you. Allow His blood to align your mind with the Father's and be in His perfect will. *You will then have every single thing your **heart** has ever desired - the fruit of the Holy Spirit. When you have that manifested in your life, everything else falls into place.*

Jesus suffered unimaginable torture when big spikes were driven through His precious hands. His hands represent all the beautiful works He did while He ministered here on Earth. *What are your hands doing today?* Are you using them to further God's plan for your life so you will advance His kingdom? Have you found your purpose? Have you tapped into your passion? If not, ask the Father to reveal it to you. Where your passion lies you will also find your purpose, your success, His perfect will for your life and the bridge that connects you to Him. Tap into your purpose and begin creating wonderful things with your hands. *Glorify your Father in Heaven with beautiful works.* You can do this any number of ways: by painting a beautiful landscape; writing a poem or novel; playing music; or by saying beautiful prayers to bless others while your hands are brought together as the words come rushing forth. You can even glorify Him by providing a great service, such as repairing cars with expert skill and upstanding ethical practices. Whatever it is, do it with the passion God instilled in you and it will bring Him glory and will bring others great pleasure and comfort. *Work as though you are working for the Lord* (Colossians 3:23).

Jesus also suffered great torment when His feet were nailed to the cross. Where do you walk these days? *Do you walk with God?* Are you in His light? Do you walk in peace and joy? Do you walk upright and dwell in His presence? Do you stand still and know He is God? Do you stand firm on His Word and trust in Him for all situations in your life? *Jesus walked in places of darkness so we wouldn't have to.* He walked in loneliness and rejection during His ministry so we wouldn't have to. He was confronted by numerous situations that would have robbed the average person of peace or faith. His example of His great faith in every storm and His ability to never waiver in God's Word is an inspiration for all of us to stand firm in God's Word. Because of our Lord's firm footing, we can have the assurance the storm will not knock us off of our tracks and blow us onto the wrong path. We can stand tall like a Roman soldier as we gird ourselves with the whole armor of God and prepare for battle, just as our Lord and Savior did. We can walk in the peace that Jesus gave us and with great faith as we follow in His footsteps. *We are more than a conqueror!*

Last, but certainly not least, I want to focus on the fact His side was pierced with a sword by the Roman soldiers to make sure He was dead. Scripture tells us that blood and water came gushing forth (John 19:34, KJV). According to Scripture, Jesus' blood is the perpetual fountain that cleanses us (Zechariah 13:1, KJV). *Thank God for covering you with His blood, as it purifies you and sets you apart, which makes you a citizen of His nation of "a holy people"* (1 Peter 2:9).

HEAVEN IS REAL

Earth and our lives as we know them are temporal. This has been revealed to me through the death of my beloved husband. To this day, his death doesn't seem real to me. Sometimes, I wonder if our wonderful life together was real or if it was just a beautiful dream. It is the strangest feeling. I began to realize this was God's revelation to me: *this life is temporal and eternity is for real. Heaven is for real*! This is what is meant by the following scriptures:

> "While we look not at the things which are seen, but at the things which are not seen: for the things which are seen are temporal; but the things which are not seen are eternal" (2 Corinthians 4:18, KJV). Furthermore: "Lay not up for yourselves treasures upon earth, where moth and rust doth corrupt, and where thieves break through and steal: But lay up for yourselves treasures in Heaven, where neither moth nor rust doth corrupt, and where thieves do not break through nor steal: For where your treasure is, there will your heart be also" (Matthew 6:19-21, KJV).

The second scripture from the gospel of Matthew tells us the things you might think are important are actually of no significance at all. *In the end, the only thing that matters is love.* I grew up in the hippie era. I was a "flower child." It was a love revolution. Peace, love, and flowers were the theme of the late sixties and early seventies. We didn't know it at the time, but we were just lost and looking for God. We wanted those things of our hearts' desires—peace and love—we just looked for them in the wrong place. Materialism didn't matter to us—we just wanted to be free. *We receive all of these things in the eternal that our heart desires in the temporal. We can also have them, however, in the here and now, through kingdom living.*

Sadly, when you are lost, you may try to fill the void through materialism or meaningless relationships. You think buying that new car or that new piece of jewelry or being in the arms of a new love will make you happy. You may feel a rush of excitement, but it is fleeting, and you'll soon be on your way to your next void-filling endeavor. You'll be greatly disappointed when things don't work out as you planned. However, when you find your Lord and Savior, Jesus Christ, He comes into your spirit and fills up the void with all the good things you have been searching for. You then cease the external search for everlasting joy and peace. This is a taste of the eternal—what Heaven will be like.

Heaven is mentioned throughout the Bible, but it is described beautifully in the book of Revelation. This description came from the Apostle John when he "was caught up in the spirit" and saw a vision of Heaven:

> "And I saw a new heaven and a new earth: for the first heaven *and the first earth were passed away; and there was no more sea. And I John saw the holy city, new Jerusalem, coming down from God out of heaven*, prepared as a bride adorned for her husband. And I heard a great voice out of heaven saying, Behold, the tabernacle of God is with men, and he will dwell with them, and they shall be his people, and God himself shall be with them, and be their God. *And God shall wipe away all tears from their eyes; and there shall be no more death, neither sorrow, nor crying, neither shall there be any more pain: for the former things are passed away. And he that sat upon the throne said, Behold, I make all things new.* And he said unto me, Write: for these words are *true and faithful*. And he said unto me, it is done. I am Alpha and Omega, the beginning and the end. *I will give unto him that is athirst of the fountain of the water of life freely. He that overcometh shall inherit*

all things; and I will be his God, and he shall be my son. But the fearful, and unbelieving, and the abominable, and murderers, and whoremongers, and sorcerers, and idolaters, and all liars, shall have their part in the lake which burneth with fire and brimstone: which is the second death" (Revelation 21:1-8, KJV, emphasis added).

Please note this last verse, actually means those who *practice* living sinful lives. If you take this verse out of context, it appears that everyone who sins is doomed to hell. However, the preceding two verses, tell us that those who receive Jesus are conquerors and are justified as God's children, which coincides with the Apostle Paul's teaching (Romans 8:37). Furthermore, if you notice the eighth verse begins with the word, "but." Jesus was emphasizing the difference between those who are saved versus those who live a life of sin, which also coincides with Paul's teaching (Galatians 5:19-21). It doesn't mean if you *occasionally* make a mistake—like, for example, if you tell a lie about something—you are going to hell. John is writing about habitual liars and people who continually sin without having any conscience about their evil acts. The verse in Revelation about all liars has been interpreted to reference the "great liars" John wrote about: "Who is the liar? It is *whoever denies that Jesus is the Christ.* Such a person is the antichrist—denying the Father and the Son." (1 John 2:22, NIV, emphasis added). I believe this is the true meaning of "all liars will be cast into hell," otherwise God wouldn't be a just or a loving God, and I know He is. Furthermore, if you interpret this scripture from the current translation, while taking it out of context, there probably wouldn't be anyone in Heaven. I'm quite sure the vast majority of us have told at least one lie in our lifetimes as there is a multitude of ways to lie.

John continues and says:

"And there came unto me one of the seven angels which had the seven vials full of the seven last plagues, and talked with me, saying, Come hither, I will shew thee the bride, the Lamb's wife. And he carried me away in the spirit to a great and high mountain, and shewed me that great city, the holy Jerusalem, descending out of heaven from God, Having the glory of God: and her light was like unto a stone most precious, even like a jasper stone, clear as crystal; And had a wall great and high, and had twelve gates, and at the gates twelve angels, and names written thereon, which are the names of the twelve tribes of the children of Israel: On the east three gates; on the north three gates; on the south three gates; and on the west three gates. And the wall of the city had twelve foundations, and in them the names of the twelve apostles of the Lamb. And he that talked with me had a golden reed to measure the city, and the gates thereof, and the wall thereof. And the city lieth foursquare, and the length is as large as the breadth: and he measured the city with the reed, twelve thousand furlongs. The length and the breadth and the height of it are equal. And he measured the wall thereof, an hundred and forty and four cubits, according to the measure of a man, that is, of the angel. And the building of the wall of it was of jasper: and the city was pure gold, like unto clear glass. And the foundations of the wall of the city were garnished with all manner of precious stones. The first foundation was jasper; the second, sapphire; the third, a chalcedony; the fourth, an emerald; the fifth, sardonyx; the sixth, sardius; the seventh, chrysolyte; the eighth, beryl; the ninth, a topaz; the tenth, a chrysoprasus; the eleventh, a jacinth; the twelfth, an amethyst. And the twelve gates were twelve pearls: every several gate was of one pearl: and the street of the city was pure gold, as it were transparent glass. And I saw no temple therein: for the Lord God Almighty and the Lamb are the temple of it. And the city had no need of the sun, neither of the moon, to shine in it: for the glory of God did lighten it, and the Lamb is the light thereof. And the nations of them, which are saved shall walk in the light of it: and the kings of the earth do bring their glory and honour into it. And the gates of it shall not be shut at all by day: for there shall be no night there. And they shall bring the glory and honour of the nations into it. And there shall in no wise enter into it any thing that defileth, neither whatsoever worketh abomination, or maketh a lie: but they which are written in the Lamb's book of life" (Revelation 21:9-27, KJV).

In Corinthians, the Apostle Paul beautifully describes the new bodies we will receive in Heaven:

"There are also celestial bodies, and bodies terrestrial: but the glory of the celestial is one, and the glory of the terrestrial is another. There is one glory of the sun, and another glory of the moon, and another glory of the stars: for one star differeth from another star in glory. So also is the resurrection of the dead. It is sown in corruption; it is raised in incorruption: It is sown in dishonour; it is *raised in glory*: it is sown in weakness; it is *raised in power*: It is sown a natural body; it is raised *a spiritual body*. There is a natural body, and there is a spiritual body. And so it is written, The first man Adam was made a living soul; the last Adam was made a quickening spirit. Howbeit that was not first which is spiritual, but that which is natural; and afterward that which is spiritual. The first man is of the earth, earthy; the second man is the Lord from heaven As is the earthy, such are they also that are earthy: and as is the heavenly, such are they also that are heavenly. *And as we have borne the image of the earthy, we shall also bear the image of the heavenly*. Now this I say, brethren, that flesh and blood cannot inherit the kingdom of God; neither doth corruption inherit incorruption" (I Corinthians 15:40-50, KJV, emphasis added).

The attributes of the bodies we receive in Heaven can further be described in the book of John. It is recorded that after Jesus was resurrected, He would suddenly appear out of nowhere: "That Sunday evening the disciples were meeting behind locked doors because they were afraid of the Jewish leaders. Suddenly, Jesus was standing there among them! 'Peace be with you,' he said" (John 20:19, NLT). Perhaps in Heaven, when we have our new bodies, we will have the same ability. Maybe all we will have to do is focus on a place, and there we will be: suddenly transported to the desire of our heart at an instant.

My favorite part about Heaven is there will be *no more tears there.* That means no more pain, suffering, or death. Everything is new. Jesse Duplantis, who states he was taken up to Heaven by an angel, describes some of the beauty he saw there. According to his experience, there is no dust in Heaven.[47] That makes sense if everything is new. All things are passed away. That must mean we won't think about the past or be bothered by things that may bother us now.

There are numerous stories of near-death experiences where people find themselves in Heaven before being revived and returned to Earth. They have vivid descriptions of their experiences. These heavenly experiences are supported by the scripture, "...to be absent from the body and to be present with the Lord" (2 Corinthians 5:8, KJV).

Bette Myers, an artist, had this type of experience. She died from cardiac arrest and found herself in Heaven with Jesus. He told her it wasn't her time yet and she would go back and paint her masterpiece. In just two hours and fifteen minutes, she painted the most beautiful picture of Jesus I have ever seen. I have shown this picture to several people who say, "That's Him!" When I show it to others, many of them experience a tingling sensation associated with a true spiritual revelation. I bought a big print of the painting. When I first unrolled it and saw His beautiful face, I wept uncontrollably. It's now hanging in my living area. His eyes seem to follow me all over the room. I truly believe that picture is what He actually looks like. I gave a small print to one of my patients. She told me whenever she looks at it, her pain would decrease. Check out Bette Myers's "The Masterpiece" on the Internet. You will be lifted up.

As I mentioned earlier, I have seen my mansion in Heaven. Jesse Duplantis says when he was taken up to Heaven he also saw his. The mansions are surprisingly similar. We both saw beautiful surroundings that comprised the interior of the two buildings. What a wonderful God we serve. *He ascended to prepare a place for us, just as He promised in Scripture* (John 14:2). *Heaven is real. You have a beautiful home*

---

47 *Close Encounters of the God Kind.* Jesse Duplantis. Jesse Duplantis Ministries, 2004.

waiting for you. It will be every single thing you have ever dreamed of. After all, the Creator of the Universe has designed and constructed it in alignment with your heart's desire.

Duplantis also describes the glory that emanates from Jesus. He said His hair looked white, but when Jesus turned His head, Duplantis could see it was light brown. He then realized the light coming from Jesus made His hair look white. Duplantis describes how Jesus' robe appeared to be completely encrusted with diamonds. When he took a closer look, He saw it was actually the glory of God emanating from Him that made the fabric sparkle. This confirms the vision I had over twenty years ago I wrote about at the beginning of the book. The two celestial beings I saw also had the same light emanating from them. It was as though their hair and robes were composed of sparkling iridescent material.

Don Piper, a minister, wrote a book called *Ninety Minutes in Heaven.* He was pronounced dead in a car accident and tells the story of how the moment he died, he found himself in Heaven. He stated all his loved ones were there to greet him. He also noticed people who were only in his life for brief periods were there also. He realized those people who were present had impacted his walk with Christ in some way. Each person was beautiful and in perfect form. They were not aged or missing body parts as they had in life. In life, his grandfather had missing fingers and his grandmother had dentures and was hunched over with osteoporosis. In Heaven, his grandfather had all of his fingers and his grandmother had beautiful teeth and stood very erect.[48] I can't wait to see my grandmother and my husband—they were the loves of my life. However, the first person I want to see is Jesus. What a glorious reunion that will be.

Soon after I rededicated myself to the Lord, I learned what we would be doing in Heaven: worshipping our Savior. At the time, that didn't sound very appealing. I was thinking I just wanted some rest

---

48 "Ninety Minutes in Heaven, Don Piper." 12 June 2013. www.youtube.com/watch?v=u8E2UAV_3w4.

and relaxation after I enter those pearly gates. So I prayed to God and asked Him to fill my heart with desire to worship Him and His Son. He answered my prayer so fully and wonderfully, I now live to worship Him. He is my everything. My mind is focused upon Him, and my heart sings His praises. Now, He is all I live for. Truly, my heart's greatest desire is to worship Him and spend every moment possible at His precious nail-scarred feet. He has become the love of my life. I would rather spend time with Him than anyone else on Earth, but I realize His will is for me to share His gospel with others so His light can shine forth to those in need. *However, when that time finally arrives and I see my Lord and Savior, Jesus Christ, I will look into those piercing eyes of love and thank Him for His tremendous sacrifice and the undying love He has for me. I will fall at His feet and wash them and kiss them over and over again. He is my beloved master, my Prince of Peace, my eldest brother, my spiritual husband, and, most of all, my Lord and Savior. I will be eternally grateful and will worship Him with all I am!*

His affirmative answer to my prayer for the desire to worship Him totally confirms the scripture when you pray according to His will, the answer is always yes (1 John 5:14). Moreover, your prayer will be answered to a degree beyond what you ever dreamed for or dared to ask (Ephesians 3:20). The best prayer you could ever pray is to be in His perfect will. Remember, He wants the very best for you, and He knows better than you what that is.

Also remember if you are a child of God, then your name is registered as a citizen of Heaven. Get this planted in your spirit and claim it now. Your home is Heaven. Earth is just a temporary assignment, which is part of an eternal journey that ends in the most beautiful destination you could ever dream of. One day you will cross that beautiful river and walk with Jesus on the paved streets of gold. He will wrap His arm around you. He will share with you great stories and mysteries. Your glory will be revealed as you stand in the light of our Beautiful King! Focus on this, and you will sense His presence. You may even get a glimpse of Him!

THE TWENTY-THIRD PSALM

God spoke to me through this psalm one day when the grief over-whelmed me. I was in my walk-in closet and two different cards fell down from a shelf where I had placed obituaries of loved ones. I opened them up and they both included this beautiful passage. I knew my Heavenly Father was telling me He was with me and would restore me because He didn't want me to hurt anymore. I feel this is such an important psalm I want to examine it here and provide you with an analysis. After reading this analysis, the meaning will become more alive for you and facilitate a deeper conviction of your divine birth-right, which David so passionately and eloquently wrote about in this beloved, timeless passage.

"The LORD is my shepherd; I shall not want.

He maketh me to lie down in green pastures: he leadeth me beside the still waters.

He restoreth my soul: he leadeth me in the paths of righteous-ness for his name's sake.

Yea, though I walk through the valley of the shadow of death, I will fear no evil: for thou art with me; thy rod and thy staff they comfort me.

Thou prepares a table before me in the presence of mine en-emies: thou anointest my head with oil; my cup runneth over.

Surely goodness and mercy shall follow me all the days of my life: and I will dwell in the house of the LORD for ever" (Psalms 23, KJV).

The most important thing I believe you should know about this psalm is the following: when the Lord is your shepherd and He becomes alive in you, you are renewed, which empowers you to operate in His will. You will then receive the fullness of who He is and every good thing He intends for you will naturally fall into place. Below is an interpretation of the verses.

The Lord is my shepherd

> When He is your shepherd, all the other blessings in this psalm will manifest in your life. The Lord watches over His flock, so we can trust Him to care for us as any good shepherd would do, but more so because His love is limitless. God is the supplier of all our needs. He knows what we need before we even ask Him. He promises to supply all our needs according to His riches and glory. It His great pleasure to give us the kingdom, just as any loving parent would want to provide for their children's needs and desires.

He maketh me to lie down in green pastures: He leadeth me beside the still waters.

> When we trust God, we then grow closer to Him and share an intimacy that helps us know who He really is—a father who loves us beyond measure. Because He loves us, God blesses us with prosperity, joy, and peace. He wants us to have what is the absolute best for us. We have to trust God to know His perfect will exceeds any plans we have for our lives. When we trust in Him, we find rest: "...come to me, ye who are heavy laden and burdened and I will give you rest" (Matthew 11:28, KJV). When we rest in and receive from Him, the cares of this world fade away and we will live a peaceful existence.

He restoreth my soul: He leadeth me in the paths of righteousness for his name's sake.

> When we follow Him, He renews us with His Word and His Holy Spirit, and we are led into righteousness. We are then strengthened, and our will is aligned with His will. Because we are renewed and His love becomes perfected in us, we repent of our sins, change our destructive behavior, and constantly

strive to be more like Jesus. This is His will for us. We now no longer desire worldly things, but our hearts are filled with longing to please Him, which is what He created us to do. We then can glorify Him by renewing ourselves in His faithful love and His beautiful countenance will shine through for all the world to see who He truly is: the God of Infinite Love and Never-Ending Blessings.

Yea, though I walk through the valley of the shadow of death, I will fear no evil: for thou art with me; thy rod and thy staff they comfort me.

Shepherds in primitive times guided and protected their flocks with a rod and staff.[49]   Jesus is the Good Shepherd. He watches over us with great concern and pays attention to the minute details of our lives. He knows that the enemy will *try* to destroy us any way he can by working on our minds, which will make us afraid of daily struggles, trials, and tribulations—even basic changes that occur in life. However, *when we accept Jesus as our Lord and Savior, He gives us His Holy Spirit: the Great Comforter, the Wonderful Counselor. The Holy Spirit's divine attributes guide and empower us to be strong, courageous, and filled with faith during our trials. We then become intimate with and trust God, which enables us to implement kingdom principles.   His perfect love casts out fear, and we can overcome* **anything** *the enemy puts in front of us* (1 John 4:18, KJV). *When we praise Him during these trials, and keep looking up instead of focusing on our circumstances; it pleases God, and He intervenes. Our trials become bearable, shorter, and less frequent.*

Praising God is what King David did during his trials, and the Lord greatly blessed him: "Thus will I bless thee while I live: I will lift up my hands in thy name" (Psalms 63:4, KJV). The Lord called David a man after His own heart. *When we praise*

---

49 Keller, Phillip. "A Shepherd Looks At Psalm 23, Part Seven." 04 July 2013. Antipas. <antipas.org>.

our Lord, He is magnified, and He takes notice and you will be filled with His loving presence. He loves to be praised when it is done with a pure and loving heart. We then can find comfort in His strength and power and can sail right through the storm and get to the other side. *Even the darkest night cannot separate us from God's love and protection. He always has His hand on us. It is those darkest hours that often draw us closer to our Almighty Defender. We then receive a deeper revelation of His loving, protective nature.*

When you are going through a trial, just profess and personalize these wonderful scriptures:

Greater is He that is in me than He that is in the world (1 John 4:4).

No weapon that is formed against me shall prosper (Isaiah 54:17).

Jesus has given me power to tread on serpents and scorpions, and over all the power of the enemy: and nothing shall by any means hurt me (Luke 10:19).

I can tell you from experience when you receive a deep revelation God is always with you, it strengthens you to withstand any storm. More importantly, when you call upon the powerful name of Jesus, the enemy *will* flee. Jesus *is* the rod and staff of the Almighty God. He is our Great Defender, our Shield, and our Great Warrior in times of trouble.

Thou preparest a table before me in the presence of mine enemies.

When we have an intimate relationship with God, we have fellowship with Him. *There is power in knowing even though you may have enemies and trials, you can come into His presence, and everything will be wonderful.* The hardships will fade into the background while you bask in His love and light. Your enemies will be diligently working their evil schemes around you, but you will be feasting in the presence of the Lord. When you are dining with the King, all your adversaries have to stand at the sidelines. They may be watching and waiting for their opportunity to strike, but you will be assured all is well as you are surrounded by great power, protection, strength, and comfort.

Thou anointest my head with oil.

This anointing is the blessing that is upon your life as a Christian that flows from the love of your Heavenly Father. When His blessing is upon you, you are highly favored. Favor shifts events so you will prosper in every area of your life. You will have the victor's crown and be an overcomer; *you will be more than a conqueror*. We can look at the life of David and see how God anointed him. He was rejected by his family and put out in a pasture to herd sheep, but God had other plans for him. David was anointed when he was a young boy to be king. He slayed Goliath, won numerous battles, led a nation, and brought the Ark of the Covenant back to Jerusalem. He was a man after God's own heart. He loved God with everything He was. All of this was part of David's life because he was anointed—he was blessed and highly favored.

All things are possible with God's blessing. With His blessing you receive and bear the fruit of the Spirit: love, joy, peace, long-suffering, gentleness, goodness, faith, meekness, and temperance. *Your anointing is His love*, from which *all* blessings flow.

My cup runneth over.

Christ came to set us free and make us prosperous. When we are in covenant with God by accepting His precious Son, Jesus Christ, as our Lord and Savior, His grace covers us; and we are in His perfect will, which includes *unspeakable joy* in all circumstances, and *peace that surpasses all understanding*. The adjectives The

Word uses to describe those two spiritual fruits are absolutely perfect. When I was deeply grieving for my husband, I never thought I would ever find any kind of happiness or peace. The joy I now have is not something I can fully describe. The peace I experience doesn't even make sense. I am truly amazed by it and so very grateful. My cup does run over! *When our cup runs over, we are operating in the kingdom, and we will have abundance in all good things. God ensures we have more than enough so we can bless others* (2 Corinthians 9:8). *We can have the kingdom in this present life because it is created from God's blessing upon our lives and the Holy Spirit within, which becomes an outward manifestation into the natural part of our existence.*

Surely goodness and mercy shall follow me all the days of my life: and I will dwell in the house of the Lord forever.

When we have an intimate relationship with God, we can expect His goodness and mercy to be upon us, which is part of His blessing. When we accepted His Son as our Savior, we were given eternal life—a life with our Heavenly Father. He lives inside of us, and we live inside of Him, and so it will be forever and always. We can access His Holy presence at any time through reverence and sincere worship. When we leave this world, we will dwell with Him for eternity because this is His greatest promise. He longs for each of us to return to Him. One day we will be worshipping Him at His throne and feasting with Him at the table. We will then go back to our homes at the end of every day, which will be a beautiful, peaceful place He created specifically for each one of us.

THE LORD'S SUPPER

Remember God's Word is multi-faceted. You can turn it around in all directions and look at it from a variety of angles. If you have a passion and/or a purpose to understand it, God will open your spiritual eyes and mind to see a deeper meaning. The following is what He revealed to me about taking the Lord's Supper.

The account of the Last Supper, on a superficial, partial level, appears to focus on Judas' betrayal, the conspiracy against Jesus, and its consequences. However, the Holy Spirit revealed to me one morning as I was reading the passages in the four gospels *the truth* of what you can receive from Him when you come to His table today, which reveals there continues to be a conspiracy around this divine birthright. The enemy doesn't want us to know the truth about communing with Jesus. He wants us to stay sick, weak, and miserable. He doesn't want us to receive healing, strength, power or any other attributes from our Savior.

When you can't receive what Jesus wants to give you, it grieves Him. Don't grieve Jesus and negate His great sacrifice by not receiving what He has done for you when you take the Lord's Supper. Don't focus on your sins, when you commune with Him during this great exchange. This is what occurred due to Judas' betrayal as noted in the following passages: "Now Jesus was **deeply troubled**, and he exclaimed, "I tell you the truth, one of you will betray me!"" (John 13:21, NLT, emphasis added). All the disciples were *distressed* and *questioned themselves about their own purity* (Mark 14:19, NLT, 1996) when Jesus told them of the impending betrayal: "It is the one to whom I have given the bread dipped in the sauce…As soon as Judas had eaten the bread, Satan entered into Him" (John 13:26-27, NLT, 1996). Plain, unleavened bread represents the righteousness of Jesus[50] who frees us from sin. Bread actually has multiple biblical meanings. Scripture tells us the following: Jesus and the Word are the same (John 1:1, 14), He is the bread of life (John 6:35) and we are to meditate on the Word day and night (Psalms 1:2). Therefore, bread can represent what we what we dwell upon—what we eat or digest (Jeremiah 15:16), whether it be inspiration from God's Word or a destructive thought pattern.

---

50 "What Does Leaven Represent in the Scripture?" Let Us Reason. 07 July 2013. <letusreason.org>

The bread Jesus gave Judas, which had been dipped in sauce, symbolizes that it had been defiled. Judas' focus was not on the righteousness of Jesus, but the sin that was taking center stage in his thoughts and previous actions that would deliver Jesus to the Roman authorities. You can only imagine what must have been going through Judas' mind at that moment: it certainly couldn't have been receiving what the Lord was offering at the table. He was, in all probability, focused on the evil he was about to do. Jesus told Judas to: "Hurry and do what you are going to do" (John 13:27, NLT). The disciples thought since Judas was the treasurer, Jesus was telling him to go *pay for* the food (Jesus is food) or give money to the poor (John 13:29). This is symbolic for those who think they must *pay a debt* of confessing all their sins or performing good deeds in order to *be worthy* to partake of the Lord's Supper. If you focus on your sin and not your Savior when you partake, you might as well be saying your sin is greater than your magnificent Savior and His great power and glory. When you focus on sin, who do you think you are magnifying? It certainly isn't Jesus, who opens the floodgate to God's blessing. Focusing on your sin creates negativity and will open the door to the enemy's devices: **"When Judas had eaten the bread, Satan entered into Him"** (John 13:27, NLT, emphasis added). Judas had *eaten* the *defiled* bread; he had *focused* on the *sin*, not His Savior and the enemy came rushing in.

When you look at the deeper meaning of the following passage, Jesus is saying if you can't receive from Him, you will live a life of torment when you block this great exchange: "For the Son of Man must die, as the Scriptures declared long ago. But how terrible it will be for the one who betrays him. It would be far better for that man if he had never been born!" (Mark 14:21, NLT). The Greek translation for betray is defined as surrender.[51] If you are unable to surrender your false beliefs about Jesus' finished work at the cross and continue to focus on *your* work of confessing sins and performing good deeds to *earn* righteousness, you will *never* have grace flowing in your life. Your life won't be one of abundance. You *receive* righteousness by *allowing* the purity of Jesus to transform you. It is impossible to earn

51 Strong's Online Concordance. EliYah.com. 7 June 2013. <eliyah.com>.

righteousness through your efforts due to the negative influences of this world that bombards your flesh. Your works are like "filthy rags" when compared to the purity of Jesus (Isaiah 64:6). So just receive from Him, and let His power transform you, instead of you trying to transform yourself.

The biblical passages in the Old Testament were a typology; they were a foreshadow of things to come. The passages concerning The Passover point to the finished work of Jesus (Exodus 12). The Israelites were instructed to eat unleavened bread for seven days to remind them of their deliverance from the "forces out of the land of Egypt." This is symbolic of Jesus' sacrifice that delivers us from destructive forces. The Israelites were told if they ate anything with yeast, it would cut them off from the community of Israel. This represents what was stated in the preceding paragraphs. Focusing on your sin, instead of your Savior, *will hinder your ability to commune with Jesus*, which is symbolic of the Israelites being cut off from their community. Throughout these verses in the twelfth chapter of Exodus, there is a pattern of multiples of the number seven. The number seven represents completion. God provided every single thing we would need in six days, and on the seventh day He rested. He rested because His work was *finished.* This is God's way of telling us to have faith in His finished work, including the work at the cross. It is finished. Your sins are forgiven. Your job is to rest in Him and receive what He has already done for you (Hebrews 4:11).

This is so simple and yet has become twisted into a ritual that diametrically opposes the intention of the redemptive covenant. If we focus on our sins instead of Jesus, condemnation *will* destroy us. When we focus on our sins, we focus on the work of the enemy. We are to focus on the finished work of Jesus. Jesus *gave* bread to the disciples. He told them to *take* it (Mark: 14:22). He is *instructing* us to *receive* from Him—receive what He's done for us.

Jesus reveals further teaching about our ability to receive from Him. This is evident in the following passages. Prior to the Last Supper, Jesus instructed His disciples to go into *the city* and *follow* a man carrying a picture of *water* (Mark 14:13). The man symbolizes Jesus, who we are to follow. We are to drink from the fountain of water that flows from Him. He will give you life: an abundant life full of all good things because He is a *life-giving* spirit (1 Corinthians 15:45). Jesus gave them further instructions that a *man would lead them into a house* and *the owner* would *provide* a guest room that was *already prepared upstairs* (Mark 14:14-15). This is symbolic for Jesus leading us into the kingdom, which prepares us for Our Father's house. Jesus tells His disciples in reference to the room that the owner had prepared, "That is the place" (Mark 14:15, NLT, 1996). He is referencing the kingdom within, our spirits communing with His, and the power we can access by receiving from Him. We are invited *without conditions* to His table to partake and receive the blessings that are already provided for us (Ephesians 1:3). Communing with Jesus will stir up the fruit and gifts of the Holy Spirit, which will enable us to access the kingdom and prepare us for the new city: the new heaven (Revelation 21:2).

Always be aware Jesus comes *every time* you partake properly: "… Go and **prepare** the Passover meal so we can eat it **together**" (Luke 22:8, NLT, emphasis added). You need to be prepared to take the Lord's Supper by meditating upon the awesomeness of His great sacrifice and expressing abounding gratitude (Luke 22:17, 19). *Each time* you partake, He reactivates and strengthens the blessing, the power, the cleansing, and the healing: "For I will not drink wine again *until the kingdom of God has come*" (Luke 22:18). If you examine this scripture, Jesus is telling you, *each time* you receive Him at His table, the kingdom that is within you (Luke 17:21, KJV) increases due to His powerful spirit communing with yours. In this way, the kingdom *has* come as Jesus then partakes of the wine again along with you while you receive the fullness of His grace and power. He has granted you this right to partake and access the kingdom (Luke 22:29-30). He deeply desires for you to do it in the proper way so that you can receive the fullness of whom He is for comprehensive salvation instead of focusing on your own efforts to save yourself (Luke 22:15, KJV). Your efforts amount to nothing in comparison with His great sacrifice and incomprehensible glory.

When I learned of the truth regarding this divine birthright, I began to take the Lord's Supper daily while focusing on the proper aspect of this sacred blessing: on the finished work of Jesus and the great exchange. The great exchange not only includes His righteousness for our sin, but His health and strength for all of the infirmities and hardships we may experience during our lifetime. It also includes what John was alluding to in the following scripture: "…greater is he that is in you than he that is in the world" (1 John 4:4, KJV). Receiving Jesus' glorified body will drive out *anything* the enemy planted within you.

Because the devil is a liar, he puts symptoms on your body, but the truth is you are healed by Jesus' stripes (Isaiah 53:5) because He already bore it for you on the cross. Paul also tells us the same power that raised Christ from the dead lives in us and gives life to our mortal bodies (Romans 8:11). The Apostle also emphasized the following to Christians:

> "The cup of blessing which we bless, is it not the communion of the blood of Christ? The bread which we break, is it not the communion of the body of Christ?" (1 Corinthians 10:16, KJV).

Let's take a look at the definition of communion from the original Greek language. It means to fellowship.[52] When you fellowship with Jesus, all of His power is present and the Holy Spirit dwelling within you is magnified. When you commune with Him daily, you will notice a supernatural shift in your life. You will be living a life blessed with miraculous healing, peace, joy, favor, protection, wisdom, knowledge, provision, and great faith. Moreover, your love for God and your fellow man will be ever-increasing.

So when you partake of the Lord's Supper, call forth this power and proclaim what you won't carry, including but not limited to illness, poverty, rejection, or anything else your Heavenly Father didn't create because Jesus already carried it for you. Declare His power that

---

52 Strong's Online Concordance. EliYah.com. 7 June 2013. <eliyah.com>.

lives in you, which makes you the same as the glorified Jesus. We are sown in corruption, but when we fully receive Jesus as our Lord and Savior, we are raised in glory and seated with Him in heavenly places (Ephesians 2:6).

After I began taking the Lord's Supper daily, my body began to heal itself. Within one week, I was able to discontinue my blood pressure medication. I was previously taking three pills per day. There was also a large sore on my back the doctor wanted to surgically remove, but it healed after seven days of taking Communion. It was a sebaceous gland that had been there for several years and had become infected. After about three weeks of taking Communion, not only did the infection go away, but the swollen gland *completely disappeared.* I also began to notice my fears became smaller and smaller with less and less time spent dwelling on negative events. There are numerous testimonies of healing due to the proper partaking of Communion.[53]

I have come to understand the entire gospel of salvation is centered on our ability *not just to believe, but to receive.* Every single good thing has already been done for us. God has told us He has blessed us with all spiritual blessings in the heavenly realms (Ephesians 1:3). We just have to transfer it into the physical realm by trusting, believing and receiving. This can be done when we commune with Jesus and by renewing our minds with His Word, which will transform us. If we are not operating in His love and are plagued with self-condemnation, then our "receivers" won't work. I truly believe the scriptures that teach us about eternal salvation can be applied to the here and now: "And with all deceivableness of unrighteousness in them that perish; because they **received not** the love of the **truth,** that they might be saved" (2 Thessalonians 2:10, KJV, emphasis added).

Remember, "***Jesus is*** the way, ***the truth,*** and the light" (John 14:6, KJV, emphasis added). *So, we have to receive Him **fully** for **comprehensive salvation** in the here and now. Jesus is seated at the right hand of His Father, just waiting for you to receive your salvation, which*

---

53 Prince, Joseph. Health and Wholeness Through the Holy Communion. Joseph Prince Teaching Resources. 2011:75.

includes your healing from all infirmities and conditions. This is what Jesus meant when He said, "But whosoever drinketh of the water that I shall give him shall never thirst…" (John 4:14, KJV, emphasis added). He is truly a river of living water. He promises when we drink from Him we will be complete in all things. *Whatever your needs may be, He will fill you up. He alone has the complete power to heal; quench loneliness; fill deep voids; bring peace and joy; and shine light into darkness. He promises He will come to us when we need Him* (John 14:18).

It's imperative that you understand the scripture in which the Apostle Paul warns us not to partake of the Lord's Supper unworthily has been misinterpreted[54] (1 Corinthians 11:34). This scripture addressed those who were hungry and would eat the bread and drink the wine for the sole purpose of physical nourishment. Paul was referring to this issue when he said, "But let a man examine himself…" (1 Corinthians 11:28, KJV). Traditionally, we have been taught we need to review all the sins we have committed and ask forgiveness during Communion, but *Jesus certainly never said we needed to ask for forgiveness when He was with His apostles during the Last Supper. He simply stated to partake of the supper in remembrance of Him* (Luke 22:14-20). His main goal was to lead us into the New Covenant of God's eternal plan of salvation, which *He, himself, emphasized* in the following scripture: "And he said to them, 'I have *eagerly desired* to eat *this Passover* with you before I suffer'" (Luke 22:15, NIV, emphasis added)—just as He *now eagerly desires* to commune with you so you can receive from Him. I know this is true because His Word tells us so: *"Jesus Christ the same yesterday, and to day, and for ever"* (Hebrews 13:8, KJV, emphasis added). *"For I am the Lord, I change not…"* (Malachi 3:6, KJV, emphasis added).

The Lord didn't tell His apostles to assess themselves before they took the bread and drank the wine. The issue of examining yourself that Paul wrote about is referring to your *true motivation* for partaking of Communion, not assessing your sins. This is plainly evident in the

---

54 Prince, Joseph. Health and Wholeness Through the Holy Communion. Joseph Prince Teaching Resources. 2011:53

following scriptures. However, false doctrine has many people focusing on their faults and weaknesses instead of the finished work of Jesus during The Lord's Supper, which *Jesus has specifically instructed* us to partake of *in remembrance of Him*, not our sins. Please pay close attention to the verses which appear in boldface italics. Not only does Paul refer to the appropriate motive for partaking, but He emphasizes those who are ignorant of the power of this great exchange are not able to receive from it. The inability to receive from Jesus *is* the sentence that people drink upon themselves which leads to sickness and infirmities:

> "So when you gather for your meetings, *it is not the supper instituted by the Lord that you eat*, For in eating each one *[hurries] to get his own supper first* [not waiting for the poor], and one goes hungry *while another gets drunk. ...So then* whoever eats the bread or drinks the cup of the Lord in *a way* that is unworthy [of Him] will be guilty of [profaning and sinning against] the body and blood of the Lord. Let a man [thoroughly] examine himself, and [only when he has done] so should he eat of the bread and drink of the cup. For anyone who eats and drinks *without discriminating and recognizing with due appreciation that [it is Christ's] body*, eats and drinks a sentence (a verdict of judgment) upon himself. That [*careless and unworthy participation*] *is the reason many of you are weak and sickly*, and quite enough of you have fallen into the sleep of death. *For* if we searchingly examined ourselves [detecting our shortcomings and recognizing our own condition], we should not be judged *and* penalty decreed [by the divine judgment]. *But* when we [fall short and] are judged by the Lord, we are disciplined *and* chastened, so that *we may not [finally] be condemned* [to eternal punishment along] with the world. *So then*, my brothers, when you gather together to eat [the Lord's Supper], wait for one another. *If anyone is hungry, let him eat at home, lest you come together to bring judgment [on yourselves]*" (I Corinthians 11:20-34, AMP, emphasis added).

These scriptures *clearly* reveal that self-examination is purely to assess your *motive*, not your past behaviors, for partaking in the Lord's

Supper. This is evident by Paul's use of the two word conjunction, "so then." He was joining his summary to all the preceding instructions he had given by emphasizing it's *the reason* we partake, not our past mistakes, which determines our worthiness for participation. Always be aware of the truth when communing with Jesus: it is your faith in His finished work, His ability, and what He has done for you that activate His power to bring you healing, strength, and wholeness.

Furthermore, the verse about falling short that results in judgment and chastisement appears to make reference to unworthiness based on sins. However, chastise in the original Greek language simply means to train or correct.[55] As previously stated, judgment means to make a determination. When Jesus determines the motive for communing with Him is not appropriate, He will help His followers with this issue. This is evident beginning in verse thirty-one, which states if we recognize and change our motives for partaking, we won't be judged. The next verse begins with the conjuction "but," which means there is a solution in the event we are judged by the improper way that we have come to the Lord's table. Paul was instructing Christians even if they do partake for reasons other than communing with Jesus, His Holy Spirit that is within them, will lead them out of this improper motive. This is evident by the use of the phrase "we may not be condemned." Paul is emphasizing the truth concerning the "Wonderful Counselor," who Jesus has placed within each of His followers. He will help the believer understand the importance of this sacred birthright of communing with Jesus, which will lead them into the abundant life that He wants all of us to have.

Therefore, when you take Communion, thank Jesus for His great sacrifice. Then, focus on what you are not going to carry any longer because He has already carried it all for you. Then transfer all those things to Him on the cross as you receive His body and partake of the bread.[56] Thank the Holy Spirit for filling you from the top of your head to the bottom of your feet. Then partake of the wine, which is the cup of the New Covenant. Thank Him for His precious and powerful

---

55 Online Strong's Concordance. EliYah.com. 11 July 2013. <eliyah.com>.
56 Prince, Joseph. Health and Wholeness Through the Holy Communion. Joseph Prince Teaching Resources. 2011:72

blood that *perpetually cleanses* you (1 John 1:7, KJV). Magnify His work of salvation instead of reviewing and asking forgiveness for each of your sins. Jesus is a life-giving spirit (1 Corinthians 15:45), so receive your health and wholeness from Him. See yourself raised in glory with Him and receive His glorified body. Declare what you are receiving from Him: His health, strength, and wholeness. Proclaim He is in you and you are in Him (John 15:5). Profess as He is, so are you in this world (1 John 4:17). Declare you are the righteousness of God through His blood (2 Corinthians 5:21) and there is no condemnation in you because you belong to Him (Romans 8:1).

I do all this in remembrance of my Savior because I *was* living in the world and was sown in corruption, but I have received Jesus and have been raised in glory with Him. *Receiving Jesus is the essence of our Father's great redemptive plan.* He wants us to receive *every part* of our Savior so we can light the way for others (Matthew 5:14) and win souls to Christ. Every time you receive Him, you will be one step closer to a complete transformation of who you were created to be: a warrior; strong, healthy, whole, healed, magnificent, powerful, and beautiful. You will be like a city set on a hill that can't be hidden and the entire world will see your light (Matthew 5:14). Your glory will be manifested and Jesus will be revealed in you. It will be absolutely undeniable.

If you are struggling with this message, refer back to the chapter entitled "Walking in Freedom." Remember, there is no way you can totally account for your sins. That is why we needed our Savior.

CHAPTER SIX

UNDERSTANDING AND UTILIZING THE DIVINE POWER WITHIN YOU

THE WORD

The Word of God was created when God *breathed life into His words* just as He breathed life into us when He created us. His breath gives energy and power to His Word: "All scripture is given by inspiration of God…" (2 Timothy 3:16, KJV). The original Greek translation of the phrase "inspiration of God" comes from the word *theopneustos,* which means "God breathed."[57] As previously stated, the word "ruach," which was also in the Greek text, means spirit, breath, or wind. Therefore *all of God's Word,* which came from His breath, *is His Spirit, as well as His essence, since Scripture tells us God is a spirit being* (John 4:24). Moreover, Jesus stated His words are life and spirit (John 6:63, KJV). The word "inspiration" has more than one meaning in the English language: to breathe; or to be encouraged to create something. We can, therefore, make the following conclusion from the analysis of these words taken from Scripture: Because God breathed life into His words; they have the power to become the catalyst for creating your world. When His Word is meditated upon

---

57 Online Strong's Concordance. EliYah.com. 7 June 2013. <eliyah.com>.

and then spoken, it becomes alive in your spirit and *empowers you to create your reality.*

God tells us in His Word everything has already been done for us. "Blessed be the God and Father of our Lord Jesus Christ, who **hath blessed us with all** spiritual blessings in heavenly places in Christ" (Ephesians 1:3, KJV, emphasis added). God has already done all the work—we just need to receive it by reaching up into the eternal and pulling it into our current existence by believing and using the power of the spoken Word.

Let's say you inherited some stocks. One day you decide you want to buy a beautiful vacation home. It's time for you to liquidate the stocks into cash. You may not have the cash in your hand, but you know you will receive the cash as soon as you sell the stocks, and then you'll be able to purchase the property you have been dreaming about. It is the same exact process with the power of the Word. *Because your blessings are already in your "spiritual account," you can transfer them into your "natural account" when you claim them by believing, declaring, and receiving.* Your faith is activated and strengthened when you believe it and declare it with the power of God's spoken Word. All you need to do is claim it, receive it, and keep your eyes focused on the blessing you are ready to receive.

Perhaps you are thinking, "What if I don't believe?" Ask God to help you with this. He wants you to have faith because that is what pleases Him the most (Hebrews 11:6) so He will grant this request. Believing in His principles is definitely what He wants for you. Keep meditating upon and speaking the Word and *it will become alive in your spirit.* Let's take a glimpse of the power of the spoken Word at work in the spiritual realm.

One day, when I was in the presence of God, He gave me this wonderful vision. I was asking Him about the mystery of His Word. I told him I understood His Word had the power to create because His divine energy is infused into the words. He showed me when we speak the words, they are sent out into other dimensions. The words are multidimensional, even though they appear flat on the page. I am assuming this is the reason different interpretations occur after reading the Word, and the same reader can obtain a totally different meaning with each subsequent reading.

In the vision I had, the words appeared to be multifaceted. They were somewhat round, but had several sides to them. They were spinning and spinning out into the atmosphere. I saw them going out and then attracting all of these different elements from other dimensions as they kept spinning. God revealed to me this is the process that creates our present existence from the eternal. He takes the elements from other dimensions and uses them to create our current reality. The characteristic of the multifaceted shape facilitates the electrical attraction between the necessary elemental properties of the creative process. The words I saw actually had an electromagnetic field around them, so, as they go out to other dimensions, they are able to attract the building blocks for our reality, which is created with the spoken Word.

The things that I saw seemed to be something out of a science fiction movie. I was having some trouble wrapping my head around it. I even heard God say more than once, "Your 3-D mind can't comprehend it." I am assuming what I saw was a very basic, simplistic illustration of a very complex process.

The following scriptures correspond with what I saw: "So shall my word be that goeth forth out of my mouth: it *shall not return unto me void*, but it shall accomplish that which I please, and it *shall prosper in the thing whereto I sent it*" (Isaiah 55:11, KJV, emphasis added). "By faith we understand that the worlds were prepared by the word of God, so that *what is seen was not made out of things which are visible*" (Hebrews 11:3 NASB, emphasis added).

Because God and His Word are the same (John 1:1), and His Spirit lives in you after you are saved, then His Word lives in you. When I was first given this vision, I saw the words as frozen balls of ice lying on the ground. The Holy Spirit revealed to me the Word that is placed within us lies frozen and dormant until we activate it by meditating upon and speaking it. A couple of days later, I heard a television evangelist talking about the Word that lies dormant within us until we learn how to transfer it from the unseen to the seen realm. I knew God was confirming the vision He gave me. Shortly thereafter, I was speaking to my patient's husband, who happened to be a pastor. He was telling me about a vision he had while he was praying. He said as he spoke, he saw the words going up into the atmosphere further and further until they were completely out of his sight. I was astounded as this directly correlated with what God had shown me about His spoken Word. The pastor shared this with me before I had told him about the vision God had given me.

During the vision when I saw the words frozen on the ground, they looked like golf-ball-sized hail. The frozen balls were lying on the ground to symbolize the Word is the *foundation* for creating the kingdom of Heaven here on Earth. *The words that have been placed inside you are like seeds that are planted deep within you waiting to be cultivated to produce an abundant harvest of all good things.* The words are essentially the will of God just lying there with great expectation to spring forth and bless you in your present existence. I believe that is what Jesus truly meant when He said the kingdom of God is within (Luke 17:21). If you analyze the word, "kingdom" it means taking dominion over your world. Jesus is telling us He gives us the power to control our external existence by tapping into our internal realm of what He has placed within us.

God tells us to meditate on the Word, both day and night, and you will be prosperous (Joshua 1:8). The Hebrew word for "meditate" is *"hagah,"* which means "to murmur in pleasure or anger or to mutter."[58] To mutter means to speak under your breath. As previously stated, Scripture instruct us to do this day and night. When you do this, it is like revving up an engine. You are preparing the Word to be propelled into other dimensions—to go out and attract the necessary substances from the eternal and bring them back to your present.

---

58 Online Strong's Concordance. EliYah.com. 12 June 2013. <eliyah.com>.

Speaking the Word one time is not sufficient. You have to speak it over and over again, which revs it up and gives it the power to go out, come back, and create your desire. The Holy Spirit revealed to me when you do this, not only are you *aligning your mind and will with God's*, you are also changing the electromagnetic field that surrounds your body from a negative to a positive state. When this happens, you are empowered to create good things for your life, as the Great Creator creates because you are now in harmonic balance with Him. You are then able to attract those elements from the eternal dimensions for the abundant life you have been promised.

Muttering God's Word repeatedly also helps it to become established within your spirit, which will increase your belief in it. You truly have to believe it before the Word can become empowered to create whatever it is you are focusing upon. If you don't believe it, and you say it without conviction, then it becomes like a car running on fumes, just puttering along until it eventually putters out.

After I was given these visions concerning the physical characteristics of the spoken Word, the next day I was shown something else. The Holy Spirit also wanted to emphasize the spiritual aspect of the Word. I was shown a peach colored window shade with stripes. He revealed to me the following: when we speak the Word, it will heal us and makes us whole, just as we are healed by Jesus' stripes (Isaiah 53:5). Speaking the Word will help us walk through the veil that was torn due to the Jesus' great sacrifice and will allow us to enter into His presence. Spending time in His presence is the primary way to access the kingdom. When we spend time in His presence, it transforms us because God *is love, and love has the power to change us.* This is what is meant by the scriptural phrase "transformed from glory to glory" (2 Corinthians 3:18). This transformation will stir up the fruit of the Holy Spirit that has been placed within us and will allow His characteristics to be manifested outward.

God answered my prayer when I called out to Him to help me understand the mystery of His omnipotent Word. He reminded me of the following scripture as I pondered the vision: "Call unto me, and I will answer thee, and show thee great and mighty things, which thou knowest not" (Jeremiah 33:3, KJV). He gave me this vision to allow us to understand the laws of physics that create our reality through the spoken Word. He also wants us to understand the spiritual importance of applying this process into our lives because *our Heavenly Father wants to bless us so we can live an abundant life in all things. His Word is nourishment for our souls. It reveals who He truly is and the power He has to change our circumstances from a life of despair to a life of joy, peace, and fulfillment.*

THE POWER OF THE TONGUE

Scripture states God's power is infused into His Word. Look closely at how this verse is phrased:

> "Who being the brightness of his glory, and the express image of his person, and upholding all things by ***the word of his power…***" (Hebrews 1:3, KJV, emphasis added).

The following commentary explains the Hebrews verse in the context of why speaking God's Word is essential for kingdom living: "Psalm 29:4 declares: "The voice of the LORD is powerful; the voice of the LORD is full of majesty." With God, words are things. Whatever He speaks - is. It IS on the basis of the power and authority of the One who speaks. From nothing came everything. And the one who spoke the words of creation, humbled Himself and took flesh, becoming the Word incarnate. Yet all things continued (and continue) to exist based on the unchangeable authority of the Word which declared them to be so. It's this power that's the foundation of our faith. Just as He spoke light into the cosmos, He also speaks light into darkened men. And the power of that Word makes it so. He spoke the stars into the Heavens, and spoke salvation into my heart. "So then *faith cometh by hearing, and hearing by the Word of God" (Rom.10:17).* "[59]

---

59 McClarty, Jim. "The Hebrews Commentary Project." 06 June 2013. <soundofgrace.com>.

Scripture also tells us that God's grace is infused into His Word:

> "Long time therefore abode they speaking boldly in the Lord, which gave testimony unto *the word of his grace*, and granted signs and wonders to be done by their hands" (Acts 14:3, KJV, emphasis added).

> "And now, brethren, I commend you to God, and to *the word of his grace,* which *is able to build you up*, and to *give you an inheritance* among all them which are sanctified (Acts 20:32, KJV, emphasis added).

These verses in Hebrews and Acts confirm when we speak His Word, His power and grace not only activate the abundant life that we long for, but can and will create miracles in our lives. You also need to be familiar with this scripture: "That the communication of thy faith may become effectual by the acknowledging of every good thing which is in you in Christ Jesus" (Philemon 1:6, KJV). This scripture tells us that we should uplift others by our faith in Christ. In order to do so, our faith has to be ever-increasing. When we profess all of the attributes Christ has placed within us, we will be able to access it. Speaking it will help you believe it so you can communicate your faith effectively to others and lead souls to Christ. Speaking God's Word is not for the purpose of moving Him to do something. As previously stated, He has already done everything for you. Speak God's Word because it will increase your faith and facilitate reception of His blessing as it is released from the eternal, which will enable you to reach out and advance the kingdom of God. You will then step into your divine destiny for which He created you. So, start declaring now that:

> "The same power that raised Christ from the dead lives in me."
> "God's grace is in me."
> "God's mercy is in me."
> "God's wisdom is in me."
> "God's knowledge is in me."
> "God's strength is in me."
> "God's blessing is in me."

"God's healing power is in me."
"God's righteousness is in me."
"God's faith is in me."
"The fruit of the Holy Spirit is in me: love, joy, peace, forbearance, kindness, goodness, faithfulness, gentleness, and self-control."

Always be conscious of your thoughts and actions. They need to line up with what you declare in order to get a hundredfold return. *What you focus on is magnified by the power God has placed within you.*

Please understand God watches over His word to perform it (Jeremiah 1:12, AMP). He is waiting for you to become His verbal partner so He can release His promises into your life. He also expects you to use His Word to advance His kingdom: "*And I have put my words in thy mouth...that I may plant the heavens, and lay the foundations of the earth*, and say unto Zion, Thou art my people" (Isaiah 51:16, KJV, emphasis added).

God tells us mysterious and wonderful things about speaking His Word:

> "For my thoughts are not your thoughts, neither are your ways my ways, saith the Lord. For as the heavens are higher than the earth, so are my ways higher than your ways, and my thoughts than your thoughts. For as the rain cometh down, and the snow from heaven, and returneth not thither, but watereth the earth, and maketh it bring forth and bud, *that it may give seed to the sower,* and bread to the eater. *So shall my word be...*" (Isaiah 55: 8-11, KJV, emphasis added).

Notice the phrases in bold. God is telling us His spoken Word has the power to create. It is the never-ending supply of seeds to create our abundant harvest. God is telling us when we line up our thoughts and words with His; great blessings will be produced in our lives. *This is the main key for kingdom living here on Earth.* We have to think and talk like Him in order to exist in heavenly places.

Proverbs 18:21 states, "Death and life are in the power of the tongue." I recently heard a sermon, based on this verse, by a television evangelist who stated God has given us the authority to determine when we die. When I first heard this, I didn't believe it. But I pondered it and realized there may be some truth to this.

Over the years, I have heard many stories of people who became ill, gave up, and died quickly. It's as though they made up their minds not to fight because they were ready to die. I worked in nursing homes during my career as a therapist. I remember a couple that lived together at one of the homes. The wife eventually died, and the husband died three weeks after her. I have heard many stories like this in my lifetime. Some people will say the remaining spouse died of grief, but perhaps it is the grief that led him or her to the make the decision to die and his or her subsequent thoughts and spoken words brought the end quicker than what had been originally planned.

I mentioned these events about death to make a valid point: our thoughts and words, which create our perceptions, are very powerful. Your soul is a combination of your mind, will, and emotions. Your soul needs to believe what your spirit believes to access the kingdom. Remember, Jesus tells us the *kingdom* of Heaven is within (Luke 17:21). He is referring to a state of being, rather than the physical location of Heaven. Since your spirit is led by the Holy Spirit when you completely surrender to God and renew your mind with the Word, then your soul will come under submission. "Your soul will be transformed to the degree you renew your mind, change your attitudes, and conform to the Word of God."[60] God's perfect will is then able to manifest in your life and you will be blessed with wonderful things. This is why it is *extremely* important to speak God's Word repeatedly. Focusing on, believing, and speaking God's Word is the *only* thing that will align your body and soul with your spirit. *His Word is your*

---

60 Wommack, Andrew. "Spirit, Soul, and Body." Andrew Wommack Ministries. 09 June 2013. <awmi.net>.

greatest weapon and your greatest source for creating an abundance of all good things in your life. This is the only way to renew your mind. Making positive statements may help, but it will not heal all areas of your life. That is what is meant by the following scripture: "But refuse profane and old wives' fables, and exercise thyself rather unto godliness. For bodily exercise profiteth little: but godliness is profitable unto all things, having promise of the life that now is, and of that which is to come" (1Timothy 4:7-8, KJV). Godliness comes by meditating on His Word. As it becomes alive in your spirit, it will help you access the love of Jesus. *When you spend a lot of time in God's Word, it will completely transform you, which can help transform others* as noted in these verses:

> "Meditate upon these things; give thyself wholly to them; *that thy profiting may appear to all.* Take heed unto thyself, and unto the doctrine; continue in them: for in doing this thou shalt both *save thyself*, and them that hear thee" (1 Timothy 4:15-16, KJV, emphasis added).

Focus on scriptures concerning God's promises, who God is, and who He says you are. *Because God and His Word are the same, when you meditate on it, it will become alive in you and align your mind and will with God's.*

I am living proof of the truth of these scriptures, which is evident by statements a beloved family member made to me. My cousin hadn't seen me in over ten years. One morning when researching scriptures for writing this book, I was prompted to contact her, which turned out to be a surprise. I learned she happened to be in town visiting family the same day I was led to connect with her. She stated she was surprised to find I now looked much younger. When she learned my husband had passed away, she was very concerned about my well-being. She knew he had been everything to me. She was amazed to see my joyful countenance and more youthful-looking appearance after suffering such a terrible tragedy. I give all the glory to God. His Word has activated His grace and power within me.

You can create with the spoken Word. God spoke the universe into existence: "And God said, 'Let there be light: and there was light" (Genesis 1:3, KJV). He created us in His image. We have power to speak things into our reality. *In order to be in God's perfect will, you have to think like God thinks and say what God says about you.* You have to believe what you say and say what you believe. You have to make your mind believe what your spirit believes so you will believe what the Word says about you. You are what you think and say, which is confirmed in the following scripture: ***"That which is born of the flesh is flesh; and that which is born of the Spirit is spirit"*** (John 3:6, KJV, emphasis added).

When something attacks you, it is going against the knowledge of God, so you need to counterattack with God's Word. When you speak God's declarations, it releases His promises into your life. God gave His Word to us. We need to believe it, declare it, and manifest it into our reality. It is the incorruptible seed (1 Peter 1:23) you sow to obtain a bountiful harvest. What determines the magnitude of your harvest is the attention you give to the seed you are planting (Mark 4:8). Your faith-filled words become the catalyst for receiving the blessings God has already created for you. The Apostle Paul tells us, "...even God, who quickeneth the dead, and ***calleth those things which be not as though they were***" (Romans 4:17, KJV, emphasis added). Remember, there is no time in the eternal. There is only now. God says He has ***already*** blessed us with all spiritual blessings in the heavenly realms (Ephesians 1:3). You just need to activate your faith by believing it, meditating upon it, and speaking it, which will help you receive it.

When you couple faith with the power of verbalizing God's Word, you can accomplish anything. *You have to be totally focused on what you believe.* You can't halfway believe it and expect to see results. You have to be single-minded. A double-minded man will be tossed around like a wave on the ocean (James 1:6). When you are single-minded, *you will then know who you truly are—a child of God, the Most High King of the Universe, and you have inherited His attributes.*

Whenever you have a problem or there is something you want to create in your life, find a scripture that applies to your situation and meditate on it. First, read it several times. Then look at each word in the scripture and focus on its meaning. *Analyze each detail of every word and phrase so your soul comes into alignment with your spirit.* Ask the Holy Spirit to reveal the meaning if you need clarification for a particular phrase. Repeat the scripture out loud over and over. Personalize it by inserting "I" or your name. Then memorize it. If it is a long scripture, memorize one section before you go onto the next section. This will help you memorize it more quickly. Don't just forget about it after that. Meditate on it throughout the day. These steps will also help you believe it and change your thought life. Write it on Post-It Notes, and plaster them on the refrigerator, mirrors, dashboard of your car, your desk at work and home, or where ever you will see it. This will remind you of the harvest you are trying to reap. Speak the scripture several times a day. When you hear something over and over again, especially if it is your own voice, it helps you believe it. This will make it firmly planted in your heart, which is where transformation takes place. Research has discovered that the heart is more than an organ to pump blood. It is a "sensory organ and acts as a sophisticated encoding and processing center that enables it to learn, remember, and make independent functional decisions that do not involve the cerebral cortex."[61] The heart's function described in this data is the medium for the fertile ground Jesus spoke of in the parable of the sower (Luke 8:4-15). Don't let anything or anyone sway your belief in your declarations. Let it transform you from the inside out. Trust God's Word and continue to speak it. Stand on His Word and watch things begin to happen.

Speaking the Word increases your faith. As Scripture tells us, "*So then faith cometh by hearing, and hearing by the word of God*" (Romans 10:17, KJV, emphasis added). The more you hear it, the more you'll believe it, and the more power those words will have as they get sown into the fertile ground of your heart. *So, talk to yourself out loud!*

---

61 McCraty, R., *The Energetic Heart: Bioelectricmagnetic Communication Within People, in Bioelectric Medicine, P.J. Rosch and M.S. Markov, Editors. 2004, Marcel Dekker: New York. P. 541-562.*

Think thoughts of God and keep standing on His Word. Put your faith to work with the power of God's Word.

*Be aware the enemy will try to steal the Word. He will do what he can to keep you from speaking it. When you speak it in Jesus name, he has to flee. Don't let him take this God-given power from you. It is a powerful weapon of destruction because if"...**God be for us, who can stand against us?**"* (Romans 8:31, KJV, emphasis added). It certainly is not some little scrawny, hairless, gremlin, slime ball like the enemy. That is how he once appeared to me. That is who he truly is in relation to Christians because Jesus gave us all authority and power over him (Luke 10:19). If you haven't been saved—well, that's another story. Seeing how powerless the enemy truly was made me laugh. Just remember "...No weapon that is formed against thee shall prosper!" (Isaiah 54:17, KJV).

Because God and His Word are the same, I was able to develop a deep love for Him when I began speaking and meditating upon His Word. I also received a deep revelation of His love for me. He is truly part of me now. *He will become alive in you,* too, when you speak His Word because they are spirit and life (John 6:63). His words are not merely text on a page—*they are truly alive.* This is one of His great mysteries. One day it will be revealed to us, but for now, *just believe and receive.* This is what Jesus meant when He said those who become like little children will enter into the kingdom of Heaven (Matthew 18:3). We have to just trust with wide-eyed wonder in His great mysteries. All the blessings then come flowing forth like a rushing river. It becomes a tidal wave of blessings and we have kingdom living on Earth.

The power of the spoken Word brings it alive within your spirit and manifests its goodness in your life. There are many things you can be saved from, including illness, stress, anxiety, depression, poor self-esteem, loneliness, addiction, and poverty. There are a multitude of scriptures for every problem that may appear in your life. You can be saved from every one of these problems by *taking authority over them* with the power of the spoken Word. Avoid talking about the problem itself. This will create fear. Instead, focus on your blessings and offer a praise of gratitude to God and He *will* deliver you out of the trial (Psalms 50:23).

On the opposite end of the manifestation of good things in your life, there are the products of negativity from fear. Speaking fear opens the door to the enemy, which will lead to destruction. Fear is what fuels him. That is why it is *imperative* to speak God's Word. Jesus warns us, "But I say unto you, that every idle word that men shall speak, they shall give account thereof in the day of judgment. For by thy words thou shalt be justified, and by thy words thou shalt be condemned" (Matthew 12:36-37, KJV). Jesus' instruction can be explained by the following example. If you are afraid of failing and you talk about your weakness, this will prevent you from succeeding toward a dream or goal. You won't accomplish your plan, or even worse, God's plan for your life. You may end up feeling like a failure and living a life of misery and making others around you miserable. Therefore, choose God's words over expressions of fear because you will be rewarded accordingly for the products of your words, in the eternal as well as in your present existence.

Have you ever been encompassed in a big snowball that rolls out of control as it grows to monstrous proportions? This is exactly what happens when you begin to verbally express your anxious thoughts. *God tells us in His Word to cast those anxieties down right away (2 Corinthians 10:5). If you feed them by dwelling on them, they will erupt into a volcanic verbal spewing of poison that corrupts your soul, as well as your outer life.*

Since we have the power of Jesus living in us; when we speak, our words have the ability to create either good or bad outcomes. There are some verses in the book of James that confirm just exactly how powerful the spoken Word is and why we need to guard our hearts and tongues:

"Therewith bless we God, even the Father; and therewith curse we men, which are made after the similitude of God. Out of the same mouth proceedeth blessing and cursing. My brethren, these things ought not so to be. Doth a fountain send forth at the same place sweet water and bitter? Can the fig tree, my brethren, bear olive berries? either a vine, figs? so can no fountain both yield salt water and fresh" (James 3:9-12, KJV).

However, when we have control over our thought life and our emotions, we have dominion. This is part of what God meant when He instructed Adam and Eve to take dominion over the Earth and subdue it (Genesis 1:26, 28). The Earth is not simply the material things that surround you, but also your mental state. Your reality consists of your perceptions and reactions to what happens around you. This concept is based on what Jesus taught in the Beatitudes: "Blessed are the meek: for they shall inherit the earth" (Matthew 5:5, KJV). Meekness often brings to mind timidity, shyness, fearfulness, or low self-esteem, but this is not the biblical meaning of this word. Meekness means power under control.[62] It is gentleness in action. Jesus epitomized this attribute. When you have brought every thought under control, surrender to God, and know who you are in Christ, you exemplify what Jesus was teaching in this Beatitude. You will then have dominion over your existence. Now don't get this concept confused with surrendering to God. His will for your life should rule over yours. However, you can take control over your reactions and perceptions to the circumstances that surround you. In this way you take dominion and you take the authority over the situation, which Christ has instructed you to do.

In order to have this attribute of meekness, you need to not only control, but change your thought patterns so they line up with the Word of God. It takes practice to focus on God's will, but it is well worth the effort. It is essential for transforming yourself into the person He created you to be.

Keep in mind *what you think will eventually spew out of your mouth like a fountain, so* "**keep thy heart with all diligence, for out of it are the issues of life**" (Proverbs 4:23, KJV, emphasis added). We are also told, "but the tongue can no man tame" (James 3:8, KJV).

---

62 Pratte, David. "Meekness and Humility: God's Cure for Pride, Haughtiness, and Egotism." Gospel Way, 8 June 2013. <www.gospelway.com>.

Therefore, be careful what you listen to, watch, think, say, and dwell upon. *What enters through your ears, eyes, and mind—and whatever you speak—becomes embedded in your heart.* Research reveals that psychophysiological information, whether it is anger or love, "can be encoded into the electromagnetic fields produced by the heart." The energy radiating from your heart can also affect others.[63] This sensitive energy has the power to impact your entire life as noted in Proverbs 23:7: whatever a man thinks; he becomes. Therefore, think and *speak faith, not fear.* Believe it and speak it so you will be blessed! "But he said, Yea rather, blessed are they that hear the word of God, and keep it" (Luke 11:28, KJV). Jesus taught this principle repeatedly:

> "While he yet spake, there came from the ruler of the synagogue's house certain which said, Thy daughter is dead: why troublest thou the Master any further? As soon as Jesus heard the word that was spoken, he saith unto the ruler of the synagogue, ***Be not afraid, only believe***" (Mark 5:35-36, KJV, emphasis added).

You choose what grows in your heart, so why not grow a Garden of Eden? You can create your own paradise with the Word of God that has been planted within you because the kingdom of God is within (Luke 17:21). You can look around all you like, but you won't find it anywhere else.

There are many stories of people who have healed themselves from terminal illnesses using the power of the spoken Word. *The spoken scriptures have the power to drive out all infirmities when they become alive in you.* For this to happen, you have to meditate on them frequently and *cast down every single negative thought* while keeping your focus on receiving the healing Jesus has provided for you. This is confirmed in the scripture: "Let thine eyes

---

63 McCraty, R., *The Energetic Heart: Bioelectricmagnetic Communication Within People, in Bioelectric Medicine,* P.J. Rosch and M.S. Markov, Editors. 2004, Marcel Dekker: New York. P. 541-562.

look right on, and let thine eyelids look straight before thee" (Proverbs 4:25, KJV).

You also have to be careful of the company you keep when you are trying to build your faith to receive God's grace. Negative outside influences may plant corrupt seeds of disbelief within your heart. *When you are growing a good garden, you don't want to allow any weeds to enter.* Some of them take extreme effort to root up. Jesus taught us to surround ourselves with those who will support our faith as noted in the book of Mark:[64]

> "And when he was come in, he saith unto them, "Why make ye this ado, and weep? The damsel is not dead, but sleepeth." And they **laughed him to scorn.** But when he had **put them all out,** he taketh the father and the mother of the damsel, and them that were with him, and entereth in where the damsel was lying. And he took the damsel by the hand, and said unto her, "Talitha cumi;" which is, being interpreted, "Damsel, I say unto thee, arise." And straightway the damsel arose, and walked; for she was of the age of twelve years. And they were astonished with a great astonishment" (Mark 5:39-42, KJV, emphasis added).

One powerful example of healing is recorded on an audio player of healing scriptures that can be purchased from John Hagee Ministries. The parents of a young child used this process to heal their daughter from a brain stem tumor. These types of tumors are usually fatal due to the location. Surgery is usually contraindicated as the brain stem controls respiration and other vital functions, including cardiovascular and digestion.

The family of the girl with the tumor saturated themselves with the Word of God and kept out anything and everyone that was contrary to His truth. Similarly, everyone that was healed in the Bible pursued healing by pursuing Jesus. They were persistent and didn't

---

64 Robertson, A.T. Commentary. Bible Study Tools. 10 June 2013 < biblestudy-tools.com. >.

give up until they were healed. *Healing means you have to let go of your belief that God has brought judgment against you as a result of some sin you have committed. This is not true. We are living under the New Covenant, and Jesus took* **everything** *for us when He went to the cross,* including all of our sins and illnesses. Refuse to use your body for sickness. Don't let the enemy condemn you for your mistakes. You have to tap into your faith and pray with great expectations of receiving your glorified Savior who is strong, healthy, and whole.

To illustrate God's promises of healing, first we should look at the definition of covenant, which was translated from the original Greek text from the word "diatheke." It is defined as follows: a contract (especially a devisory will):—covenant, testament.[65] The truth of the New Covenant bears repeating: God and Jesus have entered into a contract that enables the great exchange. This includes not only our sins for Jesus' righteousness, but also *our infirmities for his health.* Because of this New Covenant, we can receive the purity and righteousness of Jesus, who is healed, whole, strong, and glorious. Therefore, refuse to take anything Jesus already bore on the cross. *You are healed by His stripes.*

Let's take a look at what God tells us about healing with His Word:

> "My son, attend to my words; incline thine ear unto my sayings. Let them not depart from thine eyes; keep them in the midst of thine heart. *For they are life unto those that find them, and health to all their flesh*" (Proverbs 4:20-22, KJV, emphasis added).

He is telling us to *saturate* ourselves with His Word—with the essence of who He is. When He came to live in you after you were saved, *His Word was planted in you.* You have little seeds just waiting to be watered with your lips. A river of God's love will soon begin to flow through you and so will His healing power. Call forth this supernatural healing power within you and command it to heal the lying

---

65 Online Strong's Concordance. EliYah.com. 7 June 2013. <eliyah.com>.

symptoms the enemy has placed on your body. If you need something to be healed, don't talk about, receive, or claim it. Don't say, "I have cancer." Instead of making fearful statements, say things like:

> "The doctor's reports may state a diagnosis of cancer, but it is written I am healed by His stripes. I don't receive or claim this illness. This does not come from God, and I belong to God, so it has no authority over me. I call forth the power of the Holy Spirit, the same power that raised Christ from the dead, that lives in me and gives life to my mortal body. I command healing over my body by the authority vested in me by the blood of Jesus Christ. I receive the healing that Jesus has already provided for me. I rebuke and demand all spirits of infirmity leave now. Holy Spirit come and fill me up from the top of my head to the bottom of my feet! I am healed by His stripes. Amen!"

I do this every time I feel like I am getting a cold. I repeat this technique several times during the day. Every time I began to focus on the symptoms, I shift my focus and take authority over them by making declarations that line up with God's truth. The next day I am totally fine. This technique works, so use it!

I believe using the authority Christ gave us is what He meant in the following scripture. "Verily, verily, I say unto you, He that believeth on me, the works that I do shall he do also; and **greater works** than these shall he do; because I go unto my Father" (John 14:12, KJV, emphasis added). "Verily" means truly and anything said twice in the Bible means God's Word is established. *More importantly, when Jesus ascended, He gave us His Spirit to live in us (John 16:7), which includes the same power that Jesus had.*

Jesus' power in us can be further demonstrated through the exemplary life of Dodie Osteen, the mother of Joel Osteen. She was diagnosed with cancer. She researched healing scriptures and professed them. Her faith, combined with the power within her and God's spoken Word, healed her from the lying symptoms the enemy placed on her body. There are ninety-seven healing scriptures you can find in the Bible.[66] Speak them and receive the healing Jesus has already provided for you.

In addition to speaking the Word over your health, we are instructed to: "... call for the elders of the church; and let them pray over him, anointing him with oil in the name of the Lord:" (James 5:14, KJV). Do what this verse says, continue to take authority over the illness with God's Word and believe you are healed by His stripes. Receive your healing Jesus provided for you on the cross. I can testify this has worked for me numerous times.

Receiving what He has already done is paramount to healing. One day when I was praying, I asked God when He was going to heal my mind. I had a lifelong history of anxiety, paranoia, depression, negative thought patterns, and even suicidal ideations. There was always some kind of garbage going through my head; there was rarely anything pleasant in there. I heard God say, "I already did, but you're just not allowing it: you're not receiving it because of your thought life."

I asked Him what I needed to do about it. He told me not to dwell on the negative thoughts when they enter my mind, but to cast them down *immediately* and replace them with His thoughts, His words. I asked Him what scripture I should use, and He told me to say, "Casting down imaginations, and every high thing that exalteth itself against the knowledge of God, and bringing into captivity every thought to the obedience of Christ;" (2 Corinthians 10:5, KJV). I began doing this, and immediately after thinking or saying the scripture, I would speak what He says about me in His Word: *I am loved and victorious.* It was easy to get rid of those nasty thoughts with this technique.

I had previously tried a variety of interventions to cure my anxiety and paranoid thoughts: food, counseling, medication, men, meditation, relaxation, and New Age techniques. Nothing worked. *The only thing that works is renewing your mind with God's Word and being in*

---

66 "Healing Scriptures." Osteen, Dodie. Hope Faith, Prayer. 09 April 2013. <hope-faithprayer.com>.

His presence. When you stay in God's Word, you are in the spirit and your flesh will come under complete submission to your spirit, which will bring peace to your life: "For to be carnally minded is death; but to be spiritually minded is life and peace" (Romans 8:6, KJV). Two of my favorite scriptures are: "*... but perfect love casteth out fear*" (1 John 4:18, KJV, emphasis added) and "*...My grace is sufficient for thee*: for my strength is made perfect in weakness..." (2 Corinthians 12:9, KJV, emphasis added). *You need to get this planted in your heart now before your next trial. With these scriptures in your heart, you will be fully equipped to handle any situation and keep your mind free from anxiety.*

As previously stated, whatever we focus on becomes magnified and is given substance. Substance is energy in motion. This concept is referenced in the scriptures: "Now faith is the *substance* of things hoped for, the evidence of things not seen" (Hebrews 11:1, KJV, emphasis added). Let's take a look at the definition of "substance." Webster defines substance as "essential nature; *ultimate reality that underlies all outward manifestations and change;* physical material from which something is made or which has discrete existence." Since the Word refers to faith as a type of substance, you can replace the word "substance" with the word "faith," which would read "faith is the *ultimate reality that underlies all outward manifestations and change. We can surmise from this definition when we put our faith into action and focus on what we believe, it will materialize.* Because faith comes from hearing and hearing comes from the Word of God (Romans 10:17), put your faith to work with the power of speaking God's Word.

Think about how you have created things in your life because of the great attention you have given something. This is how I brought my late husband into my life. I wrote a list of all of the qualities I wanted him to have. I wanted a tall man. My couch was low to the ground, so I put blocks underneath it so he would be comfortable when he sat down. I set an extra plate at the dining room table for him, as though he were already there with me. I began to really feel in my spirit there was someone not too far away that would be coming soon. Within a year and a half, I was married to the most wonderful, tall, handsome man.

Scripture tells us why it's important to speak God's words, which I am emphasizing in the following scriptures:

> "…the words that I speak unto you they are spirit and they are life" (John 6:63, KJV).

> "In the beginning was the word, and the word was with God, and the word was God" (John 1:1, KJV).

> "And the Word was made flesh and dwelt among us…" (John 1:14, KJV).

> "So shall my word be that goeth forth out of my mouth: it shall not return unto me void, but it shall accomplish that which I please, and it shall prosper in the thing whereto I sent it" (Isaiah 55:11, KJV).

Because these scriptures tell us God and His word are the same and He is love (1 John 4:8), truth, the way, and the light (John 14:16), then so is His Word. These scriptures also coincide with the Proverb which states the *power of life and death is in the tongue* (Proverbs 18:21). God's power in you, coupled with speaking His Word, *will create His will.* His Word will transform you and the world in which you live. They also have the power to enlighten you and reveal hidden parts of yourself: "For the word of God is quick, and powerful, and sharper than any two-edged sword, piercing even to the dividing asunder of soul and spirit, and of the joints and marrow, and is a discerner of the thoughts and intents of the heart" (Hebrews 4:12, KJV).

The two-edged sword is mentioned several times in the New Testament. The original Greek translation is *distomos,* which means "two mouths."[67] Therefore, *when you speak God's Word, you are say-*

---

67 Online Parallel Bible. Bible Hub. 03 March 12. <concordances.org/greek>.

ing what He says. It is as though you are speaking together when you agree with Him and this becomes very powerful and is, therefore, sharper than a two-edged sword. It has the power to destroy and create.

So, speak the Word because it works. The following scripture alludes to this concept: "Heaven and earth shall pass away, but my words shall not pass away" (Matthew 24:35, KJV). Whenever I speak the Word, I am immediately lifted up and the negativity begins to diminish. *When we become verbal partners with the Almighty Defender, the enemy flees.* No devil in hell can withstand that kind of ammunition. God's Word *is* your weapon.

His Word releases provision in your life: "A man's belly shall be satisfied with the fruit of his mouth; and with the increase of his lips shall he be filled" (Proverbs 18:20, KJV). This scripture testifies to the power of the spoken Word, so watch what you say. You are what you say, just as you are what you eat. Whenever you dwell upon something, you mull it over in your mind. In essence, you eat it and digest it. *It becomes the fuel for the world you create.* We have the power to create, just as our Creator does because we are made in His image. Therefore, *focus only on the desires of your heart.* Magnify them with your imagination, by speaking God's Word and backing them up with your actions. Remember *thoughts are energy in motion.* Don't dwell on what you don't have. Instead, focus on what you want.

I find it quite entertaining and relaxing to transport myself to some paradise of peace and beauty. Sometimes, I see myself walking in a beautiful garden with Jesus. In fact, Scripture instructs us to do so: "If ye then be risen with Christ, seek those things which are above, where Christ sitteth on the right hand of God. Set your affection on things above, not on things on the earth" (Colossians 3:1-2, KJV).

Visualizing my desires often brings me a great deal of joy. This is how it is done. Use your imagination with every sense. Imagine how your desire looks, sounds, smells, feels, and tastes. Perhaps you are on a tropical island with the warm breeze blowing against your face. You hear the roar of the ocean's waves pounding against the shore and smell the salt in the air. You are sipping on a sweet, creamy, pineapple drink. The sand is pure white and the sky is a clear, crystal blue. When you incorporate all the senses, you are transported. Back it up with God's Word: "...it is your Father's good pleasure to give you the kingdom" (Luke 12:32, KJV).

You can also receive deliverance by professing God's Word: "The words of the wicked are to lie in wait for blood: but the **mouth of the upright shall deliver them**" (Proverbs 12:6, KJV, emphasis added). Before I began my last and final attempt at weight loss, I told a coworker, "Here, take a picture of me, I'm fixin' to get skinny." My coworker remarked that I had spoken with great conviction. I felt it in my spirit, I spoke it, and then I acted upon it by researching the best weight loss programs and documenting my "before" image. Within twenty-seven months, I had lost one hundred and ten pounds! God's promise of restoration and deliverance, coupled with my agreeing and declaring with Him, became the two-edged sword that cut the binds of a lifelong bondage. *It will destroy anything that is not in alignment with God's perfect will.* Obesity certainly wasn't God's plan for me. It was a bondage that had plagued me since childhood. I simply could not conquer it on my own; but *with God, and the power of His word, all things are possible.*

Being a victor is possible for you also when you declare and decree God's Word. Start your day by professing the following words:

"My mind and will are aligned with God's. I am in His perfect will. God's supernatural blessing is upon me. I am blessed in the city. I am blessed in the fields. I am blessed coming in. I am blessed going out. God's favor is upon me in every situation. I expect great things to happen today. I command financial prosperity over my checking, retirement, and saving accounts for myself and my family. I command the power, fruit, and gifts of the Holy Spirit to come forth and advance God's kingdom. I speak eternal and comprehensive salvation over all those I know and love. I put on the whole armor of God. I am covered by the blood of Jesus Christ and surrounded by an encampment of angels. I demand the enemy be bound and thrown into the pit of hell and burned up. He has no power or authority over me. As a citizen of Heaven, I command its power to operate over my life and my loved ones. In Jesus Name Amen."

The Aaronic blessing, noted below in bold letters, is a great declaration to speak over yourself and your family. God instructed Moses to tell Aaron to speak this blessing over his sons. This not only continues to be a current Jewish tradition, but many pastors also speak this over their congregation. *Remember God is not a respecter of persons; what is meant for one of His children is meant for all.*

"Speak unto Aaron and unto his sons, saying, On this wise ye shall bless the children of Israel, saying unto them, '**The Lord bless thee, and keep thee: The Lord make His face shine upon thee, and be gracious unto thee: The Lord lift up His countenance upon thee, and give thee peace**. And they shall put my name upon the children of Israel; and I will bless them" (Numbers 6: 23-27, KJV, emphasis added).

I have heard stories of children whose lives were completely changed when parents spoke this blessing over them. I spoke this blessing over my own son. He had a lifelong history of having a series of jobs that did not pay well or have any benefits. He was thirty-four when I prayed this blessing over him. Within a few months, he found a wonderful job with a good wage and great benefits. I know God blessed him because of His promise: "**And they shall put my name upon the children of Israel; and I will bless them**" (Numbers 6:27, KJV, emphasis added). If your child isn't receptive to this spoken blessing, do it from a distance. Personalize it by replacing the word "thee" with your child's name. Visualize your hands upon his or her head. At the age of thirteen, when rebellion may rear its ugly head and your child thinks he or she knows best; just remember our Father knows better and prayer changes things.

The most important thing I can say about the power of the tongue is this: when you speak the scriptures out loud, your love for Jesus and

His love for you become deeply rooted within your heart. *This truly is the most precious blessing the Father could ever give you. When you have this, nothing else matters, and everything falls right into place.* Whenever I speak His words, it's as though He is telling me His plans while He is watching over me. This gives me the deep revelation I am His beloved and I fall more in love with Him.

I speak the words God says about me and the words He says about Himself. When I hear my own voice saying God's words of love, life, protection, and restoration—that I am His own special treasure; His plans for me are to prosper me and never harm me; His plans for me were made before He formed me with His own two hands in my mother's womb; He rejoices over me with singing and dancing; He stores all of my tears in a bottle; my leaf shall never wither; whatsoever I do shall prosper; He has numbered every single hair on my head; His thoughts of me are more than the grains of the sand of the ocean; and He has blessed me with every spiritual blessing in the heavenly realms—*I feel His love. His words have become alive in my spirit, and He is alive in me; and I know I can overcome anything and conquer any Goliath that steps into my path.*

DOER OF THE WORD

"But be ye doers of the word, and not hearers only, deceiving your own selves" (James 1:22, KJV). Matthew Henry, an English Minister and Bible commentator, summarized the verse in James as follows: "It is not enough to remember what we hear, and to be able to repeat it, and to give testimony to it, and commend it and write it, and preserve what we have written; that which all this is in order to, and which crowns the rest, is that we be doers of the Word"

You are blessed, delivered, and freed when you do the Word: If we just go to church and listen to a sermon, but continue to live the same destructive lifestyle, then we will remain in bondage. None of God's blessings will flow through us, and we certainly won't be living the abundant, prosperous life God planned for us.

However, if we hear the Word and apply its principle to our lives, *we will be delivered from all of the old programs created from false doctrines or persons that resulted in an ungodly perception of who we truly are.* We will then be able to press forward into God's will for our lives. We will be able to advance His kingdom and fulfill our divine destiny. His blessing will overflow into and out of us so we can be a blessing to others. We will be empowered to lead others to Christ.

To be a doer of the Word, you have to know what it says. Many Christians don't read the Bible at all. Some only spend the bare minimum in the Word. This is a huge mistake. *Reading the Word is the first step to being a doer of the Word. God's Word is what changes you into the person He created you to be. It not only gives you instruction for living the abundant life, but it will give you revelations into His great mysteries and will help you develop a deep bond with Him.* Why on earth would anyone want to miss out on that? Having an intimate relationship with the Creator of the Universe is the most precious gift you could ever have.

Here's a little tidbit for you: the more you read His Word, the more God will reveal things to you, and the greater desire you will have to read it. Studying the Word then becomes self-perpetuating. God has told us, **"It is the glory of God to conceal a thing: but the honour of kings is to search out a matter"** (Proverbs 25:2, KJV, emphasis added). So, go and search it out and see how much excitement and joy you will experience. Then apply it to every part of your life. Don't just perceive doing the Word as isolated acts, rather, make it a lifestyle. Always keep your intention on the two greatest commandments: love God with all your heart and your neighbor as yourself. You will then be blessed and be a blessing to others. It is a blessing to be a blessing.

HIS POWER WITHIN YOU

I have already touched on this subject in the chapter "The Power of The Tongue." However, the concept of *His power within you* is essential for kingdom living. It is imperative I expound upon this important principle. The following scriptures can help to emphasize this point:

> "Now unto him that is able to do *exceeding abundantly above all* that we ask or think, according to *the power that worketh in us*" (Ephesians 3:20, KJV, emphasis added).

> "But if the Spirit of him that raised up Jesus from the dead *dwell in you*, he that raised up Christ from the dead shall also quicken your mortal bodies by his Spirit that dwelleth in you" (Romans 8:11, KJV, emphasis added).

> "The eyes of your understanding being enlightened; that ye may know what is the hope of his calling, and what the riches of the glory of his inheritance in the saints. And what is the *exceeding greatness of his power to us-ward who believe*, according to the working of His mighty power, Which He wrought in Christ, when He raised him from the dead, and set Him at his own right hand in the heavenly places" (Ephesians 1:18-20, KJV, emphasis added).

Now, I don't know about you, but when I think of the power God has placed within me, I get real excited. The following scripture tells us where we are in the ranks of the divine order: right under God. He has all the power, but we are directly beneath Him and he has also given us power, through the Holy Spirit. We just need to learn to access it by believing, receiving, and acting on our faith.

> "What are mere mortals that you should think about them, human beings that you should care for them? Yet you made them *only a little lower than God* and crowned them with glory and honor. *You gave them charge of everything you made, putting all things under their authority*" (Psalms 8:4-6, NLT, emphasis added).

I know one thing—I don't want to get to Heaven and be greatly disappointed because I never used all the power that was available to me. How about you? John tells us it is not just a small portion of Jesus' characteristics but the *fullness* of it that is available to us here on Earth, which astounds me: "And of **his fullness** have all we received, and grace for grace" (John 1:16, KJV, emphasis added). We are filled with His unmerited favor, His truth, and His light. Those beautiful attributes empower us to live the abundant life He came here to give us. Additionally, Paul gives us a great revelation concerning the power within us when we are filled with the Holy Spirit: "For the kingdom of God is not just a lot of talk; it is living by God's power" (1 Corinthians 4:20, NLT). Obviously, Paul was addressing the scoffers who thought the manifestation of Jesus's power in an average human was impossible. However, Scripture tells us we have the fruit and the gifts of Jesus through His Holy Spirit. This is where our power comes from.

Jesus tells us, "**But you will receive power** when the Holy Spirit comes upon you. And you will be my witnesses, telling people about me everywhere—in Jerusalem, throughout Judea, in Samaria, and to the ends of the earth" (Acts 1:8, NLT, emphasis added). Perhaps you are thinking this is just for the apostles or people who lived during Jesus' time, but I can tell you from my present experience it is not. It is for *everyone* who is *filled* with the Holy Spirit. "For the promise [of the Holy Spirit] is to *and* for you and your children, and to *and* for **all that are far away, [even] to and for as many as the Lord our God invites and bids to come to Himself**" (Acts 2:39, AMP, emphasis added). *Having the power of Jesus living inside of you is the reason you have to guard your hearts with diligence. Everything you dwell upon and speak becomes magnified when you have this power living inside you.*

So, how do you tap into all of that power? As stated in the chapter on "The Power of the Tongue," you have to align your soul with your spirit, which is guided by the Holy Spirit. You can't do this by your own volition, by sheer willpower. That is impossible. We do it through the power of God's Word.

This is an ongoing process because the world will continually bombard you with temptations of the flesh. In order to stay in the Spirit, you have to stay in the Word. This is where you want to stay because the Word accesses the power within you. Staying in the Word includes reading, hearing, speaking or meditating upon it. It may be difficult for you at first. It was for me. I simply didn't have the desire to do it. I prayed for God to give me the desire, and His answer was a definite yes. It was like I couldn't get enough of His Word. Pray about it and He will do the same for you because this is His will. God instructs us, "Let us therefore *come boldly* unto the throne of grace, that we may obtain mercy, and find grace to help in time of need" (Hebrews 4:16, KJV, emphasis added).

It is God's will for us to be just like Jesus. He wants us to tap into the power He has given us so we can have an abundant life and advance His kingdom, which will bring Him great pleasure. As the Apostle Paul wrote, "Therefore if any man be in Christ, he is a new creature: old things are passed away; behold, *all things are become new*" (2 Corinthians 5:17, KJV, emphasis added). *All* things become new—this includes the power the Holy Spirit places within you when He comes to live inside of you.

God instructs us to have faith, *which includes having faith in the power He has placed in you to do the same work Jesus has done* (John 14:12, KJV). You can't do that work if you don't believe you can. *You have to acknowledge the power within you and call it forth.* If you have any doubts, just ask God to increase your faith. *When I reconnected with God, I didn't believe all of these things I am now writing about.* That was less than two years ago. As I heard more of God's Word and prayed to Him, my faith increased and so did my ability to access the power He placed within me. You might be wondering what power I am writing about. I have provided prophetic words, which have brought healing, not only to me, but to others also. God has also made me bold in Christ so I can witness for Him. This exemplifies His power within me as my nature tends to be passive in reference to others' beliefs. I have also seen the heavenly realms in visions. I have unshakeable faith, which is a very powerful gift. When I know something in my heart, *nothing will ever* convince me otherwise. I also have the ability to hear God's voice and discern the direction of the Holy Spirit. This is also very powerful because it allows access to the spiritual realm for successful living on this Earth. All of the gifts of the Holy Spirit are powerful. They were described by the Apostle, Paul:

> "Now to each one the manifestation of the Spirit is given for the common good. To one there is given through the Spirit a message of wisdom, to another a message of knowledge by means of the same Spirit, to another faith by the same Spirit, to another gifts of healing by that one Spirit, to another miraculous powers, to another prophecy, to another distinguishing between spirits, to another speaking in different kinds of tongues, and to still another the interpretation of tongues. All these are the work of one and the same Spirit, and he distributes them to each one, just as he determines" (1 Corinthians 12:7-11, NIV).

The belief that these gifts were only meant for those living in biblical times *is non-scriptural and opposes what Jesus told us about giving us His Holy Spirit*: "Nevertheless I tell you the truth; It is expedient for you that I go away; for if I go not away, the Comforter will not come unto you; *but if I depart, I will send Him unto you*" (John 16:7, KJV, emphasis added).

Now, if you have Jesus' spirit living in you, wouldn't you have power? Your power comes from the Holy Spirit that is within you. Start tapping into that power now. *When you need something that is in alignment with God's will for you—whether it is wisdom, knowledge, healing, faith, or discernment—start calling forth your power and declaring it. Then, expect it to manifest because Jesus' Holy Spirit and the fullness of His grace resides within you if you have accepted Him as your Savior.* If you haven't, say the prayer of salvation mentioned in the first chapter of this book. Begin today!

I know from experience spending time in the presence of God also helps you to tap into His power within. When you are with Him, it changes you. You become a different person, which allows His grace to flow freely within you. Not only does this positive transformation convert your emotional and mental state, but it converts your electro-magnetic state[68] as well by altering the hormonal responses that result from your thought processes.[69] After spending time in the loving presence of God, your electromagnetic field will shift to a more positive state. This enables you to become a channel for His loving attributes, which is then easily accessed. If it is blocked by the negative charges of anxiety, anger, etc., then it is impossible to call forth that power and utilize it for kingdom living.

It is December 25, 2012 as I write these final revisions. Make it a point every Christmas to focus on His presence instead of presents under the tree. His presence is the greatest gift you will ever receive. You will be filled with His divine energy and no obstacle will stand in your way. Happy Birthday Beloved Jesus!

Now, I have to write about a topic that involves a lot of controversy in the religious community. It is my sincere prayer you will read this with a very open mind and then pray about it. I know God will answer you when the time is appropriate. When you first receive salvation, the Holy Spirit baptizes you in Jesus Christ. After you are baptized, *one of the most important things you can do to tap into His power is to ask to be filled with the Holy Spirit, which* Jesus instructs you to do in order to access the kingdom. Jesus said to access the kingdom, which is inside of you, (Luke 17:21), you have to be spirit-filled:

> "Jesus answered, Verily, verily, I say unto thee, Except a man be born of water *and of the Spirit*, he *cannot* enter into the kingdom of God. Marvel not that I said unto thee, Ye *must* be born again" (John 3:5, 7, KJV, emphasis added).

When you are spirit-filled, the Holy Spirit will provide you with one or more of His gifts. One of these gifts may include praying in

---

68 McCraty, R., *The Energetic Heart: Bioelectricmagnetic Communication Within People, in Bioelectric Medicine*, P.J. Rosch and M.S. Markov, Editors. 2004, Marcel Dekker: New York. P. 541-562.

69 Porth, Carol M. "Stress and Adaptation". *Pathophysiology.* 2nd ed. Philadelphia, Penn: J.B. Lippincott, 1986:86-88.

tongues, which is also known as the prayer language. Some religions believe speaking in tongues is the *sole* proof of being spirit-filled, but that is non-scriptural. It is *one* of the many gifts you *may* receive from the Holy Spirit, but it is *not* the *one and only* criterion for being spirit-filled.[70]

Many people argue Jesus didn't speak in tongues. They even go so far as saying that speaking in tongues comes from the enemy, despite numerous scriptural references to the contrary. This contradicts God's Word. Scripture tells us "…and His voice as the sound of many waters" (Revelation 1:15, KJV). Jesus knows all things. He *certainly* knows all languages; He created them.

Numerous scriptures tell us about the gift of speaking in tongues after becoming spirit-filled: "And they were all filled with the Holy Ghost, and began to speak with other tongues, as the Spirit gave them utterance" (Acts 2:4, KJV). Ask God specifically for this gift. I will share with you some reasons why you should ask for the ability to pray in this special language. This gift was given to me after I became spirit-filled. I didn't ask for it—it just happened. I really didn't know much about it when God gave it to me.

After first receiving this gift, I didn't use it very much. One day I was led to some scriptures that made me change my mind. We are told in this verse speaking in tongues is our spirit communicating with God's Spirit: "For what man knoweth the things of a man, save the spirit of man which is in him? Even so the things of God knoweth no man but the Spirit of God" (1 Corinthians 2:11, KJV). I figured if I could communicate with God's Spirit, then I needed to utilize this gift so I could strengthen the bond with my Heavenly Father and access the power He placed within me while living on Earth. Furthermore, some biblical scholars conclude because this is the gift of the spirit for communicating to our Heavenly Father, then the enemy is unable to interpret what is being said.

---

70 White, Rick. Sermon. Christian Fellowship Worship Center, Beaumont, Texas. 20 May 2012.

I am sure you have been in a situation in which you needed to pray for someone without knowing exactly what to pray for. Even though we don't always know what to pray for, thank God His power is beyond what we can comprehend. His knowledge is above what we could ever imagine:

> *"For my thoughts are not your thoughts, neither are your ways my ways, saith the Lord. For as the heavens are higher than the earth, so are my ways higher than your ways, and my thoughts than your thoughts"* (Isaiah 55:8-9, KJV, emphasis added).

The Apostle Paul tells us praying in tongues is actually an intercessory process, as the Holy Spirit knows what we need to pray about:

> "Likewise the Spirit also helpeth our infirmities: for we know not what we should pray for as we ought: but the Spirit itself maketh intercession for us with groanings which cannot be uttered. And he that searcheth the hearts knoweth what is the mind of the Spirit because he maketh intercession for the saints according to the will of God" (Romans 8:26-27, KJV).

Whenever I read or hear the word, "infirmities," I think of illness. However, the definition also includes weakness. *Therefore, if the Spirit is interceding for our weakness, we are given power when we pray in tongues.* When I am in a state of distress, praying in tongues comforts me. If I pray in tongues before a stressful situation, the situation usually diffuses. The stress I was facing is simply eliminated so I don't have to deal with it.

The Holy Spirit knows exactly what we need at the time we need it. He will fill in the missing blanks when we pray in the Spirit. He will complete our thoughts and desires by ensuring our prayers have the necessary petitions to create God's perfect will. In this way we will fulfill God's divine plan He designed for us before the foundation of the world.

One night, I could not go to sleep, so I began to pray in my normal language. This usually helps me to fall asleep. However, that night I heard God speak to me. He told me to get up and go pray in the living room, which I did. I knew if I didn't get enough sleep God would give me what I needed the next day to complete my work. Next, He told me to pray in tongues. As I began to do this, my prayer language increased dramatically. Previously, I had only had a few words I would utter when praying in the Spirit. After about fifteen minutes of praying with all of these new words, I heard God tell me I could go back to bed. I fell asleep quickly and rested peacefully.

I began to pray daily with my new vocabulary, which I believe opened up the door to other gifts and mysteries. In approximately one week, God began to give me visions. I shared one of them with you, which I described in the chapter entitled "The Word." I believe the following scripture alludes to the process I experienced: "For he that speaketh in an unknown tongue speaketh not unto men, but unto God: for no man understandeth him; howbeit in the spirit he speaketh mysteries" (1 Corinthians 14:2, KJV). It is definitely a mystery—this God-given gift of prayer language and it opened the door to other mysteries. I truly believe it was my increased use of prayer language that prepared me to receive and interpret such a wonderful vision.

I began to notice something else after my prayer language increased—whenever I became deeply concerned about something and I prayed in tongues, the whole vocabulary and speed of communication was entirely different. Moreover, in those moments of distress, it wasn't that I was making a decision to pray in tongues, but it was as though I had a strong urge to do so. I am not saying I had *no* control over it. I could have held it back if I was in a public place. The best way I can describe it is comparing it to a sneeze. You feel it coming on, but if you put your fingers up to your nose you can stifle it. Don't be concerned if you get this gift you will just start speaking without *any* control over it. At times, you will feel an urge to speak in your prayer language, but if the time or place is not appropriate, you have the power to be silent.

The Apostle Paul tells us that speaking in tongues edifies us: "He that speaketh in an unknown tongue edifieth himself…" (1 Corinthians 14:4, KJV). The definition of "edify" means "to enlighten or benefit, especially morally or spiritually."[71] Paul also makes additional comments concerning the necessity of using the gifts of the Holy Spirit to access the power within us: "Wherefore I put thee in remembrance that thou **stir up** the gift of God, which is in thee by the putting on of my hands" (2 Timothy 1:6, KJV, emphasis added). I have certainly been edified in spiritual knowledge through the prayer language my Heavenly Father so graciously gave me. *I have an ever-increasing faith and strength in the Lord because of this special gift.* I also know it opened up the door to the prophetic gift I have and has increased my ability to hear God's voice. If you would like to research this topic further, perform an internet search on "scriptures for speaking in tongues." You will find numerous verses and commentaries on this topic.

Another point about speaking in tongues is that it brings you knowledge and wisdom. One morning, my spiritual mentor, who spends a great deal of time in prayer, told me, "I have a word for you from God. He said you need to obtain wisdom." I asked her for clarification, but she replied that was all the information God relayed to her. So I begin to pray in my prayer language. I then asked God to tell me how I could obtain wisdom. I heard that quite voice in my head say, "Read Corinthians." I opened up the first book of Corinthians and my eyes fell upon 1 Corinthians 1:18 entitled, "The Wisdom of God." I noticed all of the notes I had written from a previous sermon about speaking in tongues in reference to obtaining wisdom. I was astounded. I am always amazed when God comes through so clearly and quickly just when I need Him the most. The following quotes are the things I had written about speaking in tongues:

> "When I pray in the spirit, I am praying about my future, which God ordained in the past. No one can take away what God has ordained" (referenced in 1 Corinthians 2:7). "Speaking in

---

71 Landau, Sidney, et al. Funk and Wagnalls Standard Desk Dictionary. Lippincott and Crowell, 1980:202.

tongues is a direct line to God. It is the highest form of inter-cession and it edifies me." "When you pray in the spirit, you are speaking mysteries, which is the hidden wisdom of God" (referenced in 1 Corinthians 2:7). "The spirit of God knows deep things of God, which is in me, so I can access deep wis-dom and get revelations from praying in the spirit." "I need to pray in the spirit when reading the Bible, so I can know God's thoughts" (referenced in 1 Corinthians 2:10-12).

It is evident all of this information confirms that speaking in tongues brings wisdom. I had wondered at times if this gift was real or if it was something I was creating because of my spiritual beliefs. I now know without a doubt this is an absolute gift from God. I now realize due to the sequence of the aforementioned events, there is no way my mind is in *complete* control of it. It definitely comes from the Holy Spirit.

THE WORKSHOP

You've heard the old saying, "idleness is the Devil's workshop." This is the absolute truth. The mind is your workshop. This is where you create your world. *If you choose to be idle or empty-headed, the enemy can and will gain control of your workshop and ultimately your life.* He places thoughts in your head. He can't read your thoughts, but he can definitely alter your thought pattern and ultimately destroy your life if you allow him to. *He operates through words and thoughts that are contradictory to God's Word.*

Because we were created in God's image (Genesis 1:27), and Jesus gave us power that He has (Romans 8:11) when He gave us His Holy Spirit (John 16:7), then we also have the ability to create with our imaginations. This is a principle that has worked in my life whenever I have put it to use consistently—which is the key to it working. One example of this principle is a treasure map, which I created as follows: I made separate pages of things I wanted to manifest in my life and then glued pictures that resembled those things. One of my pages had a picture of a group of women that were having fun together. I wrote the word "Friends" at the top of the page. Every day I would look at my pages and imagine what it would be like if all those images became reality. Within a short time, I had a wonderful group of fun-loving friends who brought me much joy.

Since the Word also tells us not to be double-minded (James 1:8, KJV), which will create instability, the opposite must also be true. A single-minded person will be prosperous in all areas of their life. Grab hold of your imaginations, focus on them daily, and cast down all thoughts that do not support the desires in your heart and do not align with the will of God. This is what Jesus was referring to in the book of Matthew: "The light of the body is the eye: if therefore thine eye be single, thy whole body shall be full of light" (Matthew 6:22, KJV).

Choose this day whom you will serve and also who you will believe - some co-worker or family member who tells you "You're not smart enough for that promotion," or "You're too fat to wear that dress," or "He will never marry you," or will you believe what God says about you? You are His child, and with God all things are possible.

In your workshop, don't allow idleness. If you are idle, havoc and destruction will show up in your life. The mind is a war zone, and this is where the enemy enters into battle with you. It can be tiring to consistently cast down all thoughts that are not consistent with God's Word. But what would you rather experience—fatigue or become totally drained? If you allow yourself to dwell upon the negative, then stress and anxiety take control, which *will* leave you void of energy. The battle takes some effort, but the end results far outweigh the expenditure. *You can't control what thought pops into your head, but you can control your attention to it.*

You are what you eat. You chew it, swallow it, and then become it. *Whatever you dwell upon becomes the center of your life.* Have you ever seen a video magnifier? It is used by those who have visual impairments. They place an object or some text under the eye of the camera. The visually impaired person turns a knob to magnify the object in order to see it. *When God becomes magnified enough in your life, when He is the main focus and you keep your eyes on Him, then your problems become so miniscule you no longer pay attention to them. All you see is God.* The problems become very small compared to your gigantic God. He will crush all of your fears with the palm of His loving hand and lift you out of the wreckage. His loving peace and joy will encompass you. Manifest God in your life by praising Him: "But thou art holy, O thou that inhabitest the praises of Israel. Our fathers trusted in thee: they trusted, and thou didst deliver them" (Psalms 22:3-4, KJV).

Sometimes you may be so distraught, you are unable to praise Him or even pray. However, when you cry for help, God will deliver you. One day when the gut-wrenching grief surfaced, I cried for God to help me. The relief was immediate. By the time I walked from my kitchen to the living room, all the pain had left. He *can and will* deliver you that quick when you cry out to Him. "Many are the afflictions of the righteous: but the Lord delivereth him out of them *all*." (Psalms 34:19, KJV, emphasis added).

I understand praising God is the last thing you feel like doing when you're in a pit, but it is the only thing that can pull you out quickly. He will deliver you. If you go back down, rise up to Him again. With each trial you face, your time and intensity in the pit will decrease and you will become a mighty warrior. Your workshop has the power to create a long-drawn out trial or one that is bearable and short-lived.

You never know what trial you may face during the day. You certainly need to end your day in a peaceful environment after encountering struggles so negativity doesn't continue to bombard your workshop. Therefore, before you leave your house, turn on worship music so a continuous praise is going up to God from your home all day long. This invites the Holy Spirit to dwell there, which makes it a peaceful haven to come home to and your mind will find rest at the end of the day.

Your workshop should be *always* filled with positive thoughts. Paul tells us to fill our heads with only good things:

> "Finally, brethren, whatsoever things are true, whatsoever things are honest, whatsoever things are just, whatsoever things are pure, whatsoever things are lovely, whatsoever things are of good report; if there be any virtue, and if there be any praise, think on these things" (Philippians 4:8, KJV).

God makes it clear not to dwell in the past. God instructs us to leave the past in the past because it will destroy you. Dwelling on hurts, regrets, or loved ones who are gone will create self-destruction. Such thoughts cause anguish, which lead to stress. Stress will affect your mind and spirit, which will eventually destroy your body. This concept is illustrated in Genesis when Lot's wife was instructed not to look back, but to move forward, so she wouldn't be consumed (Genesis 19:17). Nevertheless, she *looked back* as her hometown was destroyed. She turned into a pillar of salt (Genesis 19:26). Always be mindful it is extremely important you don't dwell on the past. God warns us of this repeatedly in the Bible:

> *"Remember ye not the former things, neither consider the things of old.* Behold, I will do a new thing; now it shall spring forth; shall ye not know it? I will even make a way in the wilderness, and rivers in the desert" (Isaiah 43:18-19, KJV, emphasis added).

> "Brethren, I count not myself to have apprehended: but *this* one thing *I do*, **forgetting those things which are behind,** and reaching forth unto those things which are before," (Philippians 3:13, KJV, emphasis added).

When you dwell in the past, it limits God's power in your present and future. When you constantly think about your past failures, you believe God can't do anything for you: "He never did before, why would He now?" As this thought becomes a stronghold, and a bitter root is planted into the fertile ground of your heart, you *will* reap a bitter harvest of undesirable manifestations because "For as he thinketh in his heart, so is he…" (Proverbs 23:7, KJV). Therefore, focus on these biblical truths: God makes all things new, but you have to let go of the past to step into the future He has planned for you. You can't be in two places at once!

As James (1:8) told us, you therefore have to be single-minded, not just about your own past but others as well. Leave it where it belongs: in the past. Don't bring it into your present. If you do, it will wreak havoc on your life. It is over with—finished and forgotten: *"As far as the east is from the west, so far hath he removed our transgressions from us"* (Psalm 103:12, emphasis added). Do you know how far the East is from the West? I don't. I can't even begin to imagine, especially if this phrase was in reference to the Universe.

Eventually, negativity *will* destroy your temple. Your body was not made to withstand sustained periods of flight-or-fight reactions. During stressful situations cortisol and epinephrine are produced. This can increase blood pressure, heart rate, and cause heart palpitations and irregular rhythms, which can eventually lead to heart disease if left uncontrolled. Heart disease is the number one killer in women.[72] Women are more susceptible to stress. We tend to be emotional beings, and our hearts are easily broken. I would assume the majority of us live in the past while we try to reconcile it with our present and future. I think it is part of our human nature: "If only I would have done this; if only he would have done that; if only I had another chance, I would do it better this time."

Allowing yourself to be idle and dwelling upon the past or negative thoughts allows the enemy to get a stronghold on you. I had a powerful revelation this morning—it suddenly occurred to me since our bodies have an electromagnetic field around them; we are negatively charged if we are consumed by negative thought patterns. This negative charge gives off a signal that attracts the enemy to attack you. I saw our bod-

---

72 "Getting the Message; Heart Disease is the Number One Killer in Women." National Institutes of Health. 15 Sept 2012. < www.nhlbi.nih.gov>.

ies like red flashing lights with a big "Open" sign. It is like we are saying, "Welcome, come on in. I am ready for your business."

The vision I had correlates to research that indicate our energy fields magnetically repel or attract others. This data also reveals we have increased vulnerability to being affected by the negativity of others when we are out of physiological balance due to negative thoughts and emotions: "When people are able to maintain the physiological coherence mode, they are more internally stable, and thus less vulnerable to being negatively affected by the fields emanating from others."[73] Keep in mind the enemy can affect you indirectly by creating negative thoughts, emotions, reactions, and behaviors in other people. Therefore, you should always guard your heart and mind to keep negativity out, which will prevent the enemy from gaining a foothold into your life.

Also be aware anything that is not created from love comes from the enemy. Fear is the opposite of love, from which all other negative feelings are derived. Fear is what the enemy uses to get a foothold into your life. This foothold (opportunity) will develop into a stronghold if you don't use spiritual warfare to combat it. A stronghold is defined as follows:

> "A demonic stronghold is anything that's compelling enough to hold you in its power. It prevents you from receiving God's love and truth."[74]

Don't allow the enemy to develop a stronghold in your life by allowing fear to dominate you. This is his main strategy. Keep in mind he often uses very subtle strategies. You won't even recognize what is going on. By the time you are in the pit, you'll be in so deep you won't care about anything. You'll just want to stay there and wallow around,

---

73 McCraty, R., *The Energetic Heart: Bioelectricmagnetic Communication Within People, in Bioelectric Medicine, P.J. Rosch and M.S. Markov, Editors. 2004, Marcel Dekker: New York. P. 541-562.*

74 Dowgiewicz, Mike and Sue Dowgiewicz. "Demolishing Strongholds." Restoration Ministries International. 03 March 2012. <www.restorationministries.org>.

sinking further and further into the abyss of self-pity and despair. He digs his claws in deep and won't let go until you get out the big guns. Then the war is on. The only thing you can do is cry out to Jesus.

God's instruction concerning letting go of the past can be exemplified by the following experience. There was a new program being developed within the community where I live to help those with addictions or people experiencing grief from the loss of a loved one. I thought due to my experiences, God would want me to help with this program. I went through the training process of becoming a group leader. This process involved exploration of my childhood, family life, and other past experiences.

Within a few weeks, the joy and peace I had received from my Savior turned into bitter sadness, anger, depression, and gloom. *When God says don't go back to the past, you should listen. It is extremely destructive.* God had healed me, and I went back and dug up all the things that had made my life a living hell. *Let dead things stay buried and move forward with God and His great plan for your life.* Trust in Him. He knows the plans He has for you. He will never harm you. His plan for you is one of prosperity. This is one of His great promises (Jeremiah 29:11).

God wants us to prosper. It's *His main desire for us*. In His infinite wisdom, He knows it's not possible if we have a negative thought life, and He tells us this: "Beloved, I wish **above all things** that thou mayest prosper and be in health, **even as thy soul prospereth**" (3 John 1:2, KJV). He has given us tools to access the kingdom of Heaven within. However you certainly can't live above what you think. Our soul, which is our internal life, has to come into alignment with God's thinking in order for us to gain prosperity internally, which then leads to external prosperity. John's scripture tells us in order to prosper in our outward life; we first have to prosper on the inside. This begins with our thoughts, which is our workshop.

Our Heavenly Father wants to extinguish our negative thought patterns. After Jesus was scourged, the cruel Roman soldiers shoved a crown of thorns down over his head, which caused him to shed blood.

This is symbolic of Jesus taking all of our negative thoughts so we would not dwell upon them. It is a strong reminder for us to crucify all negative thoughts that exalt themselves against the Word of God. *Are you going to believe the negative thoughts that go on in your head, or are you going to believe what God says about who He is, who you are, and what He wants for your life? The choice is yours. Make up your mind, and allow the greatest sacrifice ever made for you through the blood of your Savior to lift up your thought life and come into alignment with God's.* You will be more than glad that you did.

Remember these important verses:

"Casting down imaginations, and every high thing that exalteth itself against the knowledge of God, and bringing into captivity every thought to the obedience of Christ…" (2 Corinthians 10:5, KJV).

"…According to your faith, be it unto you" (Matthew 9:29, KJV).

NATURAL GIFTS

God graces us *all* with special gifts—spiritual as well as natural—not because of who we are, but because of His love and generosity. What we choose to do with those gifts is our gift to Him. I recently read an article about the "painter of light," Thomas Kinkade. He said his mother once told him God had given him the wonderful talent to paint, but what he did with that talent would be his gift to God.[75] I would say God is extremely pleased with the gift Kinkade gave back to Him. Check out his website sometime. He has painted over a thousand pieces. Each of his paintings has a description of the source of inspiration, and he gave God all of the glory.

---

75 Harper, Anthony, Rev. "Interview: Thomas Kinkade on Mirroring God's Creation." Inspire Magazine. 05 July 2013. <inspiremagazine.org>.

When you have a gift from God, you know it comes from Him when it seems effortless and it's fueled by passion and desire. That's because it's His will working within you as an outward expression of His light and magnificent power. If you have to labor over it to develop it, then it is a skill; but a gift is there waiting for you to discover it and bring it forth to share with the world. You may have to fine tune it with practice and application, but you won't have to spend endless hours struggling to achieve the end result. In essence, a gift from God is an outward expression of your spirit being in alignment with God's Spirit, which enables one of His attributes to flow through you and out of you.

I recently watched the movie, *The Bodyguard* with Whitney Houston. While hearing her sing "I Will Run to You," a tingling sensation went through my body. I frequently get this same sensation when the Holy Spirit communicates with me. This sensation also occurs if I see something beautiful in nature or whenever amazing talent captivates my attention. I asked God why I was feeling this sensation while hearing Whitney sing that beautiful song. He explained to me I wasn't actually responding to her beautiful voice, but my spirit was connecting to His Spirit. It is His Spirit that made her voice so great. It is His Spirit that makes all things wonderful and amazing. He continued to explain His gifts are expressed in the way in which He chooses His Spirit to be manifested. You might see it in a beautiful painting, a miraculous recovery due to a gifted surgeon's hand, or hear it in a beautiful voice, like Whitney Houston's.

Have you discovered your gift yet? If not, ask God to reveal it to you. If you have, don't waste it. *Use it to bring glory and pleasure to Him and assistance to others. This is what He created you for.* We are all unique—designed with a special purpose and plan by and for our Heavenly Father. *When we manifest His gifts, we are expressing the great Creator within us, which allows His brilliance to shine forth. Your gift is a blessing to all the people you touch. Be wise and use it diligently.*

CHAPTER SEVEN

OPERATING IN THE KINGDOM

SEEK YE FIRST THE KINGDOM OF GOD

"But seek ye first the kingdom of God and his righteousness, and all these things shall be added unto you" (Matthew 6:33, KJV). In this verse, not only do we find one of God's great promises to us, but we realize what the Bible is about—it is the basic instructions for daily kingdom living. Within these instructions we find the greatest role model we could ever have: Jesus.

You may be asking yourself how you seek the kingdom first. The most important thing is to be free from the bondage of self-condemnation and the illusion of unworthiness. You will then be able to love yourself, others, and your Heavenly Father. You can accomplish this when you *receive* His love and His great *gift* of righteousness through His redemptive plan of salvation:

> "...they which *receive* abundance of grace and of the *gift* of righteousness *shall reign* in life by one, Jesus Christ..." (Romans 5:17, KJV, emphasis added)

Secondly, *make God the priority in your life.* That means when you have a problem, go to Him. Pour out everything that is in your heart. Seek His advice. Listen for it. Wait for it. Trust *Him* instead of others. I'm not saying you should never listen to other people. Sometimes God speaks through others; but if what they are saying is contrary to His Word, then don't be swayed by their advice, or you will regret it.

Ask yourself in every situation, "Is this consistent with kingdom living? Is this in line with what the Word of God says? Will I be in right standing with God if I do this?" Go to the Word and find out what it says about your specific situation. Make sure you have a Bible with a good concordance, which has topics listed for practical application to daily living. I love my Touch Point Bible. It really helps guide me in my daily living, and it has a quick reference guide sorted by topics.

Praise God in *every* situation. I once heard a preacher say when you pray, angels show up, but *when you praise God, He shows up.* I know that is true because wonderful things have happened when I have praised God.

Ask God to align your mind and will with His. Ask Him to make your heart just like Jesus' heart. Ask Jesus to live in you and reproduce Himself in you so you can glorify the Father. When you have faith in your Savior and are able to fully receive His grace, you are then able to come into alignment with God's perfect will. Then, you will experience a tidal wave of blessings. His will is love, which includes *receiving* His love. When you do that, you will love Him with everything that you are. You will then love yourself, which will enable you to love your neighbor as yourself.

Letting go of negativity is a good way to fix your "receiver" so God's love can come pouring in. You need to release any resentment, anger, hatred or any other negative feelings that you may be harboring. Perhaps you have some resentment buried so deeply in your heart from long ago you have no idea it is even in there. God will reveal it to you if you ask Him. I think our feelings of fear, anger, resentment, or bitterness block love from flowing. Love feels light and uplifting—the opposite of being weighed down with negativity. When God helps you let go of the negativity and your hard heart softens, look out. It is like a dam that opens up the floodgate to all the love that has been held in over the years. My heart used to be hard from all the abuse I went through, but through the death of my husband, my heart softened. I remember driving down the highway a few months after his passing. There was a turtle in the middle of the road. He was upside down and struggling to turn upright. His legs were flailing about in a useless effort to return to a mobile position. My heart tugged at me to turn around and rescue him, which I did. As I put him down in a safe place, I began to weep uncontrollably, thinking of that poor turtle struggling to make it to safety as he crept along the grass. The old me with the hardened heart would never have felt so deeply for a turtle, but *I was a new creature in Christ and made whole with a soft compassionate heart, which was the way God had truly created me.*

Another way to seek God and His kingdom first is to *give God the glory. Always remember to acknowledge Him in all things. He is the source of all good things in your life.* Thank Him for everything. Reveal Him and His goodness to others at every opportunity. Does this mean you have to preach to others who aren't receptive to hearing His Word? No. The Bible says, "...neither cast ye your pearls before swine..." (Matthew 7:6, KJV). You can, however, state the facts when someone asks you about some blessing in your life. I found when I began to do this; more blessings flowed in my life.

Be obedient to His Word and promptings from the Holy Spirit. What does that mean? If you feel something deep inside you urging you to do something, that is usually the Holy Spirit—unless the urging does not line up with God's Word. If you are not sure about it, pray about it. If God speaks once, He will speak again. He will make it clear to you. If you don't comply, the promptings from the Holy Spirit may be extinguished, and you certainly don't want that.

Pray in all situations. Pray when you need comfort, advice, fellowship, when you are lonely, sad, hurt, depressed, or joyful. Pray when others need help. Pray for protection, wisdom, and the fruit and the gifts of the Holy Spirit to be manifested in your life. Pray for provision. When you pray, begin with praising Him and then thank Him. Tell Him you have great expectations your prayers will be answered *if you are praying according to His will because He can't say no. It is what He wants for you also.*

Prayer is important because it brings us into fellowship with our Heavenly Father and helps us to develop an intimate relationship with Him. When we become intimate with God and we walk very closely with Him, we are motivated to live a righteous life because we wouldn't want to do anything to displease or hurt Him. As previously stated, *his capacity to hurt is just as great as His capacity to love.* I was recently praying and I asked Jesus if He ever experienced deep grief over the loss of a loved one while walking on this Earth. I knew He experienced everything we do so He could have true empathy for us while acting as our intercessor as the High Priest at our Father's right hand. I searched my memory of biblical history and didn't recall Jesus experiencing the loss of a loved one with the exception of His friend Lazarus. However, He raised him from the dead. So His grief was only momentary. Then it suddenly occurred to me—the grief He feels over the eternal loss of souls is much greater than any grief we will ever experience. At least we have the reassurance of a glorious reunion with our loved ones on the other side; but for those who have totally rejected Him and will be lost forever, He will be forever separated from them. His heart will be broken over this. He tells us it is His desire that *no* man shall perish (2 Peter 3:9). It will tear Him up to say, "*...I never knew you: depart from me...*" (Matthew 7:23, KJV, emphasis added).

Jesse Duplantis describes in his account, when he was taken to Heaven and met Jesus, how Jesus' heart will be broken over lost souls. He states Jesus was imploring him to tell everyone He is coming soon. This is what Duplantis states that Jesus said with tears in His eyes:

> "On the great day of judgment I will have to tell some of the creation I love to depart from me. I dread that day. I dread it! I dread it!...Jesse, it's final. Tears flowed from my eyes the day my creation, Adam fell. But I knew I would send myself. I had

a chance to touch people. But that day is coming and it's final. Once it's said, I can't change it. I have to wipe tears from My eyes."[76]

I can only imagine how many tears Jesus has shed. I recently went to see a movie. Within the first few minutes I heard God's name taken in vain. I left the theater and as I walked away, I began to tell God how sorry I was that people hurt Him in such terrible ways. I began to weep as I felt overwhelmed by a terrible sadness inside of me. I knew God was allowing me to feel what He was feeling. Before this incident, I had believed God had a great capacity to feel pain. Now I realize just how much He can hurt. I believe He allowed me to feel this because of my intimacy with Him, which has come through prayer and seeking His presence.

One of the most important things a Christian should seek in the kingdom of God is to be filled with the Holy Spirit. This was previously addressed concerning the power Jesus has placed within you. That power will enable you to live righteously, bring glory to God, and be a soul winner for Christ.

Jesus instructs us to ask to be filled with the spirit: "If ye then, being evil, know how to give good gifts unto your children: how much more shall your heavenly Father give the Holy Spirit to them that ask him?" (Luke 11:13, KJV). When you are spirit-filled, God's spiritual gifts are manifested in you. He gives different gifts to each one of His children. Different religions have different ideas about this concept. However, I don't subscribe to any particular denomination, only to biblical principles. As mentioned previously, the Bible informs us about all of these gifts (1 Corinthians 12:4-11).

It's imperative to emphasize these gifts are meant for all of God's children, not just the apostles in Jesus' time. God's gifts, which are operating in me, is the reason I can sit down and write a book about Him without any formal theological training. He reveals things to me

---

76 Duplantis, Jesse. *Close Encounters of the God Kind.* Jesse Duplantis Ministries, 1996: 127-128.

through prophetic revelations. You surely wouldn't want to miss out on these special gifts. Ask to be filled with the Holy Spirit and it will be given to you. I asked and had to ask again and then again before I was completely filled because it's not possible to receive all of His powerful energy at once when you have been functioning in a medium of negativity. He has promised when we ask we will receive:

> "And I say unto you, Ask, and it shall be given you; seek, and ye shall find; knock, and it shall be opened unto you. For every one that asketh receiveth; and he that seeketh findeth; and to him that knocketh it shall be opened" (Luke 11:9-10, KJV).

Please know when you accept Jesus Christ as your Lord and Savior, the Holy Spirit comes to live in you. This is God's first installment of His many promises:

> "Then Peter said unto them, Repent, and be baptized every one of you in the name of Jesus Christ for the remission of sins, and ye shall receive the gift of the Holy Ghost. For the promise is unto you, and to your children, and to all that are afar off, even as many as the Lord our God shall call" (Acts 2:38-39, KJV).

While I was writing about being spirit-filled, I begin to ponder this mystery. The Bible reveals the nature of the power of God. There are several references to the danger of being in His physical presence. Moses had to hide in the cleft of the rock because of the intensity of His power as He passed by. I wondered how we could be filled with His power if Moses couldn't even stand near Him. Jesse Duplantis describes in his account of his journey to Heaven how powerful our God is:

> "The closer I got to the throne of God, the weaker I became, because of the glory of God. When people are coming to the Throne, you see God's anointing on them, that glory on them from different levels. But when you get to the Throne, nothing compares to the glory of God.

When the light from the Throne hit me I couldn't stand up: I fell down... Although I couldn't look up for very long at a time, I looked up from the floor in the direction of the overwhelming Light, and I saw Him! I saw Elohim, Jehovah God, Yahweh sitting on the Throne! But I saw His feet—only His feet. The Light was so bright that came from Him, I couldn't see His face. Now I know the Scripture says we can't see Jehovah's face and live—at least, I knew I couldn't! I had to keep looking down, the Light was so intense. But I looked again, and I saw the lower part of His hand resting on the arm of the Throne. He is so big—you can't describe Him in dimension. His hand is huge! This body, the form of it, is sort of like energy, spirit. There's a wall around the Throne, but the Throne is higher than the wall—that's why you can see the Throne from every direction, from a distance. And that power, that energy-like smoke of God, covers all around the chair of the Throne itself."

I heard a sound, *Whoooooosh!* There was a massive amount of energy in that place. That's the only way I can explain it. It was God's power! You hear that noise, then the energy goes back into Him. There is smoke and power and noise..."

The angels with wings were circling the Throne, singing and shouting, "The Great Jehovah!" Every time they circled the Throne they praised God because they saw a new facet of Him they had never seen before. And they express what they see by saying "Holy! Holy! Holy!" That's how vast God is! Even though the angels have been flying around God's Throne since the beginning of their existence, they are still seeing new revelations of His character, His love and His glory!

There was a cloud that looked like smoke going up from the Throne and I heard that massive sound, Whoosh! It was power like I've never experienced in my life. Then I saw God's finger barely move and when it moved, an angel that was flying near Him was thrown up against a wall. *Bam!* It didn't hurt the angel, but I felt if God just barely moved, a universe would be annihilated."[77]

If an angel can't withstand the power of God's moving finger, then our weak flesh certainly couldn't be filled with His power. This is what has been revealed to me: It is the same measure of power that Jesus had in the flesh that we now have in us. The only difference is Jesus understood who He was and how to utilize that power; we don't. Even if we did understand, we don't have enough faith to tap into it and believe we can do the same work that He did, although He told us we could: "Verily, verily, I say unto you, He that believeth on me, the works that I do shall he do also; and greater *works* than these shall he do;" (John 14:12, KJV). Therefore, when I write about His power being in us, it is not the full power of the great Jehovah God, but a measure of His power that dwells in us as His creations. We are extensions of His divine energy.

What is the difference between being spirit-filled and having God's Spirit dwell within you because you have accepted Jesus as your Savior? *It is the degree of the relationship you have with God and the ability to access the kingdom.* Only those who are truly spirit-filled have an intense desire for and spend a significant amount of time in the presence of God. God truly becomes the priority. People who are spirit-filled spend a great amount of time thinking about the Lord and the love they share together. I get excited when I know I have some extra time to spend with the Lord as I anticipate our time together. It is similar, but much more intense; to anticipating the time you spend with a new romantic interest. I begin to think about how I will give Him my full attention as He permeates every cell of my being and fills me with His powerful peace, joy, and love.

The Holy Spirit revealed to me that the process of being spirit-filled is similar to activating the Word. The Word and the Holy Spirit are both placed within you when you accept Jesus as your Savior. The Holy Spirit, as well as the Word, lies dormant within

---

77 Duplantis, Jesse. *Close Encounters of the God Kind.* Jesse Duplantis Ministries, 1996:112-115

your spirit until you activate them. To activate the Holy Spirit, you need to ask God to fill you from the top of your head to the bottom of your feet. Because God gives you free will, He is not going to do this until you ask. Have your pastor lay hands on you and pray for this. Don't let that Holy Ghost power just lie dormant in you for the rest of your life. Make Jesus not only your Savior, but your Lord, through the power of the Holy Spirit He has given you. *You will then withstand every battle, weather every storm, and lead others into victory!*

I think the most important point about being filled with the Holy Spirit is Jesus was spirit-filled: "John gave further evidence, saying, I have seen the Spirit descending as a dove out of heaven, and ***it dwelt on Him [never to depart]***" (John 1:32, AMP, emphasis added). Being spirit-filled also will glorify Jesus: "He will glorify me because it is from me that he will receive what he will make known to you" (John 16:14, NIV). As Christians we are to emulate Jesus. When you have the Holy Spirit dwelling within you, Jesus' characteristics will be manifested. Spirit-filled Christians will reveal His nature and help win souls to Christ.

When you are filled with the Holy Spirit, Jesus becomes not only your Savior, but the Lord of your life: "…and that no man can say that Jesus is the Lord, but by the Holy Ghost" (1 Corinthians 12:3, KJV). When Jesus is your Lord, He guides and directs you every step of the way. You look to him for wisdom, knowledge, comfort, encouragement, strength, and provision.

The Holy Spirit will also give you a new life. This is what Jesus was referring to when He said you have to be born of the spirit to enter into the kingdom (John 3:5). As I have testified in previous chapters, I was transformed from the inside out. The Holy Spirit will empower you to obtain the abundant life your Heavenly Father planned for you. His beautiful attributes will enable you to access the desires of your heart including peace, love, and joy.

You will also be a life-giver when you are spirit-filled. The Holy Spirit will become alive in you, which will empower you to help those who are not living the abundant life Christ wants them to have:

> "He that believeth on me, as the scripture hath said, out of his belly shall flow rivers of living water)" (John 7:39, KJV).

> "…But the last Adam—that is, Christ—is a life-giving Spirit" (1 Corinthians 15:45, NLT).

Christians who are spirit-filled yield to the promptings of the Holy Spirit. Just yesterday, I was driving to a patient's home, and I heard the Holy Spirit ask me why I didn't pray with the last patient I had seen. She was ill and in pain from a bladder infection. At first, I thought I was talking to myself, but then I heard the artist on the gospel station I was listening to sing, "You've got to turn around, you've got to turn around." Still, I kept driving in the opposite direction. I then began to feel "butterflies" in my stomach, which is a sign the Holy Spirit some-times uses to communicate a definite *no* when I am about to do some-thing I should not. So I turned around and drove to her home to pray for her because I realized He was communicating with me, and I never want to do anything that would grieve or quench His promptings.

The Apostle Paul instructs us in honoring the Holy Spirit God has so graciously given us:

> "And be renewed in the spirit of your mind; And that ye put on the new man, which after God is created in righteousness and true holiness. Wherefore putting away lying, speak every man truth with his neighbour: for we are members one of another. Be ye angry, and sin not: let not the sun go down upon your wrath: Neither give place to the devil. Let him that stole steal no more: but rather let him labour, working with his hands the thing which is good, that he may have to give to him that need-eth. Let no corrupt communication proceed out of your mouth, but that which is good to the use of edifying, that it may min-ister grace unto the hearers. ***And grieve not the holy Spirit of***

God, whereby ye are sealed unto the day of redemption. Let all bitterness, and wrath, and anger, and clamour, and evil speaking, be put away from you, with all malice: And be ye kind one to another, tenderhearted, forgiving one another, even as God for Christ's sake hath forgiven you" (Ephesians 4:23-32, KJV, emphasis added).

The difference between having God's Spirit dwell within you and being spirit-filled can be illustrated by the life of the disciple Peter. He denied Jesus three times prior to the crucifixion. His flesh simply did not possess the character to stand up for Jesus during that fearful time, even after walking with Jesus and witnessing all the miracles He performed. However, once Peter was filled with the Holy Spirit on the day of Pentecost, he became courageous and led the Christian movement. This resulted in his death as a martyr as Jesus forewarned:

"Verily, verily, I say unto thee, When thou wast young, thou girdest thyself, and walkedst whither thou wouldest: but when thou shalt be old, thou shalt stretch forth thy hands, and another shall gird thee, and carry thee whither thou wouldest not. This spake he, signifying by what death he should glorify God. And when he had spoken this, he saith unto him, Follow me" (John 21:18-19, KJV).

Of course, most spirit-filled Christians don't die the type of death Peter did, but his life is a testament to the fact when you are spirit-filled, you are transformed. The things that used to matter to you are no longer important, and you will desire to seek righteousness, which will glorify God and bring Him great pleasure. In order to be spirit-filled, you have to ask for the Spirit to fill you on a continual basis. It's important to emphasize you can quench the Spirit by not following His promptings, which usually manifest as a still, small voice or a feeling that won't leave you alone, indicating you should do something that is in line with God's Word. You can get more in tune with the Spirit by prayer, and reading and speaking scriptures or by being in God's presence through praise and worship.

LOSE YOUR LIFE AND YOU SHALL FIND IT

"For whosoever will save his life shall lose it: and whosoever will lose his life for my sake shall find it" (Matthew 16:25, KJV). What did Jesus mean by this? It means you should surrender to God and His purpose for your life instead of focusing on your own agenda. When you do this you will discover a beautiful biblical truth: when you pour into others, God pours into you.

To illustrate this point, let me share a little story with you. Last summer, I had a sudden onset of hip pain, which continued for several days. I had a nursing home ministry that involved visiting the facility a couple of Saturdays every month. While I was praying at the end of the sermon for the residents and the staff of the nursing home, I became overwhelmed with the presence of God and was brought to tears. As I began to walk out of the building, I noticed my hip pain was nearly gone. God had taken care of my pain as I was asking Him to care for others.

I recently saw a sermon delivered by Joel Osteen called "Sewing a Seed in Your Time of Need."[78] As he pointed out, this concept does not just apply to financial issues, but to every issue that may appear in your life. I immediately began to apply this principle. Every time an ache or pain popped up, I would pray for one of my patients or family members with the same type of pain, and then my own pain would quickly vanish. Perhaps this is God's way of reminding me to pray for others. When you pray for others, it definitely takes the focus off of you and your circumstances.

Another important point Osteen emphasized in his sermon was referenced in the following scripture: "*Trust in the Lord and do good...*" (Psalms 37:3, KJV). Osteen talked about a man who would visit his church when he went to Houston for cancer treatment. The man began to apply this scripture to his life by visiting other cancer patients in the hospital. He went up and down the halls to their rooms while pray-

---

78 "Sewing a Seed in Your Time of Need." Joel Osteen. Trinity Broadcast Network. Houston. 12 May 2012.

ing for and encouraging them. When he was retested to assess the cancer, it had gone into remission. The man trusted God and did good. He basically lost his life and found it by sowing a seed for his need. This example epitomizes the testimony of God's Word at work and the power of His healing.

I believe love is a never-ending cycle of divinity. You send it out, and it comes back to you, whether it is in the form of a smile, a kind word, a financial blessing, or some type of service you provide to someone in need. Maybe that's why Jesus said, "...It is more blessed to give than to receive" (Acts 20:35, KJV). You definitely reap what you sow. *If you only focus on your own selfish desires, you will always put yourself first and never find true happiness.* The material objects of this world only bring temporary satisfaction, but it is not true happiness. It certainly isn't joy, and it definitely isn't anything that lasts. This is what Jesus meant when He said,

> "Lay not up for yourselves treasures upon earth, where moth and rust doth corrupt, and where thieves break through and steal: But lay up for yourselves treasures in heaven..." (Matthew 6:19-20, KJV).

The only true satisfaction comes from fulfilling your heart's desire of joy and peace. Those things only come when you focus on God's love for you and your love for God and others.

Losing your life, therefore, means complete surrender to God—surrendering your will to His. When you give your life to Christ and begin to develop an ever-increasing love for Him, surrendering becomes easy because the last thing you want to do is disappoint Him. *When you have the Holy Spirit living in you—whispering to you and guiding you—your will eventually fades into the background, and His will presses you forward.*

John tells us, **"He must increase, but I must decrease"** (John 3:30, KJV, emphasis added). Keep in mind your flesh will not always want to cooperate. The Apostle Paul defines the biblical meaning of "flesh" as sinful nature in the following scripture: "The sinful nature wants to do evil, which is just the opposite of what the Spirit wants. And the Spirit gives us desires that are the opposite of what the sinful nature desires…" (Galatians 5:17, NLT). In other versions of the bible, the phrase "sinful nature" is replaced with the word "flesh." We can conclude from this scripture that "the flesh" is anything that is contrary to God's will.

Although your flesh will strive for dominance, your spirit will always want to surrender to God's perfect will. When you truly love God, your spirit gains control and will win the battle. I'm not saying you will be perfect. If you could be, you wouldn't have needed a Savior. One thing is for sure, you will never master your tongue. Things fall off of mine before I can rein them in. Then I scratch my head in confusion and think, "Where did that come from?" The Bible warns us we can't control our tongues: "***But the tongue can no man tame; it is an unruly evil, full of deadly poison***" (James 3:6, KJV, emphasis added).

Paul tells us of his struggle with the flesh: "***I don't really understand myself, for I want to do what is right, but I don't do it. Instead, I do what I hate***" (Romans 7:15, NLT, emphasis added). *We will always battle against our flesh. It wants control, but the more you practice the desires of the Spirit, the more the Spirit will be in control and the easier it will be to surrender to God's will.* The spirit is like a weak muscle you have to condition. The greater the resistance from the flesh, the stronger the spirit will become when you push against it. The more repetitions you add, the greater endurance you will have. Surrendering your will then becomes effortless as your spirit dominates over your flesh.

Surrendering to God and walking in the Spirit takes practice. It doesn't come overnight. It is a process. If you are newly saved, you have been living under the authority of your flesh for a long while, so you need to give yourself time to adjust to this new way of life, but the benefits outweigh the effort. Get in the habit of always going to Him first for everything: "***Trust in the LORD with all thine heart, And*** *lean not unto thine own understanding; In all thy ways acknowledge Him, And He shall direct thy paths*" (Proverbs 3:5-6, KJV, emphasis added). This scripture is the true essence of surrender. Notice the phrase "*all your ways.*" It may seem silly to you to ask Him about everything before you do it, but sometimes you may regret it if you don't. I certainly wished I had consulted Him before throwing a significant sum of money down the drain due to an unwise decision. I know if I had consulted God He would have given me proper direction, and I would not have regretted the consequences of my ill-conceived actions.

You need to know what He tells you to do might not always make sense at the time. It didn't make sense to me when God was directing me to give up my life, move back in with my parents, and go to college at the age of twenty-eight. I felt as though I had been kicked in the stomach when I gave up all of my belongings and privacy. I can only imagine the struggles I would have incurred had I not followed His promptings.   I have always been able to care for myself and my family, as well as be a blessing to others because of His wisdom and divine guidance. I thank Him for calling me to be a therapist and for the great blessings it has brought me. I wasn't feeling so grateful way back then, but I am completely filled with gratitude now. As I always say, *Papa knows best!*

THE KINGDOM OPERATION

Living an abundant life revolves around the principle of sowing and reaping. Jesus tells us this is the secret to the kingdom (Mark 4:11). I can tell you this principle works no matter what you sow— whether it is kindness, prayers for others, or financial aid for someone in need. I have experienced harvests that have returned the seeds I've sown one hundredfold.

I recently heard a testimony by a church member. She said the roof of her new home was damaged due to it being poorly constructed. She heard the Lord tell her to call in her seed that she had sown when her church needed a new roof.   He also said that her harvest was going to walk through the front door. She began to call in her seed by declaring she would have her roof repaired. The following Sunday someone walked through her front door and wrote a check for her roof just as the Lord had told her.

Jesus' parable of the farmer (Mark 4) tells us that our harvest depends on our ability to have faith in, receive, and focus on the Word. If you look at it on a deeper level, He is actually saying your ability to have abundance in all things and access kingdom living is directly related to the degree in which you *receive the fullness of who He is. This is true because He and His Word are the same* (John 1:1, 14). Obtaining a thirty, sixty, or a hundredfold harvest correlates with your ability to *believe who He says He is and who He says you are in Him.* Your ability to *fully receive His attributes, especially His immense faith,* and *put them to work* is the key to the kingdom (Mark 4:8).

To paraphrase the parable in Mark, Jesus describes this principle as follows: Your ground has to be fertile, which means you have to receive the Word by meditating upon it after hearing or reading it, which will plant it deep within your heart. This is your transformation center, where your inner world, which is the perception of your outer world, will lead to an outward change. This external change, which includes the electromagnetic field surrounding you, will attract the bountiful harvest you sowed into the fertile ground of your heart. If you don't tend your crop (by meditating on the Word), the soil becomes depleted, and you won't be able to grow anything. If you let the cares of this world choke out God's blessing, like a weed will choke out a plant, you won't live the life God planned for you. The struggles you face will take center stage and become bigger than Jesus, which will prevent His tender love, mercy, grace, strength, *faith*, and power from flowing in your life. Your world will be full of undesirable produce that is useless. You have to shut out all of the world's negativity and totally focus on the seed you have planted to make it bring forth your fruit. Don't let a root of regret, resentment, anger, or bitterness keep your seed from growing into a bountiful harvest of Jesus' grace. If you focus on your current circumstances, negative attitudes or perceptions from yourself or others, it will hinder your faith. If you believe anything other than the truth of

God's Word, then the enemy will succeed in stealing the power of the Word and it won't become deeply rooted within you. Don't let your *perceived* lack or past events keep you from your divine destiny of God's special plan for you. Remember, when the Word lies dormant within you, so does the gifts and power placed within you by the Holy Spirit.

You also have to use the principles outlined in the chapter entitled, "The Power of the Tongue" to reap an abundant harvest for the seed that you have sown. This is the foundation of the kingdom operation. However, the reaping depends on the motive for the sowing. If you are sowing to glorify God in some way, you *will* reap a generous harvest as the Apostle Paul writes about in the following scripture: "…He will bring to light what is hidden in darkness and will expose the motives of the heart. At that time each will receive their praise from God" (1 Corinthians 4:5, NIV).

Paul also warns us about the law of sowing and reaping: "Do not be deceived, God is not mocked; for whatever a man sows, that he will also reap. For he who sows to his flesh will of the flesh reap corruption, but he who sows to the Spirit will of the Spirit reap everlasting life " (Galatians 6:7-8, KJV). Always be mindful of your thoughts, actions, and words. They *will* one day manifest in your life, whether good or bad; therefore, sow a good seed for a beautiful garden.

To get a hundred percent return on the seed you sow, you have to *stay focused* on the Word:

> "But this I say, He which soweth sparingly shall reap also sparingly; and he which soweth bountifully shall reap also bountifully" (2 Corinthians 9:16).

Meditate on God's promises, His plan for your life, and His gifts and power He placed within you. You have to focus on who He says He is and who He says you are as His child: loved beyond comprehension and eternally lifted up in His arms. Then you will increase your faith and others will see Christ in you. This will enable you to sow the seed into others as you lead them to Jesus, which will help Him fulfill His plan of reaping a bountiful harvest of souls and increase His family.[79]

The law of sowing and reaping does not just apply to finances. *It applies to every facet of life. God wants us to know this law of sowing and reaping is a universal law that has the power to create the kingdom of God or the total opposite!* "*...choose you this day whom ye will serve...*" (Joshua 24:15, KJV, emphasis added).

Today, when I was praying, God revealed to me Jesus was His seed. The great sacrifice of His Son has brought Him a great harvest of souls. The reaping He is now experiencing from the beautiful seed He provided continues to bring Him wonderful fellowship, great joy, and comfort! His family is ever-increasing. His plan for His children, who have been adopted into His family through His Son, is being fulfilled.

FAITH AND PRAYER

Faith will increase from glory to glory when spending time in God's presence: "For therein is the righteousness of God revealed from faith to faith: as it is written, The just shall live by faith" (Romans 1:17, KJV). This scripture tells us our faith is increased when we understand His loving nature, because our trust in Him will increase. Scripture also tells us, "*so then faith cometh by hearing, and hearing by the word of God*" (Romans 10:17, KJV, emphasis added). However, the original Greek text did not state "God," but "Christos," which means Christ. This is evident in the biblical story about the man from Lystra who was born disabled but was completely healed after hearing Paul preach the Word of Christ.[80] When you saturate yourself with the Gospel of Jesus Christ, you will receive great faith and wholeness then follows.

---

79 The Four Fold Gospel, Parable of the Sower. Bible Study Tools. Salem Web Network. 09 June 2013. <biblestudytools.com. (adapted from).

80 Prince, Joseph. *Destined to Reign.* Tulsa, Ok: Harrison House Publishers; 2007:74-75.

There is one very important point I want to make about faith. I had a great deal of comfort when I learned this, so I feel compelled to share it with you. Your faith is centered in your heart, not your mind. Your mind is the gate through which all kinds of thoughts enter. If "you know that you know that you know," then those negative thoughts that try to oppose what your faith center in your heart tells you will not win. So when you are in a trial, and those thoughts try to sway your faith, just rebuke them and hold onto what you know in your heart. This is what Jesus is telling us in the following scripture: "For verily I say unto you, That whosoever shall say unto this mountain, Be thou removed, and be thou cast into the sea; and **shall not doubt in his heart,** but shall believe that those things which he saith shall come to pass; **he shall have whatsoever** he saith" (Mark 11:23, KJV, emphasis added).

Make your mind come into alignment with your heart with Christ-centered teachings. *Let go of your doubt, which will quickly stunt your spiritual growth. Let the Word cleanse all that negativity out of you. All the old programs need to be deleted that have been inputted over the years and The Word has to saturate your soul and spirit.* You can do this by listening to sermons and reading the Bible, as well as speaking scriptures. Listening to uplifting gospel music is also another way you can saturate yourself with His Word because most of the songs' lyrics come from Scripture. Gospel music will often usher in the Holy Spirit, which will make you more receptive to the truth of who you actually are.

The book of Hebrews states the following about faith: "But without faith it is impossible to please him: for he that cometh to God must believe that he is, and that he is a rewarder of them that diligently seek him" (Hebrews 11:6, KJV). I have thought about this and was given the following revelation: since Scripture tell us Jesus and His Word are the same and faith comes by hearing the Word of Christ, then the Word and faith are also the same. *Therefore, to truly be intimate with Jesus, you have to meditate on His word, which He placed within you when you accepted Him as your Lord and Savior.* Once His Word becomes embedded in your heart, your faith grows, and so does His presence within you. As this occurs, He becomes more alive in you, and you can easily enter into His Holy presence. The more time you spend in His presence, the more you can receive from Him: His grace, His tender mercy, His unfailing and overwhelming love. *Being in His presence is truly like standing in a river of living water, and when you drink from it, you will never thirst for a single thing and your faith becomes ever-increasing.*

God's greatest desire is to have an intimate relationship with you and it begins with studying His Holy Word. Now, don't confuse having a relationship with God by thinking all you have to do is accept Jesus as your Savior. Once you do that, the Holy Spirit comes to live in you. But in order to gain access to and develop your relationship with the Holy Spirit, and have true fellowship with Him, you must go through His Word. You can't just receive Jesus and then forget about it or just go to church once a week, sing a few hymns, say a couple of prayers, and then expect to access the Father. It doesn't work that way. *His Word develops the fellowship as it provides a deep understanding of how much He loves you; it's the bridge that connects you to Him. The fellowship brings Him great pleasure. Once you tap into His purpose for your life, the bridge becomes just a few steps away. You will suddenly find yourself walking closely with Him as He reveals more of Himself to you.*

Spending time in the presence of God will transform you from inside out, which Paul tells us in the following scripture. "But we all, with open face beholding as in a glass the glory of the Lord, are changed into the same image from glory to glory, even as by the Spirit of the Lord" (2 Corinthians, 3:18, KJV). I find that the quickest way to enter into His presence is to praise Him. Lift up your hands, and tell Him how wonderful He is. Meditate on His awesomeness. Put on worship music. *When you make a habit of spending time with Him, your faith and trust in Him will grow because the intimacy brings you a deeper knowledge of who He truly is—infinite love beyond our comprehension.* This revelation will bring a greater understanding of His deep concern for you, which will facilitate your ever-increasing faith in your Heavenly Father.

Since being in His presence is transforming, the things that would normally drive you crazy seem miniscule and insignificant. It changes your entire perspective on life. You will never be the same. The more time you spend with Him, the more transformed you will become. Moses was glowing when He came down from the mountain after being in the presence of God (Exodus 34:29). Jesus was transformed on the Mount of Transfiguration as He prayed to God (Luke 9:29). It is the same for us when we spend time with Him. His Holy Spirit is activated within us when we seek Him. He comes rushing forth like this great light that shines outward. People can't help but notice. This is what Jesus meant when He said:

> "Ye are the light of the world. A city that is set on an hill cannot be hid. Neither do men light a candle, and put it under a bushel, but on a candlestick; and it giveth light unto all that are in the house. Let your light so shine before men, that they may see your good works, and glorify your Father which is in heaven" (Matthew 5:14-16, KJV).

In my mind, there is no better deed than to spend time with God, so others can come to know Him through you. I was drawn to the Lord through His joy and light, which I saw manifested in another person. I knew that was what I had been yearning and searching for my whole life. I searched the entire United States. In my teens, I hitchhiked all over the country in my search. As an adult, I moved from city to city and from relationship to relationship. The ironic thing is I only needed to look inside where Jesus came to live after I received Him. There He was waiting patiently for me the entire time. There is nothing else on this Earth like spending time with the Lord. It is truly out of this world!

There is an important biblical principle about faith found in the book of James, which reads "...faith without works is dead..." (James 2:26, KJV). No, this does not mean you have to work yourself to death to please God. It means you have to act on what you believe. This is exemplified in the book of Mark:

"Since they could not get him to Jesus because of the crowd, they made an opening in the roof above Jesus by digging through it and then lowered the mat the man was lying on. When Jesus *saw* their faith, he said to the paralyzed man, "Son, your sins are forgiven (Mark 2:4-5, NIV, emphasis added).""

Notice the word in bold. Jesus *saw* their faith. You can't see a thought or belief, you can only see actions. The Word is telling us we have *to put our belief to work.* That is what James is telling us in the above scripture. Many people have interpreted this scripture to mean we have to do good works to demonstrate our faith, but that is not the correct meaning of this scripture. We need to do good works because Jesus instructs us to love each other, but good deeds are not the basis for increasing our faith. Acting on what you believe about what the Word says in reference to who Jesus is; what He has done for you; and who you are, exemplifies ways to activate your faith.

Faith is belief coupled with action, and if you don't pursue it with passion, it is dead. If you believe in prayer and you don't pray, your prayer life is dead. If you believe in God's Word, but don't speak it, it will remain dormant within your spirit. Works ignite faith. You have to act upon what you believe to manifest what you desire.

Please understand prayer is connected to faith. Pray regardless of how you feel. Recently, I sank down into the pit again. It didn't last very long. I prayed my way out of the grief. Even though I didn't feel like praying, I prayed anyway because I knew God would intervene. This exemplifies working your faith. You act on what you know. You know when you pray things will happen. Your perception and the atmosphere will shift, which will increase your faith.

I know God doesn't want me in that dark abyss that I occasionally sink back into. How can we bring Him pleasure and glory if we remain in a pit? When we understand *everything* is for His glory, our faith becomes ever-increasing. When others see His blessing manifested in our lives, it glorifies Him. Many times, this manifestation leads others to Him. This enables us to understand He *will* work it all out for good because it gives Him great pleasure to see us prosperous. When we prosper, it blesses Him because He wants us to live abundantly and be empowered to lead lost souls to Him. When He win lost souls, it brings Him the greatest pleasure of all.

Living an abundant life includes the biblical principle of preemptive prayer, which prepares you for trials and temptations. That was what Jesus was teaching us in The Lord's Prayer: "And lead us not into temptation, but deliver us from evil…" (Matthew 6:13, KJV). Don't wait for times of trouble to try to pray your way out of it. Pray now for strength, wisdom, patience, a forgiving and compassionate heart, and understanding, so you will sail smoothly upon troubled waters. I pray for protection for upcoming situations that may be difficult. Expect the prayer to change the problem you will be facing. Always pray with thanksgiving as though the event has already occurred: "Father, thank you for protecting me from all illnesses and disabling accidents." I never pray as though I am pleading for something. That would imply lack and demonstrate weak faith. Furthermore, it is non-scriptural. Our Father has already provided everything for us (Ephesians 1:3). We should therefore pray with thanksgiving. This is what the Apostle Paul instructs us to do (Colossians 2:7).

Prayer changes things. In Scripture there is the story of Hezekiah. He prayed and asked God to extend His life while he was lying on his deathbed. God granted him fifteen more years (2 Kings 20). When my husband was in a coma in the intensive care unit, I prayed for God to take my grief and turn it into something positive, which is exactly what He did. I truly believe if I hadn't prayed that prayer, I would not be alive today writing this book because the grief and devastation would have killed me.

Prayer increases your faith. When your prayers are answered, you're motivated to pray even more. Even if they don't get answered right away, you must have a great expectation God is working things out—just as He promised—and He knows best. Even if your prayer isn't answered in the way you'd initially hoped, in hindsight, you will have the revelation of God's infinite wisdom in your life. Sometimes what seems to be an unanswered prayer turns out to be the best answer you could have received. This will bring you great assurance prayers are powerful and effective. You will eventually understand He did hear and answer your prayer.

When you pray, leave some quiet time to hear God's voice. Many times, He wants to speak to us, but we can't listen when we are talking. You may hear a voice in your head or feel an intuition in your spirit when He replies. I can often hear God's voice when I focus deep in my spirit. I am able to do this by breathing very slowly and then closing my eyes and moving them downward as far as they will go. I believe this connects me to what David referred to as "...the secret place of the most High..." (Psalms 91:1, KJV). Pray from the depths of your soul because "***...The effectual, fervent prayer of a righteous man availeth much***" (James 5:16, KJV, emphasis added). Pour your heart out to Him as though you are talking to your best friend. In addition to being your Father, He *is* the best friend you will *ever* have. *When you are right with God through the blood of His precious Son, your Lord and Savior, just rest in Him, and see what happens.*

When you get an answer to your prayer, you will usually get a confirmation from some other mode of communication. God will speak again through another person, Scripture, sermon, dream, nature or any other way that He can get your attention. Keep your ears, eyes, mind, and heart open to receive what He is trying to convey to you. Once you get in tune with His voice, you will hear Him frequently, especially when you really need His guidance.

Pray the scriptures and keep God in remembrance. If you want a specific thing, find a scripture related to your need and go to God with it. Let's say you are petitioning God for a husband. Your prayer might sound like this:

> "God, you said it's not good for man to be alone. You said a man that finds a wife finds a good thing and finds favor with the Lord. I know you want to favor all your beloved children. I

know you love me and want to favor me and the husband you chose for me. I have great expectations that you will send my husband to me soon because Jesus came here to give me an abundant life, which includes the love of a godly man. Your Word says you have already blessed me with every blessing in the heavenly realm and I am standing firm on your Word. I am praying according to your will. Your Word also says that you always say yes to all of your promises. I am in covenant with you because of your son and my Lord and Savior, Jesus Christ. I have been adopted into your family through the seed of Abraham, so all the blessings you promised him are also mine. I claim them now Father. I am a faithful tither and giver. I know you know this, Father, but you said to keep you in re-membrance and I am reminding you. Thank you Father for blessing me. I have great expectations my prayer is answered and I will be married to a godly man very soon. Thank you Father for giving me the most precious husband who puts God first and me second. In Jesus Mighty Name, Amen!"

Be persistent with your prayer. When children want something from their parents they don't give up after asking one time. They continue to remind them of what they want or need until the parent supplies the provision or determines what is best for the child. Jesus tells us to be persistent in petitioning your Heavenly Father through prayer. He tells us when we keep asking, we will receive (Luke 11:5-13). Continue to thank your Father for what you are expecting to receive from Him when you pray. *Above all, thank Him repeatedly when your prayer is answered.*

Most of all, pray to always be in God's perfect will and *always* tell Him that you have great expectations your prayer will be answered. Remember that it is faith that pleases Him most (Hebrews 11:6). *Praying with faith releases the blessing for our great High Priest, Jesus Christ, to intercede on our behalf.* When you are in God's perfect will, you will learn nothing else really matters. With this understanding, you will have great faith to overcome any obstacle as you receive a deep revelation of God's perfect plan working in your life.

Always know when you pray, Jesus is standing at our Father's right hand blessing the words you are speaking, which make your prayers extremely powerful (Romans 8:34). Jesus is your prayer partner who will never fail you. Therefore, when you pray, visualize Jesus speaking your words to the Father as you say them. Know He is your faithful advocate. This will increase your faith and help you access His Holy presence as you pray. When you pray, proclaim you are entering into His presence by faith and the blood of Jesus Christ. See yourself standing in the presence of your High Priest. Know your prayers are heard, blessed, and answered if you are praying according to the Father's will. This is your divine birthright as a child of God, so claim it with every prayer as you step boldly to the throne of grace.

CONCLUSION

How *do you* sum up the Creator of the Universe? It is truly impossible. That would be another book in itself. What I do know is this: when I found myself in the abyss of darkness, His light drew me out and made me brand new. All I can say is He completely transformed me through His love, patience, and His beautiful Word, which has become alive in my spirit. He *is* His Word—not just some text on a page, but a marvelous mystery waiting to be discovered. I am now the light of the world and the salt of the earth because I am now alive in Him and He is alive in me. He was always there waiting with open arms for me to come to Him. He never abandoned me or forsook me, even when I was the worst of sinners. His undying love and His mercy truly endure forever.

Someone recently said to me, "Yeah, it's easy once you don't have to go through anything any longer." That person had it wrong. When you lose someone you have deeply loved—when you lose the only person that ever loved you unconditionally—that pain is always there. It is there when I come home and my beloved Johnny is not there to say, "Hey, baby," when I walk through the door. It is there when I get up in the morning and he is not there to say, "Good morning, baby." It is there when I roll over at night and his side of the bed is empty. It is there on my birthday and holidays, when there's no special card and gift waiting for me. It is there during the day when the phone rings and the caller ID does not speak his name. It is there at the end of the day when his laughter and loving support is absent.

It is always there. I just don't choose it. I choose God. I choose healing. I receive what He has done for me. I wake up and choose God. I choose God with whom I can share my day and I choose Him before I go to bed. When I feel the grief begin to creep in, I choose God. I cry out to Him, "Abba, come and pull me out of this pit! Don't let me stay here!" Within a moment, He reaches down and lifts me up once again because I choose God!

Choose who you will serve. You do have a choice. You can either choose God by turning to Him and believing what He says about Himself and you, or you can choose the enemy by wallowing in the misery he created in your life. *Choose God. He is the only one who can make you prosper above all things.*

From a psychological viewpoint, ignoring my grief would be considered repression. From a spiritual viewpoint, it is definitely progression because my focus is on the only one who can move me forward: *God!* After all, how much can one person grieve? I have cried an ocean of tears. At some point, you have to move forward. The psychologist would say you have to feel it to release it, but God says, "Don't look back; don't look around; just look up. Keep your eyes on me and you will win the race." Life goes on. Mine goes on with God.

So, what I want to say about my sweet Abba Father today is this: He is my King of Kings, my Lord of Lords. He is my Everything. He is the source of all good things in my life. He is the Alpha and the Omega. He is my Creator and the Keeper of the Universe. He is always there when I need Him. He never leaves me or forsakes me. He protects me in all situations. He is the Great Defender, my Strong and Mighty Tower, the one who walked on water and calmed the storm, the one who will come in a cloud of glory, the one I always run to in trouble, and the one I run to in laughter and joy. I will sing His praises for eternity and He will always dance over me with great joy. I am His and He is mine. I will never again turn my back on Him. He is my Eternal Spring that refreshes me when I am dry and comforts me when I am sad. He lifts me up when I am down and makes me laugh. He couldn't be destroyed and the world can't extinguish His light. He is the Eternal Flame in my heart and the source of my inspiration. He is the Healer of All Time and the one my soul will forever love. He is right there when I need Him. He brings me fellowship whenever I desire. He gives me wisdom and shows me great mysteries. He is my Blessing, my Father, my Daddy, and my Divine Husband. I am His own special treasure, His beloved child, and He loves me beyond measure. I will be forever grateful to Him and will dwell in His house forever. I praise His Holy Name. Blessed be the name of the Lord!

Don't ever forget that He is always with you. When you are lonely, sad, confused, angry, hurt, rejected or abandoned; He is right there by your side holding your hand. Whenever the storm rages, He will calm it. Whenever the confusion swarms, He will clear it out. You may not feel Him or see Him, but if you become very still, you will know He is carrying you when you can no longer stand on your own. He will continue to lift you up until you are strong enough to walk by His side once again. If later, you should fall, He will catch you in His loving arms, dust you off, and set you back on your path. He will never fail you, even when you fail. He will always love you even when your heart has been shattered and it seems there is not any love left. Whenever you need Him most, rest assured *He is there.* All you have to do is reach out to Him.

Always remember when Jesus looks at us, He doesn't see us in our sin, but sees us in our pain. It hurts Him deeply when we hurt. He wants us all to come to Him and receive the gift He has for us. He's standing there, waiting longingly for us to come to Him..."What's taking you so long?"

His greatest desire is for us to come to Him so we can receive, not just eternal salvation, but the *fullness* of His tender mercies and His deep eternal love. He wants more than anything to give us the *fullness* of who He is. His heart aches for this. It is His reason for existing. It is His greatest joy when lost souls come to Him. That's why He lavishes us with gifts when we *fully* receive Him and *all* He has for us.

He totally shares in all of our victories. When we win, He wins, and His joy is magnified; His peace is overflowing.

He's not focusing on our sin, but our inability to fully receive from Him because He so ***desperately*** wants us to have an intimate relationship with Him and live the abundant life He created for us. He understands it's the pain, the emptiness, and the lack of understanding of who we truly are, that influences us to make poor choices. He's rooting for us to receive a deep revelation of the love He has for us so we won't hurt and we will live the life for which He created us! What a beautiful and precious Lord and Savior we have! You are infinitely loved beyond what your finite mind can ever comprehend!

When we fully receive Him, it is a celebration: a complete and utter victory. He celebrates by giving us rewards. It's like Paul illustrates, "I have fought a good fight, I have finished my course, I have kept the faith" (2 Timothy 4:7, KJV). God is there cheering us on, and when we overcome a big hurdle, He rewards us greatly, which enables us to achieve the next victory. He continues rewarding us until we get to the finish line. He will then say to us, "…Well done, good and faithful servant…" (Matthew 25:21, KJV). Always remember, "…in all these things ***we are more than conquerors through Him who loved us***" (Romans 8:37, KJV, emphasis added).

One final thought, and then we will finish, though we will forever press forward into our divine destinies. It is God's great pleasure to give His children the kingdom. I know because I am living this biblical truth, and so can you. I am the prodigal child who was lost and finally found her way home. My sweet Abba Father kept waiting, watching, and longing for me to come to Him. *There is no place like home, and home is with the Father. When I finally did come home, I ran to Him, and He ran to me with open arms. He was there just waiting to lavish all of His beautiful blessings upon me, and that is exactly what He did and continues to do.* I have to say *"Thank you, my precious Father!"*

He wants to do the same exact thing for you. Just praise Him, give Him all the glory and gratitude, and believe His promises. *Believe who He says He is and who He says you are, and see how your world will completely change!* He will bless you beyond anything you can ever imagine. *That's who He is: a wonderful Father who wants to lavish all good things on His children, especially the ones who were lost.*

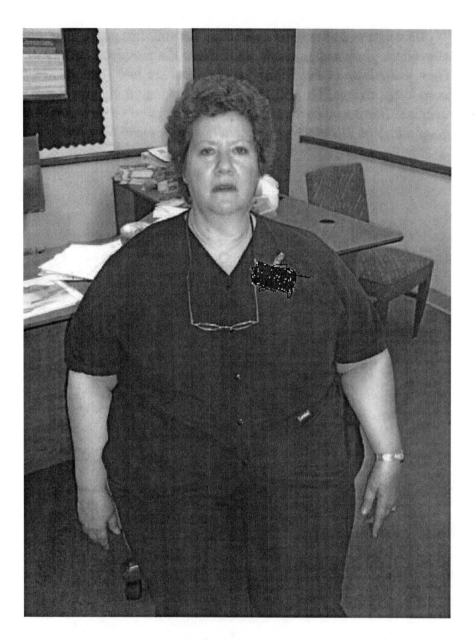

Before Christ

After Christ

TRIBUTE TO THE KING OF KINGS

Triumphantly, I stand before
My precious Lord, whom I adore
He has filled me with His grace and love,
My King of Kings, you're my Everything.

And to Him I shall pray each day
That I should always go His way.
His light shines down from up above
And fills me with His precious love.

His Spirit always dwells in me;
His truth shall always make me free
And grant me favor where I'll be.
My King of Kings, you're my Everything.

The Lord my God, my King of Kings,
My soul eternally will sing.
I praise you, Father, Your Holy Name.
My King of Kings, my Everything.

You've given me oh, everything
My heart desires, my King of Kings.
Your faithful promises that brings,
Joy and peace and loving things.

My King of Kings, my Everything,

My King of Kings, my King of Kings,
My King of Kings.

Rhonda Landry
December 20, 2010

APPENDIX

Below is a list of my favorite TV evangelists and/or websites. The TV evangelists have shows on either Trinity Broadcast or Daystar Channels. You can access free archives, webcasts, or podcasts from most of their websites. You can also purchase CDs or DVDs. Stay away from sermons that emphasize legalism and "hellfire and damnation." That will create fear and keep God's grace from flowing within you.

bishopmcclendon.com: Bishop Clarence McClendon's Ministries

http://brownbible.com—*has wonderful articles written about the grace of Jesus.*

Joni Lamb on Daystar Television

josephprince.org: Joseph Prince Ministries

redemption.org: Ron Carpenter Ministries

ronphillips.org: Ron Phillips Ministries

theblessedlife.com: Robert Morris Ministries

MUSIC

ksbj.org and air1.com: great contemporary gospel station, broadcasts approximately one-hundred-mile radius out of Houston or you can download it to your hard drive. These stations provide song lyrics to the music that is played. Air 1 also has an option to download free songs. The site below will give instructions on downloading to access radio stations on your computer. Remember, great gospel music will usher in the Holy Spirit, help you stay in the spirit, and the lyrics will help renew your mind.

www.free*download*3.com/software/gospel_music_*radio_stations*. htm

FAVORITE SCRIPTURES

I personalize scriptures by either replacing pronouns with "I" or my name.

The one I say every morning because I feel like it encompasses all things: "And he shall be like a tree planted by the rivers of water, that bringeth forth his fruit in his season; his leaf also shall not wither; and whatsoever he doeth shall prosper" (Psalms 1:3, KJV).

BLESSING

"Blessed be the God and Father of our Lord Jesus Christ, who hath blessed us with all spiritual blessings in heavenly places in Christ…" (Ephesians 1:3, KJV).

"Fear not, little flock; for it is your Father's good pleasure to give you the kingdom" (Luke 12:32, KJV).

"The Lord bless thee, and keep thee: The Lord make His face shine upon thee, and be gracious unto thee: The Lord lift up His countenance upon thee, and give thee peace. And they shall put my name upon the children of Israel; and I will bless them" (Numbers 6:24-27, KJV).

"The blessing of the Lord, it maketh rich, and he addeth no sorrow with it" (Proverbs 10:22, KJV).

FEAR

"So that we may boldly say, The Lord is my helper, and I will not fear what man shall do unto me" (Hebrews 13:6, KJV).

"Fear thou not; for I am with thee: be not dismayed; for I am thy God: I will strengthen thee; yea, I will help thee; yea, I will uphold thee with the right hand of my righteousness" (Isaiah 41:10, KJV).

"For I the Lord thy God will hold thy right hand, saying unto thee, Fear not; I will help thee" (Isaiah 41:13, KJV).

"Yea, though I walk through the valley of the shadow of death, I will fear no evil: for thou art with me; thy rod and thy staff they comfort me" (Psalms 23:4, KJV).

"The Lord is my light and my salvation; whom shall I fear? the Lord is the strength of my life; of whom shall I be afraid?" (Psalms 27:1, KJV).

"For God hath not given us the spirit of fear; but of power, and of love, and of a sound mind" (2 Timothy 1:7, KJV).

HEALING

"And ye shall serve the LORD your God, and he shall bless thy bread, and thy water; and I will take sickness away from the midst of thee" (Exodus 23:25, KJV).

"But he was pierced for our transgressions, he was crushed for our iniquities; the punishment that brought us peace was on him, and by his wounds we are healed" (Isaiah 53:5, NIV).

"Then your light will break forth like the dawn, and your healing will quickly appear; then your righteousness will go before you, and the glory of the LORD will be your rear guard" (Isaiah 58:8, NIV).

"Heal me, LORD, and I will be healed; save me and I will be saved, for you are the one I praise" (Jeremiah 17:14, NIV).

"Hearing this, Jesus said to Jairus, "Don't be afraid; just believe, and she will be healed" (Luke 8:50, NIV).

"But unto you that fear my name shall the Sun of righteousness arise with healing in his wings…" (Malachi 4:2, KJV).

"The LORD sustains them on their sickbed and restores them from their bed of illness" (Psalm 41:3, NIV).

"Bless the Lord, O my soul, and forget not all his benefits: Who forgiveth all thine iniquities; who healeth all thy diseases" (Psalms 103:2-3, KJV).

"He heals the brokenhearted and binds up their wounds" (Psalms, 147:3, NIV).

"My son, attend to my words; incline thine ear unto my sayings. Let them not depart from thine eyes; keep them in the midst of thine heart. For they are life unto those that find them, and health to all their flesh" (Proverbs 4:20-22, KJV).

"But if the Spirit of him that raised up Jesus from the dead dwell in you, he that raised up Christ from the dead shall also quicken your mortal bodies by his Spirit that dwelleth in you" (Romans 8:11, KJV).

JOY

"But let all those that put their trust in thee rejoice: let them ever shout for joy because thou defendest them: let them also that love thy name be joyful in thee" (Psalms 5:11, KJV).

"…weeping may endure for a night, but joy cometh in the morning" (Psalms 30:5, KJV).

"The hope of the righteous shall be gladness…" (Proverbs 10:28, KJV).

"Whom having not seen, ye love; in whom, though now ye see him not, yet believing, ye rejoice with joy unspeakable and full of glory" (1 Peter 1:8, KJV).

"Now the God of hope fill you with all joy and peace in believing, that ye may abound in hope, through the power of the Holy Ghost" (Romans 15:13, KJV).

KNOWLEDGE, WISDOM, AND GUIDANCE

"For to one is given by the Spirit the word of wisdom; to another the word of knowledge by the same Spirit" (1 Corinthians 12:8, KJV).

"If any of you lack wisdom, let him ask of God, that giveth to all men liberally, and upbraideth not; and it shall be given him" (James 1:5, KJV).

"But there is a spirit in man: and the inspiration of the Almighty giveth them understanding" (Job 32:8, KJV).

"But when the Comforter is come, whom I will send unto you from the Father, even the Spirit of truth, which proceedeth from the Father, he shall testify of me" (John 15:26, KJV).

"Howbeit when he, the Spirit of truth, is come, he will guide you into all truth: for he shall not speak of himself; but whatsoever he shall hear, that shall he speak: and he will shew you things to come" (John 16:13, KJV).

"For the Lord gives wisdom, and from his mouth comes knowledge and understanding.... Then you will understand what is right and just and fair—every good path. For wisdom will enter your heart, and knowledge will be pleasant to your soul" (Proverbs 2:6, 9-10, NIV).

"Trust in the LORD with all thine heart; and lean not unto thine own understanding. In all thy ways acknowledge him, and he shall direct thy paths" (Proverbs 3:5-6, KJV).

"So shall the knowledge of wisdom be unto thy soul: when thou hast found it, then there shall be a reward, and thy expectation shall not be cut off" (Proverbs 24:14, KJV).

"Teach me good judgment and knowledge: for I have believed thy commandments" (Psalms 119:66, KJV).

PEACE

"Thou wilt keep him in perfect peace, whose mind is stayed on thee: because he trusteth in thee" (Isaiah 26:3, KJV).

"Peace I leave with you, my peace I give unto you" (John 14:27, KJV).

"These things I have spoken unto you, that in me ye might have peace. In the world ye shall have tribulation: but be of good cheer; I have overcome the world" (John 16:33, KJV).

"And why take ye thought for raiment? Consider the lilies of the field, how they grow; they toil not, neither do they spin..." (Matthew 6:28, KJV).

"Take my yoke upon you, and learn of me; for I am meek and lowly in heart: and ye shall find rest unto your souls. Come unto me, all ye that labour and are heavy laden, and I will give you rest. For my yoke is easy, and my burden is light" (Matthew 11:28-30, KJV).

PROSPERITY

"Both riches and honour come of thee, and thou reignest over all; and in thine hand is power and might; and in thine hand it is to make great, and to give strength unto all" (1 Chronicles 29:12, KJV).

"Thou shalt remember the LORD thy God: for it is he that giveth thee power to get wealth, that he may establish his covenant which he sware unto thy fathers, as it is this day" (Deuteronomy 8:18, KJV).

"Be not deceived; God is not mocked: for whatsoever a man soweth, that shall he also reap. For he that soweth to his flesh shall of the flesh reap corruption; but he that soweth to the Spirit shall of the Spirit reap life everlasting. And let us not be weary in well doing: for in due season we shall reap, if we faint not. As we have therefore opportunity, let us do good unto all men, especially unto them who are of the household of faith" (Galatians 6:7-10, KJV).

"That in blessing I will bless thee, and in multiplying I will multiply thy seed as the stars of the heaven, and as the sand which is upon the sea shore; and thy seed shall possess the gate of his enemies" (Genesis 22:17, KJV).

"Every good gift and every perfect gift is from above, and cometh down from the Father of lights, with whom is no variableness, neither shadow of turning" (James 1:17, KJV).

"For I know the plans I have for you," declares the LORD, "plans to prosper you and not to harm you, plans to give you hope and a future" (Jeremiah 29:11, NIV).

"And this is the confidence that we have in him, that, if we ask any thing according to his will, he heareth us: And if we know that he hear us, whatsoever we ask, we know that we have the petitions that we desired of him" (1 John 5:14-15, KJV).

"This book of the law shall not depart out of thy mouth; but thou shalt meditate therein day and night, that thou mayest observe to do according to all that is written therein: for then thou shalt make thy way prosperous, and then thou shalt have good success" (Joshua 1:8, KJV).

"Fear not, little flock; for it is your Father's good pleasure to give you the kingdom" (Luke 12:32, KJV).

" Bring ye all the tithes into the storehouse, that there may be meat in mine house, and prove me now herewith, saith the Lord of hosts, if I will not open you the windows of heaven, and pour you out a blessing, that there shall not be room enough to receive it. And I will rebuke the devourer for your sakes, and he shall not destroy the fruits of your ground; neither shall your vine cast her fruit before the time in the field, saith the Lord of hosts. And all nations shall call you blessed: for ye shall be a delightsome land, saith the Lord of hosts" (Malachi 3:10-12, KJV).

"Therefore take no thought, saying, What shall we eat? or, What shall we drink? or, Wherewithal shall we be clothed? (For after all these things do the Gentiles seek:) for your heavenly Father knoweth that ye have need of all these things. But seek ye first the kingdom of God, and his righteousness; and all these things shall be added unto you" (Matthew 6:31-33, KJV).

"But my God shall supply all your need according to his riches in glory by Christ Jesus" (Philippians 4:19, KJV).

"The blessing of the LORD, it maketh rich, and he addeth no sorrow with it" (Proverbs 10:22, KJV).

"The liberal soul shall be made fat: and he that watereth shall be watered also himself" (Proverbs 11:25, KJV).

"For as he thinketh in his heart, so is he" (Proverbs 23:7, KJV).

"Let them shout for joy, and be glad, that favour my righteous cause: yea, let them say continually, Let the LORD be magnified, which hath pleasure in the prosperity of his servant" (Psalms 35:27, KJV).

"Trust in the LORD, and do good; so shalt thou dwell in the land, and verily thou shalt be fed. Delight thyself also in the LORD: and he shall give thee the desires of thine heart. Commit thy way unto the LORD; trust also in him; and he shall bring it to pass" (Psalms 37:3-5, KJV).

"For the LORD God is a sun and shield: the LORD will give grace and glory: no good thing will he withhold from them that walk uprightly" (Psalms 84:11, KJV).

"The righteous shall flourish like the palm tree: he shall grow like a cedar in Lebanon. Those that be planted in the house of the Lord shall flourish in the courts of our God. They shall still bring forth fruit in old age; they shall be fat and flourishing..." (Psalms 92:12-14, KJV).

"Pray for the peace of Jerusalem: they shall prosper that love thee. Peace be within thy walls, and prosperity within thy palaces" (Psalms 122:6-7, KJV)

PROTECTION

"But now thus saith the LORD that created thee, O Jacob, and he that formed thee, O Israel, Fear not: for I have redeemed thee, I have called thee by thy name; thou art mine. When thou passest through the waters, I will be with thee; and through the rivers, they shall not overflow thee: when thou walkest through the fire, thou shalt not be burned; neither shall the flame kindle upon thee" (Isaiah 43:1-2, KJV).

"No weapon that is formed against thee shall prosper; and every tongue that shall rise against thee in judgment thou shalt condemn. This is the heritage of the servants of the LORD, and their righteousness is of me, saith the LORD" (Isaiah 54:17, KJV).

"Behold, I give unto you power to tread on serpents and scorpions, and over all the power of the enemy: and nothing shall by any means hurt you" (Luke 10:19, KJV).

"The angel of the LORD encampeth round about them that fear him, and delivereth them" (Psalms 34:7, KJV).

"God is our refuge and strength, a very present help in trouble" (Psalms 46:1, KJV).

"He that dwelleth in the secret place of the most High shall abide under the shadow of the Almighty" (Psalms 91:1, KJV).

"For he shall give his angels charge over thee, to keep thee in all thy ways" (Psalms 91:11, KJV).

"My help cometh from the LORD, which made heaven and earth" (Psalms 121:2, KJV).

"The Lord shall preserve thee from all evil: he shall preserve thy soul" (Psalms 121:7, KJV).

"My goodness, and my fortress; my high tower, and my deliverer; my shield, and he in whom I trust; who subdueth my people under me" (Psalms 144:2, KJV).

"In all thy ways acknowledge him, and he shall direct thy paths" (Proverbs 3:6, KJV).

"The name of the Lord is a strong tower: the righteous runneth into it, and is safe" (Proverbs 18:10, KJV).

"And he said, The LORD is my rock, and my fortress, and my deliverer; The God of my rock; in him will I trust: he is my shield, and the horn of my salvation, my high tower, and my refuge, my saviour; thou savest me from violence. I will call on the LORD, who is worthy to be praised: so shall I be saved from mine enemies" (2 Samuel 22:2-4, KJV).

THE WHOLE ARMOR OF GOD

"Finally, my brethren, be strong in the Lord, and in the power of his might. Put on the whole armour of God, that ye may be able to stand against the wiles of the devil. For we wrestle not against flesh and blood, but against principalities, against powers, against the rulers of the darkness of this world, against spiritual wickedness in high places. Wherefore take unto you the whole armour of God, that ye may be able to withstand in the evil day, and having done all, to stand. Stand therefore, having your loins girt about with truth, and having on the breastplate of righteousness; And your feet shod with the preparation of the gospel of peace; Above all, taking the shield of faith, wherewith ye shall be able to quench all the fiery darts of the wicked. And take the helmet of salvation, and the sword of the Spirit, which is the word of God: Praying always with all prayer and supplication in the Spirit, and watching thereunto with all perseverance and supplication for all saints;" (Ephesians 6:10-18, KJV).

STRENGTH

"And he said unto me, My grace is sufficient for thee: for my strength is made perfect in weakness. Most gladly therefore will I rather glory in my infirmities, that the power of Christ may rest upon me" (2 Corinthians 12:9, KJV).

"Let your conversation be without covetousness; and be content with such things as ye have: for he hath said, I will never leave thee, nor forsake thee. So that we may boldly say, The Lord is my helper, and I will not fear what man shall do unto me" (Hebrews 13:5-6, KJV).

"Fear thou not; for I am with thee: be not dismayed; for I am thy God: I will strengthen thee; yea, I will help thee; yea, I will uphold thee with the right hand of my righteousness. Behold, all they that were incensed against thee shall be ashamed and confounded: they shall be as nothing; and they that strive with thee shall perish" (Isaiah 41:10-11, KJV).

"Have not I commanded thee? Be strong and of a good courage; be not afraid, neither be thou dismayed: for the LORD thy God is with thee whithersoever thou goest" (Joshua 1:9, KJV).

"Casting all your care upon him; for he careth for you" (1 Peter 5:7, KJV).

"For who is God save the Lord? or who is a rock save our God? It is God that girdeth me with strength, and maketh my way perfect. He maketh my feet like hinds' feet, and setteth me upon my high places" (Psalms 18:31-33, KJV).

"Yea, though I walk through the valley of the shadow of death, I will fear no evil: for thou art with me; thy rod and thy staff they comfort me" (Psalms 23:4, KJV).

"Many are the afflictions of the righteous: but the LORD delivereth him out of them all" (Psalms 34:17-19, KJV).

"And call upon me in the day of trouble: I will deliver thee, and thou shalt glorify me" (Psalms 50:15, KJV).

"The LORD is my strength and song, and is become my salvation" (Psalms 118:14, KJV).

"In the day when I cried thou answeredst me, and strengthenedst me with strength in my soul" (Psalms 138:3, KJV).

"I can do all things through Christ which strengtheneth me" (Philippians 4:13, KJV).

"What shall we then say to these things? If God be for us, who can be against us?" (Romans 8:31, KJV).

"But the Lord is faithful, who shall stablish you, and keep you from evil" (2 Thessalonians 3:3, KJV).

Who You Are - His Child: Royalty, Set Apart, Holy, Infinitely Loved, Righteous and Victorious

"For he hath made him to be sin for us, who knew no sin; that we might be made the righteousness of God in him" (2 Corinthians 5:21, KJV).

"And the Lord shall make thee the head, and not the tail; and thou shalt be above only, and thou shalt not be beneath; if that thou hearken unto the commandments of the Lord thy God, which I command thee this day, to observe and to do them..." (Deuteronomy 28:13, KJV).

"Behold, I have graven thee upon the palms of my hands; thy walls are continually before me" (Isaiah 49:16, KJV).

"But even the very hairs of your head are all numbered. Fear not therefore: ye are of more value than many sparrows" (Luke 12:17, KJV).

"But you are a chosen generation, a royal priesthood, a holy nation, His own special people, that you may proclaim the praises of Him who called you" (1 Peter 2:9, NKJV).

"How precious also are thy thoughts unto me, O God! how great is the sum of them! If I should count them, they are more in number than the sand..." (Psalms 139:17-18, KJV).

"...we are more than conquerors through him that loved us" (Romans 8:37, KJV).

CPSIA information can be obtained at www.ICGtesting.com
Printed in the USA
LVOW10s1112071013

355775LV00011B/85/P

9 780988 284463